THE TRIAL OF POPE BENEDICT

The Trial of Pope Benedict

*Joseph Ratzinger and the Vatican's Assault on Reason,
Compassion, and Human Dignity*

DANIEL GAWTHROP

Arsenal Pulp Press
Vancouver

ARSENAL PULP PRESS
Suite 202 – 211 East Georgia St.
Vancouver, BC V6A 1Z6
Canada
arsenalpulp.com

The publisher gratefully acknowledges the support of the Canada Council for the Arts and the British Columbia Arts Council for its publishing program, and the Government of Canada (through the Canada Book Fund) and the Government of British Columbia (through the Book Publishing Tax Credit Program) for its publishing activities.

Cover photograph: Corbis Images © Carlo Ferraro/epa/Corbis
Book design by Gerilee McBride

Printed and bound in Canada

Library and Archives Canada Cataloguing in Publication

Gawthrop, Daniel, 1963–
     The trial of Pope Benedict : Joseph Ratzinger and the
Vatican's assault on reason, compassion, and human dignity
/ Daniel Gawthrop.

Includes bibliographical references and index.
Also issued in electronic format.
ISBN 978-1-55152-527-3

     1. Benedict XVI, Pope, 1927–. 2. Catholic Church—
History—21st century. 3. Church controversies—Catholic
Church—History—21st century. I. Title.

BX1378.6.G39 2013   282.09′051   C2013-901720-8

FSC
www.fsc.org
MIX
Paper from
responsible sources
FSC® C103214

For Rev. John Sproule

(In memoriam: Rev. Alan Alvare, Sr. Muriel Loftus)

Contents

There is nothing more difficult to take in hand, more perilous to conduct, or more uncertain in its success, than to take the lead in the introduction of a new order of things.
—Niccolo Machiavelli

The first step toward finding God, Who is Truth, is to discover the truth about myself: and if I have been in error, this first step to truth is the discovery of my error.
—Thomas Merton

Foreword

On February 11, 2013, Pope Benedict XVI stunned the world—and, apparently, his own College of Cardinals—by announcing that he would resign the papacy and relinquish the throne of Saint Peter in seventeen days. Citing declining health—he was known to be suffering from arthritis in the knees, hips, and ankles, thus experiencing mobility issues that would have made another papal tour too exhausting to contemplate—the pope added that he was failing in spirit and in mind. "After having repeatedly examined my conscience before God," he told the hushed group of cardinals in the *Sala del Concistoro* of the Apostolic Palace, "I have come to the certainty that my strengths, due to an advanced age, are no longer suited to an adequate exercise of the Petrine ministry."

This was not your average retirement announcement. The last pope to exercise his right to abdicate was Gregory XII, who stepped down in 1415 to end the western schism in the church. By becoming the first supreme pontiff to resign in nearly six hundred years, the man who became Pope Benedict XVI was making history. In doing so, he raised questions and ignited controversy, in a manner that had become his hallmark. Although it is quite plausible that Benedict, at nearly eighty-six years of age, wanted to avoid the sad spectacle of deteriorating into incoherence like his predecessor, the Parkinson's-wracked Pope John Paul II, those who knew him well did not believe for a minute that he was growing weak "in mind." Joseph Aloisius Ratzinger had always done things his own way. He had always called the shots; always controlled the situation around him. And for all his brother Georg's insistence that he had made the decision months ago and was doing it "for the good of the Church," failing health seemed to many like an odd reason to vacate a post, and a calling, that all but two of his predecessors had pledged to serve until their dying breath. As had he.

And so, speculation began immediately that he was bailing out for other reasons; that he was forced out of office by one of the many scandals engulfing the church and threatening to swallow it up. Was it clerical child sex abuse, which had cost the church billions in lawsuits from victims and become the subject of a complaint to the International Criminal Court, with fingers pointed at Benedict for his role in the cover-up? Was it the Vatican banking fiasco, which had scared off investors like JPMorgan Chase due to revelations of fraud, money laundering, and other tawdry practices, despite the pope's best efforts to clean up Vatican finances? Was it the much-rumored power struggle with his secretary of state, Cardinal Tarcisio Bertone? Or was it fresh revelations of an underground gay priests network, revealed by an investigation Benedict himself had ordered, which confirmed that Roman Catholic officials were being blackmailed by Vatican outsiders?

Subsequent revelations in the respected Italian newspaper, *La Repubblica*, suggested that the latter scenario was the most likely: that on December 17, 2012, when Benedict finished reading a devastating report about sexual mischief and "bad fish" inside the Vatican, he decided that he had had enough. The nature and extent of the so-called "gay priests network," the leaking of information, and the embarrassment to the church had reached a point beyond his ability either to cope with the problems or provide a solution as supreme pontiff. So, on that day he made a decision he would wait until February 11 to announce: that he was saving his beloved church by leaving its problems to a younger, and presumably worthier, pope. For a man who had dedicated his life to the pursuit of power and authority over all the church's doings, it was the ultimate irony: Joseph Ratzinger, having finally assumed the throne of Saint Peter at age seventy-eight, was being forced to relinquish that power and authority as a result of events largely authored by himself.

When people ask why I wrote this book, I say it's because Joseph Ratzinger destroyed the Roman Catholic Church. When they ask why that matters, I tell them that the church, for a brief moment in our lifetime, had a rare opportunity to heal itself and become both a powerful force for good in the world and a relevant player in civic discourse. That moment was the Second Vatican Council, or Vatican II: the gathering of church clerics and theologians between 1962 and 1965 that sought to reconcile the church's mission with the realities of the modern world. Ratzinger, far beyond any other figure in the church, played a pivotal role in ensuring that the changes recommended by Vatican II would never come to pass. As a result, the church he helped create became a meaner place—a place dedicated more to controlling people's lives than to revealing the wisdom of the gospels. Rather than a force for good, it became the same divisive force of destruction it had been from the Middle Ages to the late nineteenth century. Vatican II thus represents a missed opportunity of historic proportions. Since its deliberations (and brief application by progressive clerics) had some impact in determining who I am today, I would like to share a bit of my own story before telling Ratzinger's. The two are, however distantly, connected.

On April 11, 1963, Pope John XXIII released his final encyclical, *Pacem in Terris* (*Peace on Earth*). For the first time, a papal document was addressed not only to the Catholic faithful but to everyone "of good will." Released only two years after the Berlin Wall's erection and a few months after the Cuban missile crisis, *Pacem in Terris* was mindful of the global tensions caused by the Cold War. What was foremost in this pope's mind, as he approached the end of his own life? That conflict should be resolved by negotiation and not war, that human rights were essential, and that every person, as the encyclical put it, "has the right to life, to bodily integrity, and to the means which are suitable for the proper development of life..."

Half a century later, it is hard to imagine the spirit of communion, or the general atmosphere of the Second Vatican Council, that inspired *Pacem in Terris*. By "communion," I am not referring to the eucharistic celebration but the communion of people in an egalitarian sense—as opposed to the top-down, hierarchical *Communio*[1] of blind and compulsory papalist loyalty that Joseph Ratzinger, Pope John Paul II, and their fellow conservative travelers would espouse from the end of the 1970s onward. Before Vatican II, the church was not a friendly place. "It was the tower on the mountain, condemning everyone else," a retired cleric told me recently, "the ship in which the faithful all gathered with Saint Peter while their enemies drowned in the sea." *Pacem in Terris* changed all that with its subtext of friendship. Like a charter for the conditions of world peace, it transformed the atmosphere of the church into a kind of meeting place for the "People of God," which meant everyone. This was the church I grew up in.

It is safe to say that I would not be alive today were it not for the Roman Catholic Church. I was born the sixth of seven children, the son of devout Catholic parents whose perspective changed after Vatican II. My eldest four siblings were boys; my parents wanted a girl. When they finally got one in 1960, they tried for another but in 1963 got me instead. After I was born, my parents tried once more for another girl, and this time succeeded. By this time my mother was forty-one, so she and my father agreed to cap their brood at seven. Would I have been born if they had been Lutherans? Baptists? Jews? Atheists? Absolutely not.

During the 1960s, there was a generational split among my siblings in terms of which Catholic Church we knew best. My

---

1 The quarterly review of Catholic theology and culture co-founded by Ratzinger and a group of like-minded theological conservatives.

three eldest brothers were raised on the Latin mass, Baltimore catechism, and the cane-wielding nuns of Saint Ann's Convent. But my fourth eldest brother, two sisters and I were raised on the folk mass, priests who dressed like hippies, and the left-wing social justice agenda of our bishop, Remi De Roo. Among other things, Remi encouraged his flock to get involved in parish decision-making, support women's equality, oppose the capitalist greed of multi-millionaires like media magnate Conrad Black, and stand up for Latin American peasants against the whims of US imperialism. Since by doing these things we would all be on the side of the angels, the church did not seem like a place I would ever abandon.

During my undergrad student years, it was music that kept me in the pew. Rather than somber hymns on a pipe organ, the post-Vatican II liturgy called on younger priests or seminarians to lead the faithful in spirited renditions of contemporary folk or pop songs with Christian themes. The new Catholic folk liturgy of the Saint Louis Jesuits was meant to be played on acoustic guitar with piano accompaniment. Their *Glory and Praise* songbook contained hundreds of devotional tunes with infectious melodies and a contemporary sound. Earnest? Definitely. But more sophisticated—and less cheesy—than "Kumbaya" or the gag-inducing "They'll Know We Are Christians By Our Love." Think Crosby, Stills & Nash, set to the New Testament. For a couple of years, I enjoyed singing tenor harmonies as a member of my campus parish's liturgical ensemble.

But then, just as I was floating in Vatican II's wooly embrace, reality came crashing down. One Sunday afternoon in the mid-1980s, as I stood on the altar in my usual spot between the lead guitarist and the oboe player, I found myself gazing into the congregation as I sang the first verse of John Michael Talbot's "Be Not Afraid":

> You shall cross the barren desert, but you shall not die of thirst

> You shall wander far in safety though you do not know the way

> You shall speak your words in foreign lands and all will understand

> You shall see the face of God and live

Scanning the faces of my fellow parishioners, I froze at the vision of another young man in his early twenties, whose gaze was fixed on mine: with his doe-like brown eyes, silky tanned skin, and luscious red lips—his features framed by the thick, wavy brown hair of a prince—he was like something out of a Caravaggio. All that was missing was the chiaroscuro effect from the skylight glass, which would have signaled to the congregation what a classic beauty we had in our midst. *I have seen the face of God. I shall live!*

Then his eyes darted away, and I awoke from the spell. What I had just experienced was the same lightning bolt of desperate yearning that happens to all human beings in love at first sight—the expression of which ninety percent of us take for granted and have always been entitled to openly rejoice through music, literature, and public displays of affection. Until this moment, I had taken it for granted that my own, long-delayed experience of this feeling would not be something I would ever have to hide. But now, instinct told me otherwise: within moments of that love-struck glance, I was scanning the room nervously, to see if anyone had noticed our eye contact. Within days, my paranoia would prove well founded: while I was hoping in vain to see that boy again at another mass, Joseph Ratzinger was putting the finishing touches to a Vatican document that would encourage people like us to embrace lives of self-loathing and self-denial.

As the Vatican prefect of the Congregation for the Doctrine of the Faith (CDF), Cardinal Ratzinger in 1986 released a pastoral letter to the world's bishops declaring that homosexuality was an "objective disorder." Among other things, he said that homosexuality was a "problem," and that gay unions were not "complementary" in the gender sense because procreation was neither the purpose nor the possible result of our sex. Thus, to be out and proud, I would only be confirming my "disordered" and "essentially self-indulgent" inclination. This "instruction" by Ratzinger was but one example of the new reality confronting Catholicism under his theological surveillance. Since 1981, he and Pope John Paul II had slowly undermined the pastoral credibility of Vatican II with a series of actions designed to turn back the clock. I had been pretending it wasn't happening, that we could just ignore the pope. But I could pretend no more: Roman Catholicism had become a club that no longer wanted someone like me as a member. The feeling was mutual.

But taking the boy out of the church, as we know, does not always take the church out of the boy. Although I became an "ex"-Catholic, I talked so much about Catholicism in my first few years away from its embrace that I surely gave the impression I was still in the thick of it. The first few years were a gestalt-fest of barely contained rage as I "recovered" from the shame of self-abnegation with which I had allowed the church to stifle my self-expression. Once I got over that, I moved on to righteous indignation about priestly celibacy, clerical sex abuse, and the hypocrisy of Vatican homophobia. (Wasn't the priesthood itself the largest gay club in the world?) Before long I grew bored of all that, too, and after a few years finally stopped paying attention to the church or any news coverage of it whatsoever. After eighteen years away from its powerful clutches, I was fairly confident I was free of it.

Then Pope John Paul II died, Joseph Ratzinger succeeded him, and I got drawn into the discourse once again. The fact that such a notorious autocrat and disciplinarian had been entrusted with the throne of Saint Peter seemed like a giant raspberry to Ratzinger's critics. The new pope was a career intellectual and curial bureaucrat seen by many as lacking in the qualities often associated with the office: visible evidence of personal humility and empathy with the flock, honed by several years in the clerical trenches. What's more, Ratzinger was said to have been delighted by the prospect of becoming pope—unlike many of his predecessors, who reluctantly accepted their election as a burden and an honor of which they confessed unworthiness.

But why should Ratzinger's ascension to the papacy have reignited my interest in the church? I had become an atheist, after all. Should not disgust over the new pope simply have driven me further away from it? Maybe. But I was a Catholic atheist: a Graham Greene "cultural Catholic" who, despite having left the faith, retained certain telltale behavioral traits consistent with Catholic identity. A hair-trigger guilty conscience, an abhorrence of injustice, a fondness for formal ritual around family meals and community gatherings, and a fetish for symbolic pageantry were dead giveaways of my "ex," "lapsed," or "recovering" status. A pragmatist, I also saw the church, and religion in general, as unavoidable. If pursued with reason, compassion, and dignity, they need not be argued out of existence. On the contrary, religion done smartly could still do some good in the world. So every time I saw Ratzinger, I was reminded of the man who rejected the reforms of Vatican II and took the medieval route instead.

Ratzinger himself functioned as a kind of satanic muse in my life. In New York City in 1994, it was he—and not presiding Archbishop Cardinal O'Connor—I was thinking about when I joined thousands of gay pride marchers and AIDS activists for a massive "die-in" in front of St. Patrick's Cathedral. Every time I saw another news story about yet another mind-numbing church decision, the odds were good that the policy under discussion bore his fingerprints. So all these years later, when he announced he was abandoning the ultimate seat of Roman Catholic power after an eight-year pontificate plagued by controversy, it was hard not to stifle a gag reflex. The sex abuse scandals were bad enough. But in the course of his decades-long campaign against women, gays and lesbians, liberation theologians, and religious pluralists, Joseph Ratzinger not only ruined his beloved church but created conditions for a more mean-spirited world. For all this, he must be held accountable.

Prologue

Imagine this scenario: Inside the packed main chambers of the International Criminal Court (ICC) in The Hague, all the world's news cameras are fixed on a white-haired, white-suited figure seated at the witness stand. The object of everyone's attention, the old man is staring straight ahead—his dark, beady eyes betraying none of their usual manic energy, his stony expression giving nothing away as he faces interrogation before a global audience. Standing in front of him, an ICC prosecutor spins around and gestures to the front of the gallery, pointing at a man in his mid-forties. He identifies the man as Wilfried Fesselmann. A German, like the witness, Fesselmann is an adult survivor of clerical sex abuse and one of several complainants whose cases have led to this very moment.

At age eleven in 1979, says the prosecutor, Fesselmann was attending a church-run vacation camp in Essen when Father Peter Hullermann invited him to his room. There, the Catholic priest gave the boy an alcoholic beverage, stripped him naked, and forced him to perform oral sex. Because of this, and complaints regarding three similar cases of abuse, Rev. Hullermann was sent for counseling in Munich. On January 15, 1980, the prosecutor tells the court, the witness chaired a meeting as Archbishop of Munich and Freising in which he formally approved the priest's transfer to his archdiocese. The witness also provided Rev. Hullermann with accommodation, at a parish house in Munich, while he underwent his therapy. Shortly after the therapy began—and against the advice of his psychiatrist, who told the church that the priest should not work with children—Reverend Hullermann was assigned to an unrestricted pastoral ministry at a Munich parish, which included work with children.

The prosecutor turns to the witness. "Now, you have since declared that you approved Father Hullermann's transfer to Munich for therapy but *not* his diocesan assignment; that it was your deputy, archdiocesan Vicar General Gerhard Gruber, who assigned him to a new parish, and without your knowledge. Father Gruber has confirmed as much. The question is: does this fact absolve you of responsibility?" A hush descends over the gallery as the prosecutor recounts how Father Hullermann went on to abuse boys for another six years before his arrest; how he served no jail time but was fined 4,000 deutsch marks and given an eighteen-month suspended sentence, for which he served five years' probation; how he continued working in various church posts, including for more than twenty years as a curate and parish administrator where he had regular contact with children and supervised 150 altar boys; and finally how, when he was suspended from his last religious post in March 2010, the archdiocese of Munich and Freising issued a statement saying that there had been "no evidence of recent sexual abuses, similar to those for which he was convicted in 1986"—only to retract this statement later the same month, when officials revealed a further allegation of abuse dating from 1998.

The prosecutor clears his throat and turns to the witness:

"With the utmost respect to a pope emeritus, I am afraid I have no alternative but to ask you, in the presence of this court: Why, as Cardinal of Munich, did you approve Father Hullermann's transfer to your jurisdiction, rather than defrocking him? Why, when you knew that he was a serial abuser? When you should have foreseen that, should he continue his ministry, there was a strong possibility—indeed, a likelihood—that he would abuse again, as subsequently proved to be the case? Why did you allow the vicar general to determine Father Hullerman's future, instead of taking the file yourself, thus failing to protect the young and innocent in your archdiocese? Why, Your Holiness? Why?"

At that moment, all eyes turn to the white-suited figure. In a sequence that will draw record viewing numbers on YouTube after recording the largest television audience in history, the cameras turn from the prosecutor to the witness, and then to Fesselmann in the gallery. The victim, leaning forward in his seat and folding his hands on his chin, stares straight at the witness. Eagerly anticipating his words, Fesselmann is hoping for some kind of penance that will finally bring closure to this sorry chapter in his life more than three-and-a-half decades after the fact. The cameras turn back to the witness stand, where Joseph Ratzinger, the retired Pope Benedict XVI, raises a glass of water in trembling hands, takes it to his lips, and then puts it down.

"We … we … I …," the pope emeritus stammers into his microphone, before falling silent. Then, to the general amazement of everyone, the former leader of the world's 1.2 billion Roman Catholics sits back in his chair and shakes his head, a single tear rolling down his left cheek.

Improbable? Yes. In the minds of many, the man who spent nearly eight years on the throne of Saint Peter was as likely to find himself in the dock at The Hague as was the much-reviled Henry Kissinger. Few can imagine a former pope being cross-examined in such a manner: the reality of Vatican statehood— including Permanent Observer status at the United Nations, and the diplomatic immunity extended to popes—precluded such a possibility. But if the ICC chief prosecutor ever saw grounds to proceed, or—failing that—if a convincing legal challenge arose elsewhere, it technically could happen. More importantly, many believed that it should. Whether or not it did, a case could be made that Joseph Ratzinger had much more to answer for than his own handling of the clerical rape of children.

I

Fear and Obedience

The past is never simply the past. It always has something to say to us; it tells us the paths to take and the paths not to take.

—Pope Benedict XVI, on a visit to Auschwitz, May 2006

"After the great pope John Paul II, the cardinals have elected me, a simple and humble worker in the vineyard of the Lord..."

With these words on April 19, 2005, Joseph Aloisius Ratzinger greeted the world for the first time as newly elected pope. "A simple and humble worker"? The former Cardinal of Munich, and the all-powerful prefect of the Congregation for the Doctrine of the Faith, must have been caught up in the moment to have allowed himself the luxury of such ironic cheek. For, thanks to his giant body of published work to date—and more than two decades of media coverage, which had earned him a global reputation as "God's Rottweiler" and "The Grand Inquisitor"—most of the Catholic world knew that Ratzinger was anything but "simple." And thanks to an endless reserve of self-esteem, which had allowed him to publish two memoirs *before* assuming the throne of Saint Peter (in contrast to his predecessor, Pope John Paul II, who produced none despite the second longest pontificate on record), he didn't seem all that "humble," either. Possibly the most opportunistic cleric ever to become pope, his name was more instantly recognizable and cringe-inducing to a larger number of people than that of any other cardinal in modern times. *Ratzy the Nazi. Joseph the Rat.* What had the world, never mind its 1.2 billion Catholics, done to deserve him?

By ascending to the throne of Saint Peter, Ratzinger had earned the right by antiquity to shed his troublesome surname and replace it with a venerable nickname, attached to a Roman numeral, more befitting his new stature. His choice of Benedict, Vatican observers said, was an inspired one: apart from the intrigue of ending a lengthy gap between himself and the fifteenth of his predecessors with that name, there was the fact that *benedictus* is Latin for "blessing," and "Benedict" means "the blessed." And indeed, Ratzinger appeared to have been "blessed" from the very beginning: born on a Holy Saturday, to parents named Joseph and Mary, he was baptized with the newly blessed Easter water. His long and eventful journey to the papacy also appeared blessed: while publishing his way into prominence, he had won good jobs in academia and church hierarchy alike, gained unparalleled power and influence over his peers, and had his way in just about everything. By naming himself after the patron saint of Europe—the seat of his power and the base of his influence—Joseph Ratzinger, the new pope, was placing a cherry on top of all his sweet "blessings."

It could also be said, however, that Ratzinger's choice of "Benedict" implied an indifference to public perception of him. Without a doubt, the world already knew he was "blessed" with an encyclopedic knowledge of canon law, a certain knack for making enemies, and flawlessly Machiavellian instincts. But since these could hardly be described as virtues, "Benedict" as a papal name came off at best as pretentious, at worst like parody. Eight years later, after a pontificate battered by negative headlines in the Western media—the foot-in-mouth statements offending other religions, the out-of-touch critiques of modernity, the sex abuse lawsuits and the damage control exercises to contain them, the "Vatileaks" scandal and the atmosphere of chaos surrounding it, the distasteful witch-hunt of US nuns, and even a filing with the International Criminal Court accusing His Holiness of crimes against humanity—how "blessed" could Ratzinger truly have felt as he became only the second pope in nearly six hundred years to voluntarily relinquish the throne of Saint Peter?

Just Following Orders

A native of Bavaria, Joseph Ratzinger was born in a part of Germany untouched by the Reformation: an idyllic farmer's paradise where Roman Catholicism was the foundation of community life. But when he came into this world on April 16, 1927, Ratzinger also landed in the middle of one of history's most unfortunate confluences of religion and politics: Marktl-am-Inn, the village where he was born, on the German side of the border with Austria, was only ten miles from Braunau-am-Inn, a little village on the Austrian shore of the Inn River, where Adolf Hitler was born. Despite the abundance of religious trivia about Marktl-am-Inn he provides in his memoirs, Ratzinger never does mention this little coincidence. It seems an odd omission, given the enormous implications it would have in his life.

Ratzinger was the youngest of three children of the country policeman Joseph Ratzinger Sr., a social progressive who regarded the growing presence of Nazi militias in Bavaria with increasing alarm. By 1932, with the Weimar Republic on the verge of collapse and the first persecution of Jews beginning in Munich, the Nazis had become the dominant political force in Bavaria. Ratzinger refused to spy or inform on priests who behaved as "enemies of the Reich"; on the contrary, he helped those he knew were in trouble. But the family was under increasing pressure because of his open criticism of the fanatics. At one point, Ratzinger got into an impossible confrontation with a priest who had become an ardent Nazi: the priest wanted to erect a Maypole in the village square, which Ratzinger rightly saw as a deliberate attempt to wipe out Christian influence and bring back a nostalgically patriotic sort of Germanic pagan worship. In 1937, the family moved to Traunstein and settled on a nineteenth-century farm in Hufschlag, on the outskirts of town. This is where young Joseph would spend the rest of his childhood, though it would hardly provide shelter from the coming Nazi onslaught. Before long, signs went up in the central square in Traunstein calling for citizens to boycott Jewish businesses.

Here is a brief chronology of the younger Joseph Ratzinger's teenage years, which coincide with World War II:

+ **1939**: At age twelve, just as the war is beginning, he enters the minor seminary of Saint Michael, joining his older brother Georg who started two years earlier.

✦ **1941:** At fourteen, he is recruited into the
Hitler Youth but gets a waiver allowing him
not to attend the meetings because he is in the
seminary.

✦ **1943:** On August 2, his presence is required
at a combat post. At sixteen, he is given a
Wehrmacht uniform and the assignment of
defending a BMW factory in southern Bavaria.

✦ **1944:** In September, he is assigned to a
labor camp between the borders of Austria,
Czechoslovakia, and Hungary. One night, he
and his group are pulled out of bed and gathered outside. An SS officer has each of the boys
step forward to be humiliated with "voluntary"
recruitment into the SS. Ratzinger and a few
others say they are planning to become Catholic
priests; after being insulted, they are sent on
their way.

✦ **1945:** On his eighteenth birthday, he is required
to report for basic military training with the
German infantry. With the Third Reich only
days away from total collapse, he decides to
desert. Although serving the German infantry
is virtually an act of suicide by this point, his
decision does suggest some courage: summary
executions for desertion are still common,

right up to the bitter end. Luckily, the only two soldiers he encounters on the road are as sick of the war as he is; noticing that his arm is in a sling, they let him go. He makes it home to Traunstein, and the loving arms of his parents, safely enough. But shortly afterward the US forces arrive, and he is arrested. He is marched down the road in full uniform to a prisoner-of-war camp, where he remains for several weeks. On June 19, 1945, he is freed. When his missing brother Georg is returned in mid-July, and both brothers are back in the seminary by November, the war may be said to be well and truly behind him.

When Pope Benedict's critics referred to him as "Ratzy the Nazi," they were speaking less about his wartime experiences than of his management style at the Vatican.[2] Most people are less interested in the moral decision-making abilities of a teenager in World War II than in the same person's decisions as a post-war adult with real power. One of Ratzinger's contemporaries, Günter Grass, has admitted in recent years that he was

---

2 On the other hand, one cannot help noting Pope Benedict's little gaffe in March 2009, when he invited back into the fold the Holocaust-denying bishop Richard Williamson. Pope John Paul II had excommunicated Williamson and three other bishops after the fascist Marcel Lefebvre ordained them as bishops for his separatist church in 1988. Benedict claimed that Vatican staff were unaware of Williamson's claims that no Jews were killed in Nazi gas chambers. He added, somewhat lamely, that they should have consulted the Internet before recommending that his excommunication be lifted.

a member of the *Waffen-SS* during World War II. But his life after the war took a different turn from that of the Bavarian seminarian. Much of Grass's literary output is concerned with German guilt over the war, so the blowback he suffered for having tucked away a few skeletons was not of the fatal variety. As for Ratzinger, he did himself no favors with his recollections of those years. In some instances, his memoirs provided ammunition to his critics.

First, his portrait of the war years is silent on some important issues and gratuitous on other, less important ones. For example, his memoirs say nothing about his cousin with Down Syndrome who was taken away by the Nazis. Nor do they mention that, while he was at the BMW plant, he saw detainees from Dachau being treated with brutality when brought in to perform menial tasks. Avoiding unpleasant memories is an all-too-human instinct, but Ratzinger's rose-tinted focus on the bucolic Bavarian countryside, and of the war being far away most of the time, smacks of the ostrich. "Because of the war," he says at one point, "the international public could no longer come to the famous music festival, and so one could get rather good tickets at a very low price. So it was that we were able to go to performances of Beethoven's Ninth Symphony, Mozart's Mass in C-minor, and a concert by the Regensburger Domspatzen." The *Anschluss* as cultural opportunity? Yes, thanks to Nazi Germany's annexation of Austria, the Ratzingers enjoyed the arts like never before.

Second, when it comes to historical figures in the Catholic Church, Ratzinger is lavish with praise where he could be critical. No one can fault him for admiring his great uncle Georg, a nineteenth-century Catholic politician and author who would make it onto a list of the 1,000 most important Bavarian personalities of the past 1,500 years. Georg supported the development of a state based on Catholic principles as an alternative to both Marxism and capitalism. This he would do through the *Bauernbund*, or Farmers' Party, a political alternative to defend the interests of the poor. Unfortunately, the *Bauernbund*'s populist protectionism lent itself to a virulent form of anti-Semitism: Georg Ratzinger blamed the Jews for the suffering of his rural Bavarian constituents. The published record of his bigotry—an embarrassing stain on Georg's legacy—is something his famous great-nephew might have acknowledged. But in *Salt of the Earth*, a book-length interview with the German author and journalist Peter Seewald about a wide range of topics, including his own upbringing, Joseph Ratzinger said nothing of it. Georg's "achievements and his political standing," he concluded, "made everyone proud of him."

The archbishop of Munich, who would one day ordain him and his brother Georg, he similarly praises as a worthy moral example. But Cardinal Michael von Faulhaber is another ethically challenged mentor figure. In 1936, a year after the Nuremburg Laws were passed, Faulhaber had an opportunity to intervene and save the lives of abducted Jews. But the only Jews on whose behalf he was willing to plead were those who had converted to Catholicism. "The state has the right, within its own jurisdiction, to move against the abuses of Judaism," said Faulhaber, adding this partisan caveat: "especially when the Jews, when they are also Bolsheviks and communists, threaten the order of the state." On October 1, 1938, the day Nazi Germany annexed the Sudetenland, Cardinal von Faulhaber ordered the following telegram to be sent to Hitler: "The German episcopacy feels it is its duty, in the name of all Catholics in every diocese, to extend its respectful congratulations and gratitude, and to order that this coming Sunday the church bells be rung in celebration." According to Ratzinger's account in *Milestones*, the church was the only refuge from the dreadful reality of the Third Reich; "the alternative" to its "destructive ideology" that had "stood firm with a force coming to [it] from eternity." Was Cardinal Faulhaber's the "firm" stand he was thinking of? Or Pope Pius XII's concordat with the Nazis his "force from eternity"?

Third, and most problematic, is Ratzinger's argument that resistance to the Nazis was "impossible." In fact, some Catholics did resist, but his memoirs do not acknowledge them. Some of the most courageous resistance in Traunstein came from the local Communists, but they aren't mentioned either. His biographer, longtime Vatican observer John Allen Jr, has perhaps put it best: "There is no shame in being unwilling to risk one's life; but equally, the urge to self-preservation is not the same thing as impossibility." Allen provides a useful contrast between the lessons Ratzinger brought away from World War II and those of Bernard Häring, a Redemptorist priest and moral theologian. Häring's experience of witnessing "the most absurd obedience by Christians toward a criminal regime" led him, after the war, to return to moral theology and teach it. Its core concepts, he said, "would not be obedience but responsibility, the courage to be responsible." For Ratzinger, on the other hand, obedience would become the dominant, Hobbesian theme of his life: from his own strategic obedience to the Third Reich and doctrinal obedience to the word of God, to others' religious obedience to the all-powerful church and, ultimately, to Joseph Ratzinger.

A "Truth-Seeker" Is Born

In 1947, Ratzinger completed his two-year study of philosophy and transferred to the Herzogliches Georgianum, an ancient Bavarian theological institute associated with the University of Munich. The star of the faculty was Friedrich William Maier. More than three decades earlier, Maier had been banned from Catholic teaching for a reason that now seems laughable by Ratzingerian standards of heresy: his "two source theory" of the Gospels—that Mark is the source for later Gospels according to Matthew and Luke—contradicted ancient tradition that saw in Matthew the oldest Gospel, said to have been written by the apostle "in a Hebrew dialect." This transgression was seen as a surrender to liberalism, so Maier had to leave the world of Catholic teaching. During World War I, he served as a military chaplain. Later, he worked as a prison chaplain. After returning to the fold in 1924 to teach the New Testament at Breslau, he was understandably bitter about his lengthy time in purgatory.

Maier was forced to leave teaching for no other reason than that his challenge of a second-century tradition was deemed "a threat to the very foundations of faith itself," as Ratzinger puts it in his memoirs. In retrospect, he regarded Maier's example as a warning to all who dare to question church orthodoxy—despite the fact that Maier's theory is now "accepted by almost everyone." As his student, Ratzinger was less than dazzled, perhaps because Maier represented "those who look upon dogma, not as a shaping force, but only as a shackle, a negation, and a limit in the construction of theology." By this time, Ratzinger was well on his way to becoming dogma's greatest defender.

As a theologian, he showed much philosophical vigour, as conversant in Kant and Heidegger or Plato and Aristotle as he was in Aquinas or Augustine. One of his mentors at this time was Gottlieb Söhngen. Söhngen belonged to a metaphysical tradition that had a passion for truth-seeking and, as Ratzinger put it, "asking unrelenting questions about the foundation and goal of all the real," including "the basic question concerning the relationship between rationality and mystery." He was not a mere positivist, and "always developed his thought on the basis of the sources themselves." Under Söhngen's influence, Ratzinger developed a sense that "dogma was conceived, not as an external shackle, but as the living source that made knowledge of the truth possible in the first place." He was also a big fan of Henri de Lubac's Catholicism. Recalling de Lubac's influence on him in his early twenties, Ratzinger in *Milestones* sounds almost Marxist. "De Lubac was leading his readers out of a narrowly individualistic and moralistic mode of faith and into the freedom of an essentially social faith, conceived and lived as a we," he wrote in his memoirs. "A faith that, precisely as such and according to its nature, was also hope, affecting history as a whole, and not only the promise of a private blissfulness to individuals."

On June 29, 1951—fittingly, the feast of the apostles Peter and Paul—Georg and Joseph Ratzinger were ordained together as priests in the Freising cathedral. The ceremony was conducted by the aforementioned Cardinal Michael von Faulhaber. A month later, Joseph began his ministry as an assistant pastor in Bogenhausen, the upper-class district of Munich, in the parish of the Precious Blood. The daily demands of parish life must have taken some adjustment after all that time in the ivory tower. His weekly duties included sixteen hours of religious instruction at five different levels; two masses and two different sermons every Sunday; an hourly confessional from six to seven a.m. (four hours on Saturday afternoons); several burials a week; youth ministry needs; and other ceremonies such as baptisms and weddings, etc.

His memoirs speak fondly, if not entirely convincingly, of this period: life as a parish priest must have been drudgery for a cloistered academic unaccustomed to the workload demands of an entitled, upper-crust parish. Ratzinger lasted only a year at Precious Blood before reporting to the seminary in Freising on October 1, 1952. By the fall of 1953, he had his first PhD in theology, from the University of Munich. At this point, his career was almost derailed by his first exegetical run-in with another theologian. For his *habilitation* (the degree qualifying one to teach at a German university), Ratzinger shifted his study area from Augustine to the Middle Ages, with Saint Bonaventure and the concept of revelation as his focus. Revelation, he said, "now appeared no longer simply as a communication of truths to the intellect but as a historical action of God in which truth becomes gradually unveiled."

One of Ratzinger's advisors, professor Michael Schmaus, said that his *habilitation* did not meet the scholarly standards; he dismissed it as "modernist." Ratzinger's version of the story, years later, was that he had been forthright in a manner "not advisable to a beginner": he had written that the study of the

Middle Ages in Munich—mainly represented by the works of Schmaus—had "come to almost a complete halt at its pre-war state." The frostiness between Ratzinger and Schmaus would not dissolve until the 1970s, by which point the former student would be singing from the same conservative song sheet as his erstwhile advisor. In any event, Ratzinger's *habilitation* was ultimately approved.

On April 15, 1959, he began lectures at the University of Bonn as a professor of fundamental theology—the chair once sought in vain by Gottlieb Söhngen. Looking back on this period, Ratzinger relished the memory of addressing a large and "very full" lecture hall, where the students "reacted enthusiastically to the new tone they thought they could hear" in his words. One of them, Horst Ferdinand, said that his lectures "were prepared down to the millimeter. He gave them by paraphrasing the text that he'd prepared with formulations that at times seemed to fit together like a mosaic... In some lectures, as in the pauses in a concert, you could have heard a pin drop." Said another student, Viktor Hahn: "The room was always packed, the students adored him. He had a beautiful and simple language. The language of a believer." It was this quality, and his growing reputation as a published scholar, that ultimately won Ratzinger an invitation to the Second Vatican Council as theological consultant and ghostwriter to Cardinal Joseph Frings of Cologne.

II

Augustine's Apostle

Auctoritas, non veritas, facit legem. (*Authority, not truth, makes law.*)
—Thomas Hobbes

Half a century later, Vatican II (1962–65) is today regarded as a groundbreaking event in the 2,000-year history of the Roman Catholic Church. A sweeping review of the world's largest religion, the Council covered both the church's internal workings and its relationship to the outside world. Unlike the First Vatican Council, best known for its declaration of papal infallibility before it was abruptly adjourned by the Franco-Prussian War in 1870, Vatican II sought a much more progressive mandate. Because the second Council sought to address real inequities and bring the church into the modern world, the presiding pope became the most significant of the twentieth century simply by opening it.

Angelo Roncalli, as Pope John XXIII, was determined to move the church away from Biblical literalism and toward a more pluralistic view of Catholicism. By emphasizing the church's role as an agent of change, Pope John hoped to reconcile modern human experience with Catholic precepts. A practical progressive, he was ahead of the 1960s curve. He knew the church was facing new challenges driven by political, socio-economic, and technological change; it needed to adapt to these changes in order to remain relevant. It was time, he said, to open the windows and let in some fresh air. He called it *aggiornamento*, or "bringing up to date," a sort of ecclesiological equivalent (decades before the fact) of Soviet *perestroika*.

Vatican II was not without its flaws. The proceedings were plagued from the start by wrangling between the Council and the Roman Curia, whose members were trying to keep the Council under its control. Pope John's decision to appoint curial cardinals as presidents of the individual council commissions and curial theologians as both general secretaries and secretaries of the commissions often led to political gridlock.[3] The list of taboo subjects for discussion included divorce, marriage of priests, a new order for nomination of bishops, reform of the curia, and reform of the papacy—including a review of infallibility. Pope John's death in 1963, less than a year after Vatican II's opening, didn't help matters: one discussion by the cardinals, involving a comprehensive policy on birth control, would be halted by his successor, Giovanni Battista Enrico Antonio Maria Montini (Pope Paul VI), and referred to a papal commission.

Despite all this, the Council did produce a significant new mandate for change. For example, it superseded Pope Pius XII on a range of issues including ecumenism, liturgical reform, freedom of religion, and the church's troubling record of anti-Semitism and "Red"-baiting. Vatican II resulted in a much more

---

3 Recalled Hans Küng, who was invited by Pope John as an expert participant: "It was as if, in parliament, the parliamentary committees of an investigation were completely controlled by the controlling ministers themselves and their helpers."

constructive attitude toward Islam and the other world religions, and it recognized that "salvation" was possible outside of Christianity—even for atheists and agnostics, if they acted in accordance with their conscience and in a manner consistent with the gospels. Perhaps most importantly, the Council's Constitution on the church replaced its eleventh-century image as Holy Roman Empire with the more egalitarian principle of the "People of God": everyone belonged to the church, from the newly christened baby to the lay educator. According to this concept, office-holders in the church did not stand above the People of God but were part of them; they were not rulers of the faithful but their servants. Cynics and far-right clerics would scoff at this New Age privileging of warm and fuzzy "spirituality" over the cold, hard orthodoxy of "religious truth." Ratzinger would eventually become one of its fiercest critics.

An Apostle for "Truth"

To understand the young theologian's thinking when he arrived at Vatican II, it helps to examine his ecclesiology. One can learn a lot about a theologian from the saints he reveres, and Ratzinger's favorite was Aurelius Augustine (354–430). Given the facts of Augustine's life, and what we know about Ratzinger/ Benedict today, the similarity between the two thinkers is striking. Saint Augustine's campaign for a universal Catholic Church to solve a schism between two rival faiths (the Catholic Church was spread over the entire world and was numerically the largest, he argued, so it was therefore the best) has echoes today in Ratzinger's peculiar Roman Catholic chauvinism. And *The*

Rule of Augustine, particularly Chapter VII ("Governance and Obedience"), might be said to have Ratzingerian overtones in its subordination of the individual to the church as institution. "The superior should be obeyed as a father with the respect due him so as not to offend God in his person, and, even more so, the priest who bears responsibility for you all," said Augustine. "It is by being more obedient, therefore, that you show mercy not only toward yourselves but also toward the superior whose higher rank among you exposes him all the more to greater peril."

Augustine's belief that violence against heretics and schismatics could be theologically justified can be seen in some of Ratzinger's comments urging "understanding" towards gay-bashers. Augustine's reading of a phrase from Jesus's parable of the banquet, *Coge intrare*, as "Compel [rather than invite] those outside to come in" is similar to Ratzinger's "orders" rather than "suggestions" when meting out discipline. Throughout the ages, says the liberal theologian Hans Küng, Augustine "became the key witness for the theological justification of forcible conversions, the Inquisition, and holy war against deviants of all kinds." Some would say this applies equally to Ratzinger.

We also have Saint Augustine to thank for the doctrine of original sin. This idea tries to explain the sin of every human being as having its origins in the Biblical story of the fall of Adam, which was based on "primal" or sexual sin. Yes, even newborn babies fall victim to eternal death—until they're baptized—all because of Adam's lack of restraint in the Garden of Eden. Saint Augustine believed that sexual pleasure for its own sake (i.e., not for procreation) was sinful and to be suppressed. Finally, his view of world history could be reduced to a series of dualistic, us-and-them distinctions—or, as Küng put it, "a great clash between belief and unbelief, humility and arrogance, love and the quest for power, salvation and damnation." Ratzinger's enforcement of the faith many years after Vatican II would begin to reveal a certain logic when considered in the full light of his Augustinian outlook.

At thirty-five years of age, Ratzinger was one of the youngest theological experts invited to Vatican II when he accompanied Cardinal Frings as an advisor. A member of the Central Preparatory Commission for the Council, Frings was sent drafts of texts (*schemata*) that were to be presented to the conciliary fathers for their discussion and vote after the assembly had convened. He sent Ratzinger the texts for criticism and suggestions for improvement. Although the documents gave the young Ratzinger "an impression of rigidity and of insufficient openness, of an excessive link with neo-Scholastic theology, of thinking too much professorial and too little pastoral," as he would put it in *Milestones*, he found no grounds for "radical rejection" of what was being proposed. On the contrary: when he arrived at Vatican II he was still seen as a leading figure in the *liberal* wing of the German church—an impression only reinforced by the events of November 8, 1963.

On that morning, Cardinal Frings delivered a blistering attack on Cardinal Alfredo Ottaviani, the leading conservative voice at Vatican II and prefect of the Holy Office of the Roman Curia (otherwise known as the Inquisition, later renamed the Congregation for the Doctrine of the Faith). The strategy behind this assault—which painted the Inquisition and Cardinal Ottaviani as unjust, undemocratic, and author-itarian—was to pre-empt any move by the curial cardinals to rubber stamp the Vatican II documents before a full discussion of them had taken place. "The Holy Office does not fit the needs of our time. It does great harm to the faithful and is the cause of scandal throughout the world," said Frings, speaking words written by Ratzinger. And then this: "No one should be judged and condemned without being heard, without knowing what he is accused of, and without having the opportunity to amend what he can reasonably be reproached with."

The conciliary fathers erupted into applause several times during Frings' address. If only they knew who had written these lambasting words, and what would become of him. If only they knew that, eighteen years later, Joseph Ratzinger would have Ottaviani's job and be accused of much the same things; that his passionate call for due process in 1963 would be abandoned, all those years later, in favor of a punitive approach that would make Ottaviani's modus operandi seem quaint by comparison.

There were two principal tracks for discussion at Vatican II, as Ratzinger put it in his memoirs: "the interior life of the Church" and "the Church vis-à-vis the world." As far as the former was concerned, reform of the liturgy was the main issue—although this was not exactly controversial among the conciliary fathers. Cardinal Montini (who, as Pope Paul VI, would take over the presidency of Vatican II after the death of Pope John XXIII on June 3, 1963) saw liturgical change as one of the less substantial tasks on the agenda. In Ratzinger's view, the real drama began when *The Sources of Revelation* (on scripture and tradition) was presented for discussion. The problem, he recalled later, was that the "historical-critical method" of Biblical interpretation favored by liberals had become the dominant Catholic theology in the climate of the Council. "By its very nature, this method has no patience with any restrictions imposed by an authoritative Magisterium," Ratzinger recalled in *Milestones*. "In other words, believing now amounted to having opinions and was in need of continual revision."

Of course, *real* liberals, such as the German Jesuit Karl Rahner, saw things differently. Where Ratzinger spoke of "revelation" and the "authoritative Magisterium," Rahner's thought was sprinkled with words like "grace," "mystery," and God as a "possibility" that was up to the beholder to see. Rahner's theology was based on the idea that all human beings have a latent awareness of God in any experience of limitation in knowledge or freedom as finite subjects; such experience he described as "categorical" in the Kantian sense, because it was the "condition of possibility" for such knowledge and freedom. Given their subsequent differences, it is noteworthy that, at Vatican II, Ratzinger and Rahner collaborated on a schema about revelation for Cardinal Frings. According to Ratzinger, the second, "more developed" version that the two men produced was more Rahner's work than his. The collaborative experience revealed that the two theologians "lived on two different theological planets": Ratzinger was from the Munich School of Scriptural Literalists; Rahner was from the Heidegger School of Reasonable Doubt. Or so the former implied in his memoirs. "[Rahner's] was a speculative and philosophical theology in which Scripture and the Fathers in the end did not play an important role and in which the historical dimension was really of little significance," wrote Ratzinger. "For my part, my whole intellectual formation had been shaped by Scripture and the Fathers and profoundly historical thinking."

It was during this period—between the summer of 1963, when Ratzinger was approached by the University of Munster and invited by dogma specialist Hermann Volk to take his chair, and the Bamberg Conference of 1966, when he sounded the first warning bells about "false renewal"—that Ratzinger's position hardened into conservatism, and he began to see Vatican II more as a destructive force for the church than a positive one. "The impression grew steadily that nothing was now stable in the Church, that everything was open to revision," he would later write. Vatican II was like a great church parliament that could "shape everything according to its own desires." The faith, he added, "no longer seemed exempt from human decision-making but rather was now apparently determined by it." It was in this vein that a kind of elitism began to take hold in Ratzinger, fueled by fear of the times he was living in. He was not excluding himself when he penned the following: "The role that the theologians had assumed at the Council was creating ever more clearly a new confidence among scholars, who now understood themselves to be the truly knowledgeable experts in the faith and therefore no longer subordinate to the shepherds."

By "the shepherds," Ratzinger was referring here to the bishops. In his view, the bishops—along with parish level priests— had been fiddling with the faith by advancing all manner of touchy-feely nonsense in their post-conciliary ministry. What really made his blood boil about Vatican II was "the idea of an ecclesial sovereignty of the people in which the people itself [sic] determines what it wants to understand by Church, since 'Church' already seemed very clearly defined as 'People of God.' The idea of 'The Church from Below,' the 'Church of the People,' which then became the goal of reform particularly in the context of liberation theology, was thus heralded."

Seeing what had happened to his native East Germany under the Iron Curtain—or hearing from family and friends who still lived there, once he had left—frightened Ratzinger. The fear of Communism, endemic in eastern Europeans with first-hand knowledge of its atrocities, has often led to a deterministic tendency to conflate all "leftist" ideas, anywhere in the world, as part of the same dystopian nightmare. Although the reality of Eastern bloc Communism had no equivalent in the so-called "West"—no matter how fervent its leftist student movements— any discussion of theology based on even the thinnest strand of Marxist analysis was beyond the pale for Ratzinger, regardless of how or where such ideas might be applied. In his view, Western society was on a slippery slope to the gulag; entirely susceptible to the Stalinist horror show. Thus, to prevent the faith from being supplanted by totalitarianism, it was absolutely vital for Ratzinger that the church become a champion of its absolute truths. This was more of a gradual awakening than a Road to Damascus moment, but it would become a life-long and unshakable conviction for him. Fear, by the mid-1960s, was becoming his new watchword; a loyal companion to obedience.

Oddly enough, this hardening of Ratzinger's theological outlook was not yet sufficiently evident to cause alarm for Hans Küng, who came knocking on his door in the summer of 1966 to offer him a position at Tubingen University. The two had met in 1957 at a congress of dogmatic theologians in Innsbruck, just after Ratzinger had completed reviewing Küng's doctoral work on the Protestant theologian Karl Barth. Küng's piece was an ecumenical tour de force that nicely bridged the gap between Protestant and Catholic conceptions of salvation. Ratzinger had read it with pleasure, even though Küng's theological style was different from his own; it was Küng's "winning openness and straightforwardness" that impressed his colleague. Küng had arrived at Tubingen in 1960, after leaving the Sorbonne in Paris, to take the chair in fundamental theology. At Vatican II, a personal friendship had developed between him and Ratzinger; a friendship, the latter has noted, that not even a "rather serious argument" about conciliar theology could jeopardize. So when the chair in dogmatics came open at Tubingen, Küng didn't bother writing up a *terna*, the usual list of three candidates for the position. Ratzinger was his only choice, and he phoned him in Munster to confirm acceptance. The faculty approved this protocol breach, happy to have landed such a star.

Things went smoothly for Ratzinger's first few months at Tubingen. On good terms with everyone in the faculty, he would later describe his colleagues as "first-rate." During this time, liberal Catholics he could still count as friends included Küng, Rahner, and the Flemish Dominican Edward Schillebeeckx. But in 1967, shortly after Tubingen celebrated the 150th anniversary of its Faculty for Catholic Theology, the outside world began arriving at Ratzinger's doorstep. The nascent student movement of the 1960s was comprised of a much more confrontational core than the compliant, pistol-whipped youth of Ratzinger's upbringing during World War II in Germany. What was worse, he thought, was that the current youngsters had been captured by "modern" pop culture and politics. "At almost a moment's notice," he would recall, "there was a change in the ideological 'paradigm' by which the students and a part of the teachers thought." Suddenly, the influences of Rudolf Bultmann's theology and Heideggerian existentialism were "replaced by the Marxist ... The Marxist revolution kindled the whole university with its fervor, shaking it to its very foundations."

What upset Ratzinger the most was that the theological faculties were no longer serving as "a bulwark" against "the Marxist temptation" but, at Tubingen, were suddenly becoming "its real ideological center." In his view, the theologians were allowing the destruction of the faith through a "Marxist messianism" that was "eliminating God and replacing him with the political activity of man." By 1968, the student protests that had exploded in the streets of Paris and spread across Europe were reaching Tubingen. Ratzinger described these protests as "manifestations of a brutal, cruel, tyrannical ideology." Students held sit-ins at his lectures, where they shouted "Accursed be Jesus!", condemned the crucifix as a symbol of sado-masochism, and snatched a microphone from his hand. "With the spirit of utopia, forced by the events of 1968 ... the better future world suddenly became the sole object of faith. Or better: there was no more 'object of faith,' but rather only the projection of a hope, which in its turn signified action," Ratzinger recalled in *Milestones*. "Even Christians stopped talking about redemption through the cross, about the resurrection of Jesus Christ, and about our hope in eternal life. They, too, came to speak almost only of our society, for the better civilization that would be born. Utopia became the only dogma that inspired thought and action. [But] the all-dominant utopia was unmasked as an empty phantom: staring at the void in a dreamy state, we lose sight of reality."

Apart from his theological objections—the sense that ideology was being presented in the name of the faith and that the church was being "used as its instrument"—Ratzinger was also emotionally rattled by the confrontation. He couldn't stand the heat of the student protests but preferred the cool, solitary comfort of his own thoughts (interrupted only by the effortless transmission of his words to the empty vessels of young believers' minds). By this point, his opposition to Vatican II was of a piece with his virulent anti-Marxism and anti-liberalism, which was only reinforced by the protests.

For Ratzinger, there would be no relief from the Age of Aquarius—not even after he left Tubingen in 1969 and retreated to his native Bavaria to become the chair in Dogmatics at Regensburg. "The waves of Marxist revolt naturally pounded against our young Alma Mater too," he wrote. "Particularly within the circle of assistant professors there were many determined leftists." Increasingly isolated politically, he turned his back on Küng and the other progressive theologians from this point on. He no longer agreed with them, and he thought they had betrayed the church by siding with the students. No matter: he would soon find new allies. Shortly after his arrival at Regensburg, Pope Paul VI appointed him to the International Papal Theological Commission. Also on the Commission were Jorge Medina and Hans Urs von Balthasar. These men, and others, would form a circle of like-minded conservatives who would support Ratzinger's view of the church. Together, they would take back the church and redefine it on their own reactionary terms.

Going on the Offensive

In Regensburg, Ratzinger removed himself somewhat from the daily rabble of classroom politics. With thinkers such as Balthasar and Medina, he had found two kindred spirits who saw in the Council the same flaws he did. Thus he was able to spend more time preparing a theological counter-offensive to Vatican II. Balthasar, who hadn't been invited to the deliberations in Rome, was looking for new solutions, as Ratzinger put it, "to divert theology from the partisanship toward which it was more and more tending." One of his main targets was *Concilium*, a quarterly magazine of liberal and progressive Roman Catholic thought. Founded in 1964 while Vatican II was in session, its goal was to support and continue the Council's work. Ratzinger had been among its early contributors, but by the late 1960s he and Balthasar had grown disenchanted with its editorial direction, and in the early '70s began opposing its liberal stance. Ratzinger thought *Concilium* was trying to undermine the magisterium by proposing a vision of the church more in keeping with the anarchy of 1968 than with the recognized traditions of Rome. And so in 1972, he launched a new magazine to rival it. In a sense, *Communio* (from "communion") was a perfect title for it—a kind of rebuttal to the "People of God" concept of popular sovereignty. For the next five years, Ratzinger would use it as his bully pulpit—and his launching pad to bigger and better things.

On July 24, 1976, Cardinal Julius Dopfner, the archbishop of Munich, died suddenly. Rumors began circulating that Ratzinger, by now the vice-president of Regensburg University, was a candidate to replace him. But he didn't take these rumors seriously. "My limitations with regard to health were as well known as my inability in matters of governance and administration," he wrote in *Milestones*, clearly not imagining that he would still be going strong as supreme pontiff more than three-and-a-half decades later: "I knew I was called to the scholar's life and never considered anything else." The position sat vacant for several months. On March 24, 1977, Pope Paul VI named Ratzinger the archbishop of Munich and Freising. Four days later, he was ordained bishop. Then, on June 27, he received his cardinal's red cap in Rome. Nearly a quarter of a century after completing his one and only year in the priesthood, he was once again a man of the cloth. It was a giant leap, going from assistant pastor of Precious Blood to full cardinal of Munich and Freising. For his episcopal motto, Ratzinger chose a phrase from the Third Letter of John, "Co-worker of the Truth."

As Ratzinger made his way up the career ladder, things went from bad to worse with Hans Küng. For years, he had publicly berated his old friend and former colleague who had gotten him the plum job at Tubingen. In 1970, Küng published *Infallible? An Inquiry*, which challenged the 1870 declaration of papal infallibility at Vatican I, dismissing its theological foundations and describing the ruling as a disaster for ecumenism. Ratzinger was a theological advisor to the German Bishops Council that denounced the book and made no secret of the fact. Two years later, Küng nonetheless invited him, all expenses paid, to a graduate seminar on infallibility at Tubingen. Ratzinger gladly accepted, before carving up his host in public. In 1974, he dismissed Küng's masterpiece, *On Being a Christian*, as "undisguised arrogance," its theology a "rootless and ultimately nonbinding" form of certitude that "lands ultimately in the abstruse" and "leads nowhere."

Five years later, as Cardinal of Munich empowered by the new right-wing pope, Ratzinger went after Küng in earnest. In the spring of 1979, Küng had written an introduction to another author's book on papal infallibility, apparently breaking an agreement he had made the previous year to say nothing more on the subject. In September, he published a highly critical account of John Paul II's first year as pope that received broad international media coverage. The gloves were off. In early November, the pope summoned Ratzinger and the other German cardinals to Rome to discuss Küng's fate. Afterward, Ratzinger told the German Catholic news agency that Küng could not teach Catholic theology while holding the views that he did. A month later, the German bishops held a press conference announcing that Küng was no longer a qualified Catholic theologian, and his *mission canonica* was withdrawn. On December 31—the last day of the 1970s—Ratzinger justified this high-profile expulsion in terms that now seem highly ironic. "The Christian believer is a simple person," he said. "Bishops should protect the faith of these little people against the power of the intellectuals."[4]

---

4 Küng was clever enough to find a way around his discipline. Since he could no longer teach at Tubingen's College of Catholic Theology, he simply transferred the Institute (of which he was director) to the University of Tubingen itself—a state institution. He thus remained a full professor of ecumenical theology.

III

The Smiling Pope

I have noticed two things that appear to be in very short supply in the Vatican: honesty and a good cup of coffee.

—Pope John Paul I, to a friend from northern Italy

Two months after receiving his cardinal's red cap from Pope Paul in June of 1977, Joseph Ratzinger was enjoying his first holidays at the diocesan seminary in Bressanone when he received a surprise guest: Cardinal Albino Luciani, Patriarch of Venice. Ratzinger would later tell interviewers how "unworthy of such a visit" he had felt at the time; that he was humbled by the gesture because he saw Luciani as a man of exceeding "goodness," "luminous faith," "exquisite courtesy," "great simplicity," and "wide culture." Nonetheless, the two men enjoyed each other's company like equals and shared fond reminiscences of their respective seminary days. Exactly a year later, at the papal conclave of August 1978, they met again. This time, following the death of Pope Paul VI, the church was at a crossroads. In the five weeks that followed, both men would play key roles in the drama. They likely didn't know it at the time, but they represented opposing forces.

❧

Albino Luciani's life story offers a stark and telling contrast to Joseph Ratzinger's personal narrative. It also serves as a poignant reminder of the road *not* taken by the Vatican, or Ratzinger himself, since 1981.[5] He was born into poverty on October 17, 1912. His life-long lack of any sense of entitlement was probably due to the fact that food was so hard to come by in the small mountain village of Canale d'Agordo, about 120 kilometres north of Venice, where he was born and raised. His father, Giovanni Luciani, was an itinerant laborer who frequently traveled outside Italy to find work as a bricklayer, electrician, or mechanic. The poverty of their rural mountain community—the Luciani home was a converted barn whose only source of heat was a wood-burning stove—was one reason he became a committed Communist. When Giovanni decided to run in local elections for the Socialist party, Albino endured the catcalls of traditional Catholics who deplored Communism. He would never forget his mother's dread at seeing her husband's face on Socialist party posters around the village. To avoid the teasing of other village children, he buried himself in books and became a voracious reader. By age seven, he had devoured the works of Twain, Dickens, and Jules Verne[6]—not bad in a country where half the adults were functionally illiterate. He entered the seminary at age eleven and was ordained at twenty-three,

---

5 I am indebted to David Yallop's *In God's Name* (New York: Carroll & Graf, 2007) for much of the biographical material that follows.

6 His love for these writers would much later result in the publication *Illustrissimi*, a collection of letters to various literary and historical characters. Each letter comments on an aspect of modern life designed to appeal to the "recipient," along with some thoughtful advice on prudence, responsibility, humility, and charity. Among many others, Luciani wrote "to" Twain, Dickens, Walter Scott, Goethe, and Marlowe.

completing his PhD in theology at Gregorian University in Rome. His thesis was entitled *The Origin of the Human Soul According to Antonio Rosmini*. Toward the end of World War II, when the seventeen-year-old Joseph Ratzinger was being press-ganged into service by the Nazis in Bavaria, the thirty-two-year-old Luciani was brushing up on his German so he could hear the confessions of captured Third Reich soldiers.

Unlike Ratzinger's journey to Rome, Luciani's was marked by continuous priestly ministry. In 1949, he published his first book, a scholastic work that would cement his reputation, for some, as one of the finest teachers of the Catholic catechism in the twentieth century. In 1958, at age forty-six, he was ordained Bishop of Vittorio Veneto by the newly crowned Pope John XXIII. In celebration, he read aloud Chapter Twenty-Three of Thomas à Kempis's *The Imitation of Christ*, which emphasizes four principles of humility—the first three of which most Christians, especially popes, seldom achieve:

1. Try to do another's work, not just your own.

2. Choose to have less rather than more.

3. Choose the lowest place and be less than anyone else.

4. Long and pray that the will of God may be fully realized in your life.

Leading by Example

For his investiture as bishop, Luciani was offered money, food, and gifts from the priests of his diocese. He turned them all down. He also turned down a luxurious apartment, choosing instead a more spartan existence in the Castle of San Martino. As for his leadership style, Luciani believed in power sharing. When it came time to establish a new Presbyterial Council, he decided not to submit nominations but instead allowed a democratic election with no interference from his office. He also placed great importance on accountability. In August 1962, two priests in his diocese were convinced by a real estate seller to get involved in property speculation. One confessed to Luciani that the amount of money they'd sunk into the investment was more than two billion lire. Rather than excuse the priests or hide behind ecclesiastical immunity, Luciani displayed some first-rate damage prevention skills. First, he went to the city's major news daily, told the editors what had happened, then pleaded with them not to treat the story in a sensationalist manner: he was going to call a meeting of his 400 priests and hold the diocese accountable. "I intend to sell ecclesiastical treasure," he told his priests. "I further intend to sell one of our buildings. The money will be used to repay every single lira that these priests owe. I ask for your agreement." He got it.

Luciani was not so easy to politically pigeonhole. Over the years, the right would accuse him of being in thrall to his Communist roots; the left mistrusted him as a theological conservative or, at best, a cautious reformer.[7] Regardless, it was not

---

7 While he was Patriarch of Venice, Luciani was accused of disbanding a student

until he was invited to the Second Vatican Council and experienced the conciliar declaration *On Religious Freedom* that he had his own Road to Damascus moment: his realization that the anti-modernist theology of Pius X, which he had taught his students in the catechism, was wrong. The key issue for him was birth control. On April 23, 1966, the pontifical commission on the family, which Pope Paul VI had established in order to study the church's position on contraception, finally released its report. By sixty-four votes to four, a group of theologians, legal experts, historians, sociologists, doctors, obstetricians, and married couples recommended that the church support some form of contraception.

Luciani agreed with the report, but His Holiness was not prepared to move on it. Despite a persuasive argument supported by a broad range of Catholics, Pope Paul sat on the commission report for two years, preferring to wait for a minority report from a group of conservatives before making a decision. In April 1968, Luciani sent his own submission to the pope, a personal plea that spoke of the widespread misery the birth control ban had caused. Contraception was an issue of poverty and social justice, not morality, he wrote; he himself had seen firsthand the consequences of church doctrine for his own brother, Eduardo, a devout Catholic who struggled to support his family of ten children. Luciani concluded by recommending the anovulant pill, developed by the American biologist Gregory Pinkus,

group that was in favor of relaxing divorce laws. In fact, all he did was remove a priest who had been advising the group: Luciani was concerned that the group had misused Vatican II documents, as well as misinterpreting Church authorities and theologians, in building its case to support liberalized divorce laws.

as the official Catholic birth control pill. He received no reply.

Three months later, on July 25, 1968, *Humanae Vitae* was released. The papal encyclical ignored the majority opinion of the papal commission, reaffirming that artificial birth control was contrary to God's law. Pope Paul recommended abstinence or the "rhythm method" for married couples who preferred not to procreate when they copulate. Despite widespread hostility toward *Humanae Vitae*, Luciani did not openly condemn the encyclical, as some priests did. Instead, he urged strength among lay Catholics and compassion in clerics dealing with those who violated the church's order. The pope was so impressed by this show of moderation that, in September 1969, he offered Luciani the position of Patriarch of Venice upon the death of Cardinal Giovanni Urbani. But Luciani turned him down. Three months later the pope repeated the offer, and this time he accepted.

Upon assuming office on February 8, 1970, Luciani was presented with a donation of one million lire from Vittorio Veneto, in gratitude for his decade of service as bishop. He turned it down. He also canceled a planned gala celebration for his arrival, calling it decadent. Instead, the new cardinal arrived in Venice carrying only some linen, small furniture, and books. Nor did he replace the robes left for him by his predecessor; instead, over the years, his nuns would mend and re-mend them. Meanwhile, his generosity became legendary. In one example cited by David Yallop, a diocesan priest who was a landowner raised the rent on one of his houses, forcing the eviction of an unemployed schoolteacher. Luciani first offered the use of a house that had been reserved for him as Patriarch. But the Vatican blocked the move, so instead he wrote a cheque for three million lire. Soon, crowds of poor people began showing up at his office.

In 1971, Pope Paul nominated Luciani to attend the World Synod of Bishops. For one of its two subject tracks, Justice in the World, the Patriarch of Venice offered his own suggestion of how to help poor countries: the more fortunate churches could tax themselves and pay one percent of their income to the Vatican aid organizations. In September 1972, Pope Paul visited Venice and addressed a crowd of 20,000 faithful in Saint Mark's Square. At one point, he removed his stole and placed it on the shoulders of his host, a gesture of respect for Luciani's righteousness. The crowd went wild. "Pope Paul VI made me blush to the roots of my hair," Luciani would later recall. "Never have I blushed so much!" Six months later, in March 1973, he became Cardinal of Venice.

Married to the Mob

One of the issues that gnawed at Luciani's conscience was the church's shoddy treatment of people with disabilities. Even priests from his own diocese displayed un-Christian mean-spiritedness by protesting his decision to give First Communion to a group of disabled parishioners. ("These creatures do not understand," they told him. He replied by ordering them to attend the event.) In 1972, he decided it would make sense to help society's unfortunate through the "priests' bank," Banca Cattolica del Veneto, which had always provided low-interest loans to the Venetian clergy to do good works. But there was a problem: the low-interest loans had recently stopped, and the priests were told they now had to pay full interest on any future loans—no matter how righteous the cause.

It turned out that the bank had been sold, and at a huge profit, without Luciani or anyone from Venice being consulted. The seller? Paul Marcinkus, head of the Institute for Works of Religion (the Italian acronym is IOR), otherwise known as the Vatican Bank. The buyer? Roberto Calvi of Banco Ambrosiano in Milan. The bishops of the region approached Luciani and asked him to raise holy hell at the Vatican. Luciani decided to seek more information first, so he approached Monsignor Giovanni Benelli, the number two under Secretary of State Cardinal Jean Villot. Benelli came back with even worse news: the sale also involved tax evasion and illegal movement of shares. When Luciani returned to Venice to tell his bishops what had happened, they all pulled their money out of the Banco Ambrosiano.

In May 1973, Benelli visited the newly minted Cardinal Luciani to inform him about an unusual delegation he'd recently received at the Vatican: a US Department of Justice official responsible for organized crime and racketeering, the strike force chief from New York's southern district, and two FBI officials. What the Americans told Benelli's staff at the Secretariat of State was sobering, to say the least: a police investigation of the New York mafia had led to Rome and the discovery that $14.5 million in counterfeit US bonds had gone to the Vatican Bank. Someone with financial authority in the Vatican—Paul Marcinkus—had ordered the fake bonds, and the $14.5 million was merely a down payment on $950 million in counterfeit bonds. Marcinkus and Italian banker and businessman Michele Sindona, an underworld figure who became an adviser to the Vatican Bank after Giovanni Montini's ascendancy to the papacy, wanted the bonds so that they could buy Bastogi, a giant Italian company with wide interests including property, mining, and chemicals.

By early 1976, Sindona's empire was crumbling. Banks were collapsing in Italy, Switzerland, Germany, and the US. The Italian media were claiming that the Vatican had lost more than $100 million USD. Meanwhile, the Don Orione School for the handicapped in Venice did not have enough money for schoolbooks. In one issue of the diocesan magazine, Luciani encouraged his parish priests and sanctuary rectors to sell their gold, necklaces, and precious objects, and donate the proceeds to the school. He himself would sell the bejeweled cross and gold chain that had belonged to Pius XII and which Pope John had given him when he was made a bishop. He would also sell to the highest bidder a pectoral cross with a gold chain, and a ring of Pope John, which had been given to Venice by Pope Paul during his September 1972 visit.

On August 6, 1978, Pope Paul died after a lengthy illness. The conclave to choose his successor would not occur for nearly three more weeks. On August 13, a group of Catholics calling themselves the Committee for the Responsible Election of the Pope (CREP) held a press conference at the Columbus Hotel in Rome. Father Andrew Greeley fielded questions from more than 400 reporters. Greeley was not a committee member but was part of a group of theologians who, on behalf of the committee, had written up a job description for the ideal pope. What was needed, they said, was "a man of holiness, a man of hope, a man of joy. A holy man who can smile. A pope not for all Catholics but for all peoples. A man totally free from the slightest taint of financial organizational wheeling and dealing." The job description also made reference to the contemporary media environment; the fact that the new pope was likely to be followed by television cameras wherever he went. It was critical, they said, that the new pope understand how his "'media image' [would] have a profound effect for good or ill on his followers and on others, regardless of whether he knows it or approves of it." So what was required, in addition to those other virtues, was a "media personality par excellence."

At this point, the unassuming Luciani was not considered a serious candidate. "I am at best on the 'C' list for pope," he told the Italian press. At the conclave, he told all the cardinals who would listen that the time was right for a pope from the Third World. His own vote was for Cardinal Aloisio Lorscheider, Archbishop of Fortaleza, Brazil. But Lorscheider himself, and an increasing number of the cardinals, began throwing their support behind Luciani. The appetite for a non-curial candidate—or, at least, someone who was *not* a scheming Vatican careerist—was growing stronger. By the first ballot on August 26, Luciani's supporters even included Krakow's Karol Wojtyla—an early sign of the Polish cardinal's knack for knowing which way the wind was blowing. When the fourth ballot concluded with Luciani the clear winner, the Patriarch of Venice nearly turned it down. "May God forgive you for what you have done in my regard," he told Cardinal Villot, when asked if he would accept his canonical election. He called himself John Paul, in honor of the popes who had made him archbishop and cardinal, respectively, and in homage to Vatican II, which he pledged to enact in full. In an odd twist, he added the suffix "I" after his name.

On August 31, *Il Mondo,* Italy's leading economic periodical, issued a challenge to the new pope that would seem quaintly earnest a few decades later. In a long open letter entitled, "Your Holiness, Is It Right?" the journal asked Pope John Paul I to "restore order" to the Vatican's financial dealings, which included "speculation in unhealthy waters." It asked pointed questions that no Roman Catholic—especially one of Albino Luciani's moral fiber—could simply brush off. "Is it right for the Vatican to operate in markets like a speculator?" *Il Mondo* asked. "Is it right for the Vatican to have a Bank whose operations help the illegal transfer of capital from Italy to other countries? Is it right for that Bank to assist Italians in evading tax?" Good questions, all—and John Paul I was already on the case. Four days earlier, over dinner with Cardinal Villot, the new pope first turned down the Secretary of State's request to retire and asked him to remain on the job a while longer. Then he instructed Villot to begin an investigation into the entire financial operation of the Vatican. "No department, no congregation, no section is to be excluded," he told him.

A Revolutionary Pontificate

Pope John Paul I was turning heads with his unconventional approach to his office. First he dispensed with some of the ancient customs, rejecting the traditional six-hour coronation ceremony in favor of a more humble investiture. He refused to be crowned: there would be no jewel-festooned tiara and no ostrich feathers. The *sedia gestatoria,* the ceremonial chair used to carry the pope, was ordered back into the lumber room—at least until the Curia convinced John Paul that the crowds couldn't see him without it. Finally, there was this telling quote: "We are the objects of undying love on the part of God ... He is our father; even more he is our *mother* [emphasis added]. He does not want to hurt us ... "

The curial cardinals hated all this. They deplored John Paul I's eschewal of ostentation for a more pedestrian approach to the papacy, and they thought his personal touch and use of the vernacular diminished the office of supreme pontiff. They also had deep concerns about some of his more heretical views. It was becoming apparent, for instance, that the new pope was in favor of artificial birth control. Tellingly, of all the statements and encyclicals from Pope Paul VI that he quoted in his various addresses, there wasn't a single mention of *Humanae Vitae*. For his draft acceptance speech, prepared by the Secretary of State's office, Luciani removed all glowing references to it. A few months earlier, he had refused to attend an international congress in Milan celebrating its tenth anniversary. (Another cardinal who did attend, and vocally supported it, was Karol Wojtyla.) Now Cardinal Villot began pestering Luciani about it, trying to convince him that the rhythm method might be acceptable. John Paul I smiled wearily. "Eminence," he said, "what can we old celibates really know of the sexual desires of the married?" When Villot persisted, the pope cut him off. "Eminence," he began, "we have been discussing birth control for about forty-five minutes. If the information I have been given, the various statistics, if that information is accurate, then during the period of time we have been talking over one thousand children under the age of five have died of malnutrition. During the next forty-five minutes while you and I look forward with anticipation to our next meal a further thousand children will die of malnutrition. By this time tomorrow thirty thousand children who are this moment alive, will be dead—of malnutrition. God does not always provide."

The Roman Curia had to put a lid on this kind of talk. It was of utmost importance that Luciani's more radical comments to Vatican aides and friends, and even remarks intended for public consumption, never see the light of day. The Curia controlled the Vatican media, so they made sure that the official news bulletin, L'Osservatore Romano, polished or altered Luciani's thoughts until they reflected the Vatican line. A special edition of the bulletin, released hours after the election results were known, featured a full biography of the new pope that described someone even more conservative than Paul VI. As far as Humanae Vitae was concerned, the voice of the Vatican declared, the new pope had always believed "that its teaching was beyond question." John Paul I's speeches to the Wednesday general audiences were recorded by the Vatican, but the Curia deleted sections of them that were deemed unacceptable—such as the pontiff's plea for drug addicts to be treated with the same virtues of Faith, Hope, Charity, and Love with which all Catholics treat their own children. Meanwhile, the published text of the papal speeches restored the royal "we."[8]

The Curia might have had serious reservations about John Paul I, but the media and the masses loved him. Here was a

---

8 Luciani was the first pope to drop the royal "we," the monarchial first-person plural, and always use "I" when relating a personal tale in public addresses.

pope whose smile and warmth were genuine, whose head and heart were connected, and who had an instant rapport with the people; a clerical populist whose words even children could understand; a religious figure with an uncanny ability to relax his listeners and make them laugh. After Pope Paul VI's austere and reclusive leadership following 1968, the new pontiff easily attracted crowds by the tens of thousands in Saint Peter's Square. With his broad smile and naughty sense of humor, the "Smiling Pope" looked a bit like Peter Sellers. But the comparison was not a compliment, as far as the Curia were concerned; it made him a buffoon. And behind the scenes, Luciani's struggles with the Curia didn't make for good comedy.

Among the dozen heads of state and other foreign representatives at the investiture ceremony on September 3 were three men whose appearance greatly upset Luciani: Argentinian dictator Jorge Raphael Videla, Chilean foreign minister Hernán Cubillos Sallato, and a son of long-time Paraguayan president Alfredo Stroessner. The three men were from countries with atrocious human rights records. The media criticized John Paul I for their presence in Rome—not knowing that it was Cardinal Villot who had sent out the invitations without consulting the pope. After the Mass, General Videla—the de facto president of Argentina since a coup d'état two years earlier—had a private audience with His Holiness. John Paul I quickly dispensed with the diplomatic niceties and began asking his guest about *los desaparecidos*, the thousands of left-wing trade unionists, students, journalists, Marxists, Peronist guerrillas, and other activists who had been wiped off the face of the earth thanks to the state-sponsored terrorism of Videla's military dictatorship.

By the end of his fifteen-minute grilling by the new pope, the general was wishing he hadn't come.[9]

The days and weeks of John Paul I's pontificate were filled with a sense of urgency, and passed quickly. Luciani, having recovered from the initial shock of his election, was inspired by Pope John XXIII's first 100 days and wanted to emulate his great hero. There was much to do beyond the routine requirements of the office, but John Paul managed to fulfill his every pontifical duty. Between August 26 and September 28, in addition to the *Urbi et Orbi* (his first message to the College of Cardinals and to the world, given at the end of Mass in the Sistine Chapel on August 27), and the investiture ceremony he would give five Sunday masses including the Angelus at Saint Peter's Square, four general audiences, two homilies, and nine speeches. There were events to plan, places to go, delegations to see. Before Christmas he was hoping to visit strife-ridden Beirut. In October, there was an important conference in Puebla, Mexico, on liberation theology, for which he set dates and an agenda. He was hoping to attend himself but decided to cancel when the date conflicted with a more important meeting at the Vatican on October 24 with a US congressional delegation reporting on ways for the church to endorse birth control and accept the use of oral contraceptives.

---

9 At that time, a forty-one-year-old Jesuit priest caught up in Argentina's "dirty war" refused to publicly support priests targeted by Videla for their promotion of liberation theology. Jorge Mario Bergoglio's actions during this period would come under intense scrutiny on March 13, 2013—the day he became Pope Francis.

Throughout all this, John Paul somehow found the time to write letters—including one to Cardinal Joseph Ratzinger of Munich. Ratzinger had seemed genuinely pleased with Luciani's election to succeed Paul VI. He empathized with Luciani's shock at having been chosen, and with his sense of the enormous weight this new responsibility represented. He would later tell others that Luciani "wasn't a man who was after a career but thought of the posts he'd had as a service and also a suffering." The last time they met, on September 3, 1978, Luciani approved Ratzinger's visit to Ecuador as the papal delegate to the Marian Congress in Guayaquil. The pope, extending his blessings as he sent Ratzinger on his way, said he looked forward to his report on the Congress. Had things turned out differently, perhaps the two men would have enjoyed many more conversations over the next several years—although it is likely that these conversations would have become increasingly animated by a growing mutual awareness of their theological and political differences.

Meanwhile, the investigation of the Vatican Bank that John Paul had ordered at the beginning of his pontificate was nearing completion. On September 28, Secretary of State Cardinal Villot returned with its results. That evening, the pope met with Villot to share his decisions on the matter, which were to be announced the following day. For starters: John Cody, the Cardinal of Chicago, who had amassed a personal fortune through corruption, was to be sacked. Cody's diversion of church funds had bankrolled a house for his mistress in Boca Raton, a luxury car, expensive clothes and furs, and holiday cash presents. A few months earlier, Pope Paul had sent an emissary asking him to leave—but Cody had told him to go to hell. This time, the Cardinal would simply be relieved of all his duties whether he was willing to leave or not.

In another decision, Paul Marcinkus, head of the Vatican Bank, was also to be sacked. Marcinkus had approved the order of $950 million USD in counterfeit bonds while presiding over several instances of tax evasion and illegal movement of shares. He had also allowed Michele Sindona, Roberto Calvi, and a host of other unsavory figures to influence church decision-making—as well as allowing an illegal Masonic lodge to establish Vatican links. As well, there were to be several other appointments and transfers that would result in the Vatican being entirely cleansed of Masonic influence. This included acceptance of Cardinal Villot's early retirement request and his replacement by Cardinal Benelli. Villot's final task as Secretary of State was to carry out these orders.

When Roman Catholics woke up the next day to greet September 29, their new pope was dead. Gone, after a pontificate of thirty-three days. Within hours, rumors began to circulate that he had been poisoned. The debate would rage on for years, with Yallop and others who have investigated Luciani's death concluding it was murder. Despite the Vatican's persistent denials (including a book by John Cornwell, written with the Vatican's support, to discredit any notion of conspiracy and repeat the official line of death from heart attack), the pope's personal physician repeatedly confirmed in subsequent years that Luciani had no heart condition and was in excellent health when he went to bed on September 28, 1978.

Clearly, something happened during those critical hours that will never be explained. Thanks in no small part to Cardinal Villot's thorough cleansing of the papal apartments, there was no trace of Pope John Paul I's worldly existence (never mind a clue to explain his untimely demise) only a few hours after his death. Equally troublesome was the Vatican doctor's brief external examination and declaration of a time and cause of death, and the fact that John Paul I's body was embalmed with no autopsy, in accordance with Pope Paul's 1975 law. What could be said for sure was that Luciani had been using the liquid medicine Effortil to counter the effects of low blood pressure. Given the threadbare security detail in the papal apartments in those days, it would not have been difficult for a hired killer to enter the pope's bedroom when he wasn't there, add a fatal dose of digitalis to his medicine bottle, and then slip out of the room undetected. When John Paul I was found in his bed the next morning, he was clutching the notes for his big assignment shuffle.

Was he done in by "the Italian solution"? Who knows? But if Pope John Paul I was indeed killed by a plot, then the alleged conspirators covered their tracks very well. With the passage of time, it has become impossible to prove what happened on September 28–29, 1978. What we do know is that, after Pope John Paul I's death, none of the orders on his "To Do" list were carried out and none of his initiatives fulfilled. Cardinal Villot, already in poor health, continued on as Secretary of State until he, too, died a few months later. Over the years, misfortune befell most of the other characters of interest in the pope's sudden death.[10] All except for Paul Marcinkus, that is.

Four years after his death, Pope John Paul I's attempt to fire the Vatican Bank chief was finally vindicated when Marcinkus was indicted as an accessory in the $3.5 billion USD collapse of the Banco Ambrosiano. The wily American knew he would be arrested and put on trial the moment he stepped on Italian soil. So, thanks to an immunity agreement based on the Lateran Treaty (see Chapter IX), he received a clemency deal from Pope John Paul II that allowed him to avoid extradition to Italian authorities. Marcinkus managed to hide out in Vatican City, remaining in charge of the IOR for nearly a dozen more years before quietly retiring to an exclusive gated community in Arizona. There he would live for another sixteen years, quietly working on his golf handicap, before finally meeting Saint Peter. As for Cardinal Benelli, instead of becoming Secretary of State, as Pope John Paul I intended, he carried the torch of Luciani's memory into the next conclave as his potential successor. During the early ballots, he came within nine votes of the papacy. The eventual winner, Poland's Karol Wojtyla, took the name John Paul II. However, apart from providing a simple crypt in the Vatican grottoes beneath Saint Peter's Basilica, Wojtyla would not honor Luciani in any significant way throughout the twenty-six-and-a-half years of his papacy.

---

10 To name just two: the Banco Ambrosiano's Roberto Calvi was found hanged under Blackfriar's Bridge in London in 1982. Four years later, Michele (The Shark) Sindona, while serving a twenty-five-year sentence for murder, was poisoned in his cell by cyanide in his coffee.

❧

As the shock of John Paul I's sudden and premature death continued to sink in, Roman Catholics around the world wondered what kind of pope he might have turned out to be. Having released no major encyclicals or passed significant edicts (other than a sweeping review of seminaries, which he inherited from Pope Paul), he was still in his ecclesial honeymoon period—a fact that can lead to the kind of retroactive, romantic theorizing that tends to idealize the tragically fallen. Some Vatican observers have tried to disillusion John Paul I loyalists by suggesting that their hero opposed liberation theology and was an anti-Marxist. But there is no evidence to suggest that Luciani would have approved either a canonical crackdown on individual theologians or the complete destruction of the movement itself. One must also wonder how an opponent could have voted, as Luciani did, for an outspoken advocate of liberation theology at the conclave that ended up choosing him instead, or could have broken with diplomatic protocol by grilling an Argentinian dictator whose invitation to his papal investiture he had not approved.

In any case, everything about Albino Luciani's journey to Rome, what he found there and what he tried to do about it in the little time he had, suggests the promise of a progressive new Catholicism unfulfilled—or, at least, a genuine interest in advancing the goals of Vatican II. But there would be no nostalgic lament for John Paul I from Joseph Ratzinger. The cardinal of Munich would mourn Luciani's passing for the required two weeks before turning his thoughts to the next conclave. When asked later what "message" could be derived from Luciani's death after only thirty-three days as pope—that is, for the best interpretation of the Holy Spirit's intentions—Ratzinger replied that "a turning point had been reached" and that "something absolutely new was needed." Few could have guessed that, by "absolutely new," what the cardinal from Munich intended was a decisive turn to the right that would ultimately put the torch to Vatican II.

IV

A War on Liberation

When Catholic theologians see their name in Ratzinger's footnotes, they might want to consult a good canon lawyer.
—Vatican observer John L. Allen Jr

Within the space of three months in 1978, the "Year of Three Popes," the leadership of the Roman Catholic Church effectively passed from a dithering curial loyalist (Paul VI) to a boat-rocking progressive (John Paul I) to a right-wing, orthodox traditionalist (John Paul II). As if to imply that their choice in August of the pro-Vatican II Albino Luciani as new pope had been a mistake, the cardinals did a total about-face during the next conclave in October. By choosing the cardinal from Krakow, Karol Wojtyla, to be the next pope, they went with a social conservative who embraced the ultimate authority of canon law. What kind of message did this send to the world about the church's future direction—especially its intentions around Vatican II?

It would be some time before the answer was clear. Meanwhile, one cardinal in particular who had voted for Wojtyla in the conclave stood to gain the most from his election. Wojtyla had always liked Joseph Ratzinger. The two men agreed on most theological issues, shared a similar affection for the Virgin Mary, and were both virulent anti-abortionists. Within months of becoming pope, Wojtyla, impressed by Ratzinger's sharp mind and doctrinal discipline, began lobbying the German cardinal to join him in Rome. In 1980, he asked Ratzinger to take over leadership of the Congregation for Catholic Education, but Ratzinger politely demurred, asking to remain in Munich.

But a year later, the pope made Ratzinger an offer he couldn't refuse: to replace the retiring Cardinal Franjo Seper as prefect of the Congregation for the Doctrine of the Faith (CDF). Founded in 1542 by Pope Paul III as the Holy Congregation of the Roman and Universal Inquisition (or the Inquisition), the CDF was the oldest of the nine congregations of the Roman Curia and one of the most durable Vatican institutions. Its purpose, according to the Apostolic Constitution on the Roman Curia approved by Pope John Paul II in 1988, is to "promote and safeguard the doctrine on faith and morals in the whole Catholic world. So it has competence in things that touch this matter in any way." It was an office Ratzinger knew all too well, having demonized its authoritarian excess eighteen years earlier in a ghostwritten attack on its then prefect, Cardinal Ottaviani. Now he was being offered a chance to make it his own. This time, he said "yes" to Rome.

On November 25, 1981, at age fifty-four, Ratzinger succeeded Cardinal Seper as CDF prefect. The seventy-six-year-old Seper would enjoy neither a lengthy retirement nor the opportunity to see how his replacement measured up: he died only a month after Ratzinger assumed his duties. Another previous holder of the office who would not live to see Ratzinger's reign was Cardinal Ottaviani, whose stewardship of the Holy Office during Vatican

II the young theologian had eviscerated in self-righteously liberal terms. The always acerbic and quote-worthy Ottaviani, who died two years before Ratzinger arrived at the CDF, knew an ambitious up-and-comer when he saw one. Some years after Ratzinger's Vatican II appearance, when his liberalism had all but disappeared in the rear view mirror, an aging Ottaviani nicely captured the young theologian's opportunism. "Ratzinger first came to Rome with a group that was seeking new horizons," he said. "Then, however, he understood the presumption of those theologians, and he rid himself of their company."

Together at last in the Vatican, Pope John Paul II and Cardinal Ratzinger established a sort of Good Cop, Bad Cop routine. While His Holiness basked in the glory of positive headlines—touring the world like a rock star, kissing babies, addressing football stadium crowds, developing a CNN-friendly television presence while being credited with saving eastern Europe from Communism—Ratzinger got stuck with all the heavy lifting: alienating liberals, clashing with dissidents, and meting out discipline. Showing, in effect, the unfriendlier face of the church. John Paul II's choice of Ratzinger for CDF prefect sent a clear message that the church would no longer tolerate dissent and would do everything in its power to impede the progress of Vatican II. Ratzinger was more than up to the task.

Foremost on his agenda was ridding the church of as many liberal theologians as possible while imposing his own vision of

Catholicism on the world. As the Vatican's gatekeeper of religious orthodoxy, he would spend the next twenty-four years turning "People of God" into a euphemism for Communist excess. Over the course of his term at the CDF, Ratzinger would expel at least 107 theologians through defrocking, removal of teaching privileges, or official silencing through denouncement. Many others he would call on the carpet to "instruct." His first major target would be a social justice movement led by left-wing priests in Latin America.

Backward, Christian Soldiers!
More than a quarter-century after his official "instruction" on liberation theology, one finds at least two tragic ironies in Ratzinger's successful efforts to stamp out this popular grassroots movement. The first is the brilliance with which he conflated the evils of Stalinism in Eastern Europe with the pedagogy of the oppressed in Latin America. In so doing, he adopted the red-baiting logic of Ronald Reagan to reject the concept of "social sin" in a part of the world whose socio-cultural and historical realities bore little resemblance to those of the continent on whose Marxist example he relied to build his case. The second irony is how, in "correcting" a pope who did not completely share his views on liberation theology, he blinded John Paul II to the church's double standard with regard to "people power." In Wojtyla's native Poland, the church sided with the workers, thus allowing priests and bishops to help overthrow a Communist dictatorship. But in Latin America, the church sided with the state military and the corporations, thus rendering clerics

impotent and exacerbating poverty. Thanks to the church's support of right-wing dictatorships or their elected, corporatist equivalents, hundreds of thousands of human lives were sacrificed on the altar of religious orthodoxy that Ratzinger—and, to a lesser extent, John Paul II—espoused.

What was Ratzinger's problem with liberation theology? What was wrong with bishops, priests, and theologians joining with civil society to improve the plight of the poor and challenge the political oligarchies responsible for their oppression? Was it not the church's duty to defend the world's disadvantaged and work to secure their redemption? Well, no, according to the CDF prefect, it wasn't. First, a liberation theology based on Marxism only replaced the Christian promise of redemption through Jesus with a "messianism" based on materialism; it substituted a reward in paradise with revolution. This was wrong, said Ratzinger: the only redemption possible was individual salvation through Christ. Second, liberation theology challenged the internal hierarchy of the church by aligning priests with the poor and allowing earthly political realities, not Rome, to drive the pastoral agenda.

Liberation theology was inspired by Vatican II ecclesiology. *Gaudium et Spes* instructed the church to "take on flesh" by joining with social movements to build a society that reflects human dignity. In 1968, an assembly of Latin American bishops in Medellin, Colombia, endorsed a "preferential option for the poor," an imperative for the church to align itself with the underprivileged against powerful elements defending the status quo. Throughout the ages, the church had perpetuated feudalism in Latin America—from the missionaries who evangelized for the European conquerors to contemporary church leaders who always sided with the elites. Now its leaders were prepared to switch loyalties and, by supporting the poor, do "what Christ would do."

One of liberation theology's earliest proponents was Gustavo Gutiérrez, a Dominican priest who served as theological advisor at the Medellin conference. His book, *A Theology of Liberation: History, Politics and Salvation* (1971), became the movement's seminal text. In it, Gutiérrez spoke of liberation theology as an indigenous movement particular to local conditions in the nations where it arose. But Ratzinger saw it as an ideological import from Europe, leftist pablum that was being force-fed to the ignorant masses by intellectuals who had "read too much German theology." The movement's practitioners frequently quoted Johann Baptist Metz of Munich, the founder of "political theology," and Jurgen Moltmann of Tubingen, founder of the "theology of hope." Metz saw Vatican II as a clarion call for Christians to read the "signs of the times" in social and political movements, to align themselves with those seeking to improve the human condition. Moltmann was a Lutheran who embraced a more radical vision of Christ as fearless rebel for social transformation. Ratzinger also noted that liberation theology's most influential figures had studied in Germany or elsewhere in Europe: Gutiérrez at Louvains, Lyons, and Rome; Brazilian Franciscan Leonardo Boff at the University of Munich; and Uruguayan Jesuit Juan Luis Segundo at the University of Paris.

Notwithstanding the European training camp for its intellectual standard bearers, the ideas behind liberation theology were not imported. They were the product of indigenous popular movements tied to pastoral work in Latin America and inspired by experiences of the local poor. To begin with, there were the "base communities": small groups (usually ten to thirty people) of poor Christians who met to discuss social issues in the context of the Bible. Throughout Latin America there were said to be tens, possibly hundreds, of thousands of these small groups. Sometimes they met under the guidance of a priest, but usually they were lay-led. The scriptural study and reflection was goal-oriented: it was supposed to lead to action. Liberation theologians aligned themselves with base communities rather than with the institutional church, its hierarchy or its upper class supporters. In progressive dioceses, being part of a base community was a critical part of doing one's job as a priest.

Another liberation theology concept native to Latin America was "social sin," which expanded the concept of sin from the individualistic (i.e., personal transgressions such as lying and stealing) to the collective (i.e., institutional corruption, police violence, neocolonialism). The forgiveness of sin by Jesus Christ thus involved far more than the redemption of individual souls; it also meant transforming unjust social realities. This was crucial to liberation theology's core belief in what it meant to be a good Catholic. What kinds of actions did this involve? Everything from eucharistic strikes (withholding the sacraments from politicians, village headmen, or army officials who had "sinned" against the people) to revolutionary violence (only as a last resort when all other means to social justice had failed).

The church had always enabled *social* violence by condoning the status quo; it had enabled *state* violence by turning a blind eye to military repression. So how could it condemn the desperate violence of the poor who needed food, housing, and jobs?

The problem, as Ratzinger saw it, was ideology. While liberation theologians saw the historical Jesus as champion of the marginalized, the CDF prefect saw only Che Guevara and the Baader-Meinhoff gang. In his view, a theology based on Marxism could only lead to terrorism. Who could trust it, after all, if even the Medellin conference of bishops—with its "pastoral reflection on poverty," as Gutiérrez put it—was unwilling to renounce violence? Priests such as Father Camilo Torres, a Colombian leftist killed in 1966, had, in fact, taken up arms, joined guerrilla movements, been killed, and then celebrated as martyrs. Liberation theology by definition supported leftist political movements, some of which were proudly Marxist and a few of which advocated violence in building a just society. Ratzinger also thought that liberation theologians relativized Christian doctrine through *orthopraxis*, the privileging of "correct action" before "correct belief."

By the time of his ascension to the papacy, Karol Wojtyla's ideas about Marxism had moved some distance from those of the thirty-three-year-old priest who had written *Catholic Social Ethics* (1953). Back then, young Karol recognized the validity of class struggle and acknowledged that Marxism contained elements of truth. But by the late 1970s, the grim realities of life in Soviet-controlled Poland had hardened him against Communism. And this complicated his views on liberation theology once he became Pope John Paul II. On one hand, he had given strength to the Solidarity movement in Poland and was thus disposed to have sympathy for priests and laity who may have identified as "socialist" but were confronting unjust governments. Even in Latin America, there would be instances where he spoke in favor of liberation theology, at least in theory. But the prospect of a Communist "solution" to the struggle turned him off. He soon became ambivalent about the movement, confused in his messaging about it, and thus incapable of leadership on the issue.

Early in 1979, John Paul II attended the conference on liberation theology in Pueblo, Mexico, that had been rescheduled after John Paul I's death. The meeting was dominated by conservatives. Cardinal Alfonso Lopez Trujillo[11] of Colombia wanted the final statement to include a condemnation of liberation theology, contradicting the Medellin statement. With the conservatives' anti-Marxist rhetoric still ringing in his ears, the pope told the priests: "You are not social or political leaders or officials of a temporal power." He urged them to embrace a "Christian idea of liberation," not an "ideological" one. In the end, the Puebla Declaration affirmed the "option for the poor" but warned against revolution.

---

11 Trujillo (1935–2008) was the Vatican's leading voice in defence of traditional family values and in opposition to abortion, contraception, and gay marriage. He was also notorious for his long association with infamous drug lord Pablo Escobar. This included joint membership in a civic association called Medellín sin tugurios (Medellín without shantytowns), "widely seen as a smokescreen for Escobar's illegal activities," Vatican reporter John Allen has noted.

In February of 1980, the pope received a visit from Oscar Romero, Archbishop of San Salvador. Romero was in Europe to receive an honorary doctorate from the Catholic University of Leuven, in recognition of his courageous work as a human rights advocate in a country where the slogan "Be a patriot—kill a priest!" was all too often taken literally. Stopping in Rome, he met with John Paul II to express his concerns about what was happening back home. Romero urged the pope to condemn the Salvadoran government for legitimizing terror and assassinations.[12] His Holiness was unmoved: opposing the junta meant supporting the Farabundo Marti National Liberation Front (FMLN), the Marxist guerrillas. Romero returned home disappointed, unaware that he had been hung out to dry. In fact, the Vatican had opened a file on him and was already monitoring his activities.

For Romero, who had begun his episcopacy as a theological conservative, conversion to the left occurred only a few weeks after he was named archbishop. On March 12, 1977, a progressive Jesuit priest and personal friend, Rutilio Grande, was assassinated. Seeing Grande's dead body, Romero committed himself to joining the base communities with which Grande had worked. Continuing his friend's fight for social justice, in January 1979, Romero excommunicated the president of El Salvador, Carlos Humberto Romero (no relation), for failing to stop the killing of priests and laity. In spring of

---

12 The same month, Romero had written to US President Jimmy Carter, pleading with him to stop funding the junta government. But Carter—regarded today as a sage of peace, shuttle diplomacy, and fair elections—ignored Romero's letter and kept funding the junta, helping to seal Romero's fate.

that year, Georgetown University in Washington announced that it would award the archbishop with an honorary degree. The Holy See tried, but failed, to convince the university to cancel the plan.[13]

On March 20, 1980, Cardinal Seper—Ratzinger's predecessor at the CDF—along with Cardinal Sebastiano Baggio of the Congregation for Bishops, and Cardinal Silvio Oddi of the Congregation for Clergy, attended a Vatican meeting about the future of the archbishop of San Salvador. Concerned that Romero's constant criticism of the government and his political advocacy for the poor was dividing the Salvadoran church, they decided that he must be replaced. The pope agreed; the order was to come down later in March. During his Sunday mass on March 23, Romero dedicated his homily to the country's security forces. It was against God's law, he said, for Salvadoran soldiers, national guardsmen, and police to kill their brothers, the peasants. Urging them to disobey any order to kill, he then uttered liberation theology's most famous plea from the pulpit: "In the name of God, in the name of this suffering people whose cries rise to heaven more loudly each day, I implore you, I beg you, I order you in the name of God: *Stop the repression!*" The next day, Romero was assassinated with a single shot from a sniper's rifle as he celebrated mass in a small chapel. In the years to come, John Paul II would refuse to acknowledge him as a martyr or consider him for beatification—rather odd for a pope who canonized

---

13 A Jesuit in residence at Georgetown, Timothy Healy, traveled to San Salvador to bestow the degree—thus ensuring a place on the right side of history.

almost three-quarters as many saints as all of his predecessors combined.[14]

By 1980, more than 800 priests and nuns had been murdered in Latin America. John Paul II was not unmoved by their heroism in resisting state authority. (How could he be, given what was happening in Poland?) But he drew the line when it came to bishops, priests, and laity challenging the hierarchy within the church. (And, of course, there was his little hate-on for Communism.) So when Ratzinger arrived at the CDF, it wasn't hard for the new prefect to convince his pope that demands for internal reform in Latin America were the product of Communist infiltrators bent on weakening the church. Ratzinger had held this stance for quite some time—at least since the Marian congress in Ecuador, to which he was sent to represent John Paul I. After Luciani's death, Ratzinger gave an interview to Munich's *Suddeutsche Zeitung* about the Ecuador trip. "Where the much-discussed theology of liberation is blended with Marxist presuppositions," he said, "the door is opened to ideological means of struggle." He went on to blame liberation theology for the gains made by Jehovah's Witnesses and Mormons in Latin America: it was the failure of Marxism and revolution to meet the spiritual needs of the people, he said, that led to these conversions.

---

14 For many Catholics, the idea of freezing out Romero from sainthood—or, at least, delaying his beatification indefinitely—while fast-tracking Opus Dei founder and fascist sympathizer Josemaria Escriva into the club says a lot about John Paul II's politics, as well as Ratzinger's. (Escriva's repugnant sex life—dominated by child rape, bigamy, and incest—is recounted in Chapter VIII, along with Pope Benedict's much-welcomed though belated decision to defrock him.)

To be fair, Ratzinger was hardly alone in his desire to stamp out liberation theology. Many in the Latin American clergy shared his views; in some cases, local conservative opposition to the movement predated Ratzinger's position. As well as the aforementioned Cardinal Trujillo of Colombia, conservatives like Cardinal Eugenio Sales and Bishop Boaventura Kloppenburg of Brazil would assist the CDF prefect in identifying which liberation theologians posed the greatest threat to the church. Kloppenburg, for instance, had a special loathing for Leonardo Boff, a flamboyant left-wing Brazilian he had once groomed to be his successor as theology chair at the Franciscan university in Petropolis. By the late 1970s, Boff had drifted from his orbit; while Kloppenburg became one of liberation theology's biggest enemies, Boff became its most prominent advocate.

Boff had studied at the University of Munich under Karl Rahner from 1965 to 1970. When he delivered his PhD dissertation, *The Church as Sacrament in the Horizon of World Experience*, Rahner suggested he show it to a colleague. Joseph Ratzinger liked the thesis so much that he helped Boff find a publisher. By the time he began at the CDF, however, Ratzinger and Boff had moved in opposite directions. In 1984, Ratzinger had a bulging dossier on the Brazilian's heretical theology and embrace of Marxism. On May 15 of that year, the CDF prefect sent Boff a six-page letter asking him to clarify his views, especially as they concerned the challenge to hierarchical authority from the "church of the people." The letter accused Boff of a "pitiless, radical assault" on the institutional church. Meanwhile, the archbishop of Rio de Janeiro withdrew the *missio canonica* from Boff's brother Clodovis and a colleague, accusing both of using Marxist analysis.

On September 7, 1984, four days after the official release of the CDF's *Instruction on Certain Aspects of the "Theology of Liberation"* (of which more later), Boff attended a colloquy with Ratzinger at the Vatican to discuss the CDF's objections to his book *Church: Charism and Power*. Given that September 7 is Brazilian Independence Day, Boff had written the CDF asking for the meeting to be held in Brazil, but Ratzinger refused. So when Boff arrived in Rome, he held an impromptu press conference at the airport. To avoid further breaches of secrecy, Ratzinger arranged for his private secretary to pick up Boff and return him to his Franciscan residence. None of Boff's Franciscan colleagues were allowed to accompany him to the colloquy, and Ratzinger turned down three members of the Brazilian hierarchy who had asked to attend, including Cardinal Aloisio Lorscheider.[15] The colloquy broke up with no mention of punishment, so the Brazilians thought they had won the day.

On March 11, 1985, the CDF issued formal notice on Boff's *Church: Charism and Power*. The book, said Ratzinger, endangered the faith with its concept of dogma, its understanding of sacred power, and its overemphasis on the prophetic role of the church. On April 26, he accused Boff of "ecclesiological relativism" and sentenced him to a year of "obsequious silence." The formal silencing prevented Boff from publishing, teaching, or speaking publicly. Many saw the punishment as heavy-handed.

---

15 Lorscheider, the reader will recall, was Albino Luciani's preference for pope at the 1978 conclave that elected Luciani. After some negotiation, Ratzinger allowed the Brazilian group to join the second part of the conversation.

Ratzinger, ever the spin doctor, had a different take on the situation. "Well, rather than a year of silence, I would describe it as a year's sabbatical," he said. "It offers Father Boff, as a theologian, a writer, and a thinker, a long time of leisure for thinking. I, too, in solidarity with Father Boff, wish that I could have a chance to spend a year in silence."

When Boff traveled to a remote Amazon village during his silence period to participate in a religious retreat, it took only three days for word to reach the Vatican. Meanwhile, a Catholic publishing house in Brazil was planning to issue a book containing all the correspondence between Ratzinger and Boff, plus a transcript of the colloquy in Rome. Ratzinger, catching wind of it, intervened to stop publication. When Boff's silence was lifted just before Easter, 1986, some supporters saw it as a victory. But over the next few years, Ratzinger kept chipping away at the Brazilian, ordering him to clarify, modify, or disavow his own views until he finally packed it in.

In 1987, the CDF blocked publication of another of Boff's books, *Trinity and Society*. By this time, the radical Franciscan was calling for the dissolution of the Vatican's national sovereignty and the recall of all papal nuncios. In 1991, Ratzinger demanded that Boff step down as editor of the Franciscan journal *Vozes*. Boff accepted the verdict, a signal that his resolve was weakening. The following year, Ratzinger issued a second silencing order, this time banning Boff from teaching and imposing pre-emptive censorship on all his writings. Boff, Ratzinger declared, had still not cleansed his ecclesiology of the dissent and internal class struggle that had been at issue in 1984. This was the last straw. On May 26, 1992, Boff announced that he was leaving the Catholic priesthood. "Ecclesiastical power is cruel and merciless," he said, in a parting shot at his tormentor. "It forgets nothing. It forgives nothing. It demands everything."[16]

Then there was Gustavo Gutiérrez. Ratzinger's persecution of liberation theology's founding thinker began in 1983 when he sent a letter to the Peruvian bishops, asking them to investigate Gutiérrez. To assist them, Ratzinger checked off a few of his target's chief sins:

+ Marxist view of history and perversion of the gospel

+ selective reading of the Bible, overemphasizing the poor

+ treats Holy Spirit as source of revelation separate from church tradition and teaching office

+ class-ridden theology

+ emphasis on building the kingdom through class

---

16 In 1999 Boff noted that, having received no paperwork from the Vatican formalizing his departure, from a canonical point of view he thus continued to be a priest and a friar. He still considers himself a member of the church today, but "more Franciscan than Roman Catholic."

struggle, while changing structures of the church

* turns church into partisan group, "which puts in jeopardy the hierarchy and its legitimacy"

* neglects beatitudes

By March of 1983, Gutiérrez knew something was up. When he contacted Ratzinger directly and asked for a meeting, Ratzinger agreed. Reportedly, the CDF prefect was pleasant, but their meeting at the Vatican was discouraging. By June, Gutiérrez submitted a sixty-page defence of his work to the Peruvian bishops. He had to wait until January 1984 before the bishops finally voted, thirty-one to fifteen, in favor of some kind of criticism—but without agreeing on a text. In March, Karl Rahner—two weeks before his own death at age eighty—stepped forward to defend Gutiérrez. Cardinal Landazuri of Lima received a letter from Rahner dated March 16. "I am convinced of the orthodoxy of the theological work of Gutiérrez," Rahner wrote. "The theology of liberation that he represents is entirely orthodox. A condemnation of Gustavio Gutiérrez would have, it is my full conviction, very negative consequences for the climate that is the condition in which a theology that is at the service of evangelization may endure. Today there are diverse schools and it has always been thus ... It would be deplorable if this legitimate pluralism were to be restricted by administrative means."

The following September, Gutiérrez and the bishops met with the CDF in Rome. Ratzinger was hoping to see some kind of condemnation from the bishops for Gutiérrez's Marxism, for his overemphasis on "social sin," and for his refusal to disavow violence. Gutiérrez countered by quoting Paul VI's *Populorum Progressio*, which refused to rule out violence as a final option against a "manifest, long-standing tyranny." In the end, the bishops issued no condemnation. Their concluding document, released on November 26, praised liberation theology as a movement "born on our soil" that had led to "spiritual deepening." Score one for the forces of light: this marked one of the few occasions that Ratzinger ever lost an argument while at the CDF.[17]

Gutiérrez would be back in the Vatican doghouse soon enough, however. In August 1985, he visited Nicaragua to express solidarity with Miguel D'Escoto, the Sandinista foreign minister and defrocked priest. D'Escoto had launched a hunger strike to protest US-sponsored violence against Nicaragua. Gutiérrez voiced his agreement that "the big threat to Nicaragua" came from the US. This was hardly a controversial stance: the existence of the contras, and the lengthy history of US bullying of the country, was well documented by this point. But Ratzinger condemned the visit nonetheless.

---

17 He was hardly a sore loser in this case. In 2004, Ratzinger's final year as CDF prefect, he approved Gutiérrez's latest article on ecclesial communion, which was published in the Angelicum university's scholarly review. And on February 21, 2007, Pope Benedict annointed Gutiérrez, with ashes on his forehead, during an Ash Wednesday liturgy.

"Silencio!": The Status Quo Wins

The death knell for liberation theology rang in 1983, when Pope John Paul II stopped in Nicaragua during a pastoral visit to Central America. News coverage of the visit revealed a Polish pope who was rattled by all the sloganeering around him—especially the mix of religion and politics that confronted him in Managua during an outdoor mass for 700,000 on March 4. At the mass, the pope was greeted with banner messages such as, "Thank God and the Revolution." John Paul had come prepared to talk about church unity, but his warnings not to succumb to "ideological compromises and temporal solutions" did not go over well with the crowd. Less than halfway into his homily, shouts began to drown out the polite, supportive applause. Soon the pope could no longer hear himself above the chanting of, "We want a Church that stands with the poor!", "We want peace!", "Between Christianity and the revolution there is no contradiction!", and finally: "Power to the people!" Seething with rage, His Holiness paused a moment before bellowing three times into his microphone: *"Silencio!"* Then, scolding the crowd like an embattled schoolteacher trying to stop a food fight, he protested: "The Church is the *first* to promote peace!" For Catholics who had been expecting their pope to declare himself on the side of the Latin American poor, *"Silencio!"* was a big letdown, a betrayal of Archbishop Romero's "Stop the repression!" plea of three years earlier.

The other enduring image from John Paul's Nicaragua visit occurred in the first few minutes after his arrival in Managua. The pope was making his way through the receiving line, accepting official greetings, when he was confronted by the sight of Ernesto Cardenal, the Minister of Culture—one of three priests in the Sandinista cabinet he had ordered to resign. Cardenal had refused. Now here he was, embarrassing the Holy Father by showing up in his diplomatic capacity. Cardenal greeted the Pope by dropping to one knee and attempting to kiss his ring. But John Paul pulled his hand away and wagged a finger at Cardenal. "First you must make good your dealings with the Church," he said.[18]

In 1980, a policy paper prepared by key advisors to Ronald Reagan had sounded the alarm about liberation theology in Latin America, which the Republican presidential candidate regarded as an example of a broader Soviet–Marxist attempt to corrupt the "soft underbelly" of the Western hemisphere. The so-called "Santa Fe Document" urged the US to take action to undermine the influence of liberation theology. Using the black-and-white language of Cold War duality, it painted the issue with an us-versus-them simplicity that appealed to Reagan's Armageddonist Christianity and drew no objection from the pope. Marxist-Leninist forces, the document said, "have used the church as a political weapon against private ownership and the capitalist system of production, infiltrating the religious community with ideas that are more communist than Christian."

US "assistance"—unopposed by the Vatican—began with tacit approval of police pressure and military brutality and quickly expanded to direct military assistance and CIA-sponsored covert ops, including illegal funding of the contra

---

18 In December 1984, Fernando Cardenal (Ernesto's brother), the Sandinista minister of education, was dismissed from the Jesuits. Ernesto and another priest, Edgar Parrales, were involuntarily deprived of their status as priests (Parrales willingly so). Sandinista foreign minister Father Miguel D'Escoto, referred to earlier, was expelled.

rebels in Nicaragua and support of the military in El Salvador and Guatemala. Throughout all this, Ratzinger was wise enough to see that these tactics would eventually backfire, alienating more Catholics and drawing more support for liberation theology. He knew that the best way to crush the movement was to use his office to deprive liberation theology of credibility and, thus, institutional support.

Ratzinger's assault on liberation theology began in 1984, about the same time he began targeting Boff. On March 14 that year, he published an essay in *30 Giorni* (the Italian house journal of the conservative Communion and Liberation movement) that condemned liberation theology as not only dangerous and unorthodox, but heretical as well: its adherents, he wrote, apply different content to the ideas of redemption and grace. That same month, the CDF met with the Latin American Bishops Conference in Bogota. Their concluding statement praised liberation theology but rejected Marxist analysis. That set the stage for the first Vatican encyclical on the issue, Ratzinger's *Instruction on Certain Aspects of the "Theology of Liberation"* (September 3).

In its account of struggle against "totalitarian" regimes, the *Instruction*'s overall message and sense of history appealed more to the eastern European than the Latin American church. "Millions of our own contemporaries legitimately yearn to recover those basic freedoms of which they were deprived by totalitarian and atheistic regimes which came to power by violent and revolutionary means, precisely in the name of the liberation of the people," Ratzinger wrote. "This shame of our time cannot be ignored: While claiming to bring them freedom, these

regimes keep whole nations in conditions of servitude which
are unworthy of mankind. Those who, perhaps inadvertently,
make themselves accomplices of similar enslavements betray
the very poor they mean to help." (Astute readers of Ratzinger's
work would see a code word for "Communist" here in his use of
"atheistic.")

Instruction on Certain Aspects of the "Theology of Liberation"
marked a significant departure from the 1977 statement of the
International Theological Commission. While the ITC document reaffirmed the Vatican II teaching of Gaudium et Spes, that
in God's kingdom "not only love will remain, but love's labor as
well" (a nod to the concept of healing "social sin"), Ratzinger's
1984 instruction called most forms of liberation theology "a
negation of the faith of the church." As Vatican reporter John
Allen has noted, the concern over excessive reliance on Marxist
analysis had occupied one paragraph in the 1977 document. In
Ratzinger's instruction, it comprised more than 4,000 words of
a 10,000-word report. Gone from the Ratzinger document were
key points in the ITC's statement noting that the church "inevitably makes political commitments, or that it should employ
these commitments on behalf of the poor."

Despite its negative tone with regard to Marxism, the
Instruction managed to pull the wool over the eyes of several
liberation theologians. Perhaps in deep denial—as some would
soon find themselves in Ratzinger's crosshairs—many thought
that the document either did not apply to them or had no serious implications for their future practice as theologians. They
did not regard themselves as Marxist, after all, and they had not
rejected Christ's grace. Some even praised the Instruction as a

reinforcement of their own work. Clearly, they were oblivious to the fact that Cardinal Ratzinger did not care how they self-identified politically; his point was that their theological assumptions were dangerous, whether or not they recognized it. But not everyone was so gullible. The Belgian Dominican Edward Schillebeeckx, another Ratzinger target (for reasons other than liberation theology), responded to the *Instruction* of 1984 by saying: "The dictators of Latin America will receive [it] with joy because it will serve their purposes. Whether it was intended to or not, this instruction is, in fact, being turned into a political instrument in the hands of the powerful in Latin America who, in turn, are being supported by the great foreign powers in order to consolidate the system that keeps the poor submissive in favour of some of the rich. Is this the good news we might have expected from Rome?"

Juan Luis Segundo, also, was not being fooled. In 1985, he published *Theology and the Church: A Response to Cardinal Ratzinger and a Warning to the Whole Church*. In this book, Segundo made it clear that liberation theologians could not disregard the *Instruction* as if it did not apply to them. On the contrary, the document was an attack on their work that had to be taken seriously. Schillebeeckx and Segundo would turn out to be right.

In the meantime, it appeared that Ratzinger may have overstepped his authority with the *Instruction*. On reading the document, the Vatican secretary of state, Agostino Casaroli, said that he had not been consulted about it. He regretted its "negative" tone, and concluded that a positive document would have been "preferable." Even worse, the pope was rumored to be unhappy about it. At the time, John Paul was still fighting Communism in Europe and trying to free his native Poland from Soviet rule. However, he wasn't ready to embrace Ratzinger's outright dismissal of Marxism, which contradicted ideas he had expressed in *Catholic Social Ethics* so many years earlier. Furthermore, he had assumed that the document had been discussed by the doctrinal commissions of the Latin American bishops. When he learned that this was not the case, he suggested it be regarded as a "working paper of the doctrinal congregation." He then assigned the head of the Pontifical Council for Justice and Peace to begin drafting a more positive statement—thus undermining his CDF prefect.

Ratzinger's next statement, the *Instruction on Christian Freedom and Liberation* (March 1986), said pretty much what the first had—but without so much Red-baiting. It at least seemed to be positive. It reaffirmed support for the poor, applauded base communities as a "source of great hope for the church," and even accepted armed struggle as a final solution to "prolonged tyranny." Leonardo Boff, welcoming the document, actually addressed the CDF prefect as a comrade ("Dear Brother Ratzinger") in a letter hailing the new instruction as a "decisive and historic" reinforcement of liberation theology. "Now there can no longer be any doubt," he said. "Rome is at the side of the oppressed and all those fighting against injustice." His letter to Ratzinger was co-signed by his brother Clodovis—this even after the CDF prefect had disciplined them. But the brothers Boff were in denial: they somehow missed the part in the new *Instruction* about the importance of resisting Marxism: the CDF, Ratzinger ruled, had found it necessary "to draw attention to 'deviations, or risks of deviation, damaging to the Faith and to Christian living.'"[19]

Meanwhile, events apart from Leonardo Boff's silencing were beginning to reveal which way the church was headed. In 1985, Lopez Trujillo and his circle of conservative clerics gathered for an ad hoc meeting outside Santiago, Chile. Here they produced the *Andes Statement*, which denounced liberation theology as a Marxist perversion of the faith. The *Andes Statement* drew coverage on Pinochet-controlled state television and was cited in defence of the government's arrest of Father Renato Hevia, editor of the progressive journal *Mensaje*. That same year, Ratzinger fired Archbishop Dom Helder Camara, replacing him with a compliant right-winger who proceeded to reorganize the diocese and carry out interrogations and purges of other liberation theologians.

From this point on, the chronology of events becomes a litany of defeat for liberation theology:

- **November 1987**: The Conference of American Armies (comprised of the armies of fifteen Western hemisphere nations, including the US and El Salvador) meets to discuss its report on liberation theology. It condemns the movement and names certain supporters as hard-core Marxists who advocate Communist revolution.

---

19 In 2008, Leonardo and Clodovis Boff had a public spat over liberation theology, with the former attacking his brother's rejection of the movement and embrace of Pope Benedict's view.

+ **September 1988:** Ratzinger silences Pedro Casaldaliga, Bishop of Sao Felix da Araguaia, Brazil, accusing him of supporting liberation theology. The CDF prefect sentences him to compliance with the magisterium and a period of silence, also ordering him not to interfere with other dioceses in his travels.

+ **November 1989:** The Berlin Wall comes down. In El Salvador on November 16, the decade ends as it began—with leftist martyrdom. At the University of Central America in San Salvador, six Jesuit priests, their housekeeper, and her daughter are murdered by a right-wing death squad. One of the Jesuits is Ignacio Ellacuria, who was on a list of liberation theologians iden-tified as a threat by the Conference of American Armies (see above).

+ **February 25, 1990:** The Sandinistas are forced out of power in Nicaragua. Franciscan Uriel Molina, who led the revolutionary Catholic Church during the 1970s and '80s at Santa Maria de Los Angeles parish in Managua, is expelled from the Franciscan order. The Vatican orders him out of the parish.

+ **1991:** In Haiti, the Vatican shocks observers by being the only "nation" in the world to recognize the military regime after it assumes power in a coup. As in El Salvador, where the twelve-year civil war resulted in a death toll of 70,000, Ratzinger's warnings about liberation theology's terrorist nature ring rather hollow with Haitians, who see the Vatican's support of the coup as an endorsement of systematic terror.

✦ **October 1992:** For the fourth assembly of the Latin American Bishops Conference in Santo Domingo, the Vatican insists that its own appointees, Secretary of State Angelo Sodano and Chilean cardinal Jorge Medina Estevez, chair the session. Medina is on friendly terms with Augusto Pinochet, which suggests that liberation theology might get a less than sympathetic hearing.[20] The final document of the Santo Domingo assembly formally denounces any identity of the kingdom of God with any sociopolitical arrangements. The kingdom can only be glimpsed through mysterious connection with Jesus, not in any social order, the assembly decides.

---

20 In 1999, when Pinochet was detained in London on possible human rights abuse charges, it was Medina who convinced the secretariat of state to intercede with the British government on the aging fascist's behalf.

Throughout all this, Pope John Paul II responded to liberation theology with all the consistency of a weather vane—adjusting his position depending on his audience and on political mercury levels of the day. In January 1986, he declared from Rome that the only real liberation was individual liberation from sin. Two months later he told his bishops: "Purified of elements which can water it down, liberation theology is not only orthodox, but necessary." (He repeated this theme in a letter to the Brazilian bishops conference: liberation theology was "not only opportune, but useful and necessary.") In 1996, during a visit to El Salvador, His Holiness announced: "the era of liberation theology is over." But in January 1999, the weather vane shifted back and forth on a trip to Mexico. During his in-bound flight, John Paul was asked about the uprisings in Chiapas. "The church obviously does not agree," he said, with "substituting liberation theology with indigenous theology" based on Marxism. Then, once landed, he referred to "social sins" and criticized neo-liberalism with a leftist fervor worthy of Leonardo Boff.

Ratzinger, on the other hand, suffered from no such ambivalence. From the beginning, he and the liberation theologians were at loggerheads over the life-and-death questions of *praxis*. Their bottom line was freeing the Latin American poor from the chains of poverty and hunger; Ratzinger's was defending the faith from ideology. In his view, there was no saving the Latin American poor if it meant casting one's lot with the leftists. Anyone who disagreed with him on this was simply denying transcendence, denying God, or making the question of God irrelevant; denying the "truth." What the cardinal was proposing to the Latin American poor was a simple choice not unlike that facing German citizens and other victims of the Nazis, a recurring theme in Ratzinger's life: speak out and risk the ultimate punishment, or remain silent and live. Obey, and all shall be well. Ratzinger's insistence that liberation was an individual experience of Christian grace—not a collective imperative to make the gospels work for everyone—became the prevailing wisdom in the Latin American church after the 1980s. Through his persuasive opposition to liberation theology, Ratzinger exacerbated socio-economic apartheid in Latin America, thus increasing inequality. By siding with right-wing governments, he enabled the ideology of neoliberalism (freer trade, less taxation, smaller government) that widened the gap between the rich and poor. It is a testament to his legacy that, in 2006, when Daniel Ortega and the "new look" Sandinistas were returned to power in Nicaragua after sixteen years in political exile, Ortega claimed to be a changed man. The once-and-future president declared that he had moved from Marxism to Catholicism—making it a foregone conclusion that, as per Ratzinger, the two were mutually exclusive.

On March 28, 2012, Pope Benedict ended a three-day visit to Cuba by sitting down in Havana for a half-hour chat with Fidel Castro. The former Communist leader, looking frail six years after relinquishing power, was on his best behaviour. As the flashbulbs popped away, the Jesuit-educated altar boy-turned-revolutionary asked Benedict about changes in the liturgy since Vatican II, the canonization of Mother Teresa and

Pope John Paul II, the role of the pope, and larger philosophical questions. Benedict, for his part, showed diplomatic aplomb by criticizing the US for continuing its fifty-two-year trade embargo against the Communist state. But this was after a public homily in which he denounced Communist "fanaticism." And, in front of the world's media, he couldn't resist a little one-upmanship with his erstwhile ideological adversary. When Castro, also in his mid-eighties, joked about their advanced age, His Holiness quipped: "At least I still carry out my duties." This was a boast, of course, that would turn out to be short-lived.

V

From Ecumenism to Empire

A tyrant is more afraid of good people than of bad people.
—Saint Thomas Aquinas

Regensburg University: September 12, 2006
It should have been his golden moment—and it was, while it lasted: Pope Benedict XVI, leader of the world's 1.2 billion Roman Catholics, had returned in triumph to the place where his plan to recapture the church had really begun—the think tank from which his ambitious younger self had begun to plot the Augustinian revival. Decades after captivating his students at Regensburg, Ratzinger as pope now had the entire world as his audience while speaking from the same stage. In his address, he spoke about rationality and violence—and of the responsibility of both academe and the church to condemn violence. It wasn't a bad speech, really. In 5,545 words, His Holiness managed to capture some of the tensions between reason and faith (while deploring violence justified by faith) that would interest a non-believing audience of "representatives of science." The speech wrapped up with a nice appropriation of Socrates that illustrated the importance of keeping an open mind to the possibility of God's existence.

Recalling the great philosopher's comment to Phaedo about the many false philosophical opinions that had come up in their earlier conversations, he quoted: "It would be easily understandable if someone became so annoyed at all these false notions that for the rest of his life he despised and mocked all talk about being—but in this way he would be deprived of the truth of existence and would suffer a great loss." Ergo: when we abandon the search for meaning, our lives become meaningless. This was Benedict's answer to the Dawkins/Hitchens crowd—not a bad riposte, if that was in fact what he meant.

Unfortunately, this being the age of the sound bite, only thirty-two of those 5,545 words got much coverage. The pope's sound bite that day was from a centuries-old quotation: "Show me just what Muhammad brought that was new, and there you will find things only evil and inhuman, such as his command to spread by the sword the faith he preached."

These were the words of Manuel II Paleologus, one of the last of the Byzantine emperors. As Benedict explained to his audience, Paleologus was speaking with an educated Persian on the subject of Christianity and Islam, possibly in the year 1391, when he said this. The pope introduced the quote by referring to the emperor's "unacceptable" and "startling brusqueness"; he also noted that the emperor went on to explain why spreading faith through violence was "incompatible with the nature of God and the nature of the soul." His own point was raised in the question: "Is the conviction that acting unreasonably contradicts God's nature merely a Greek idea, or it is always and intrinsically true?"

Fair enough, on the face of things. But Benedict's one

mistake—in media optics, if not in logic—was that he was caught red-handed, scoring points for Jesus at Muhammad's expense. Instead of expanding on the Byzantine emperor's brief reference to the Koran (that "there is no compulsion in religion" for holy war), or offering examples of Christian violence to balance things out, he added fuel to the fires of the emperor's bigotry. First, he referred to eleventh-century Andalusian polymath Ibn Hazm's contention "that God is not bound even by his own word" and that, "were it God's will, we would even have to practice idolatry." Then, to remove all doubt as to his Christian triumphalist agenda, Benedict placed Ibn Hazm's "capricious God" in direct opposition to the Catholic faith. With much subtlety, he invoked Ephesians 3:19 (roughly: the love of God is *logos*, or reason) and Romans 12:1 (Christian worship is worship in harmony with the eternal word and with one's reason) to celebrate the "inner rapprochement between Biblical faith and Greek philosophical inquiry." This, he said, was the decisive "event" that created Europe and built its foundations. In other words: Christianity as civilizing force, the go-to religion for salvation.

Given the power of his office and strength of his intellect, could His Holiness truly have been surprised that his comments would send the entire Muslim world into an uproar, sparking ten days of violent demonstrations that would culminate with the murder of an Italian nun in Somalia? Or that Pakistan's parliament would adopt a resolution condemning his "derogatory" comments about Islam and seeking an apology? The Grand Imam Sheikh Mohamed Sayyid Tantawi of Cairo, the leading cleric in Sunni Islam worldwide, described the manner of the pope's citation of Paleologus as "a huge religious and scholarly mistake." In Britain, the head of the Muslim Council wondered why Benedict didn't "act and speak with responsibility" and denounce the Byzantine emperor's bigotry "in the interests of truth and harmonious relations between the followers of Islam and Catholicism." But it was in Turkey, a moderate democracy seeking European Union membership, that Benedict was most condemned.

Turkey's long-delayed entry into the EU was a sensitive process, to put it mildly; something that required the best diplomatic behavior from all "state" representatives with an interest in it. The pope's reference to present-day Istanbul as "Constantinople"—the city's name until 1923, when the modern Turkish state was formed—could at least be passed off as the quaint eccentricity of an esoteric intellectual, nostalgic for the days before the city was conquered by Muslim Ottoman Turks. But Turkish critics found something sinister in Benedict's willingness to give Paleologus a pass on his statements about Islam and violence. Salih Kapusuz, deputy leader of the Islamic-rooted governing party, told Turkish state media that the pope was a "poor thing" who "has not benefited from the spirit of reform in the Christian world. It looks like an effort to revive the mentality of the Crusades."

It would be easy to comment on the sad irony of all this, to argue that the religious violence inspired by the pope's denunciation of religious violence merely reinforced his argument. However, such frankness would put His Holiness in an awkward position: for the leader of the world's 1.2 billion Roman Catholics, it is more important to promote peace and harmony than to win an argument in front of the world's media. And for a man who loved winning arguments and was all too accustomed to doing so, the notion of being forced by diplomacy to apologize must have been excruciating. Despite heavy pressure on Benedict to issue a personal apology, it was only after ten days—following the death of a nun and some clumsy attempts by Vatican officials to apologize on his behalf—that he finally spoke up, and then sought meetings with Muslim officials.

However, the Socratic tone of his invitations was not entirely appreciated. "It is extremely weird," said Ahmed el-Tayeb, president of al-Azhar University and a former mufti of Egypt, "to see someone who insulted you asking for a delegation to go to him to explain reasons behind his insults."[21] After one meeting in Rome, a representative of Italy's Muslim community said: "We were invited for a dialogue, but it was a monologue." The substance of that "monologue," interestingly enough, was an invitation by the pope to join him in opposing modernity and the evils of the same Enlightenment he so championed in the Regensburg address. "In a world marked by relativism and too often excluding the transcendence and universality of reason," Benedict told the Muslim clerics, "we are in great need of an authentic dialogue between religions and between cultures, capable of assisting us, in a spirit of fruitful cooperation, to overcome all the tensions together."

Was this really an olive branch to the Muslim world? Quite possibly, but not necessarily for the best of reasons. The year before he became pope, on May 13, 2004, Cardinal Ratzinger

---

21 Al-Azhar also rejected a Vatican proposal to invite Benedict to Cairo to deliver a speech on Islam.

delivered a speech at the Library of the Italian Senate on the history of the European continent from Herodotus to Toynbee. As with many of his speeches, this one took the form of a warning: unless Europeans reversed the trend of atheism plaguing the continent and gained a new appreciation for Christianity, all those values they held dear—human rights, democracy, equality, justice—would be dashed. The West would be doomed to unrestrained greed, with money the ultimate value. To whom could the Europeans turn, to find their way? To what shining example could they be inspired to rediscover Christianity as a daily reality in their lives? Why, Islam, of course!

Far from being anti-Muslim, it's quite possible that Ratzinger was coming out of the closet here as a moderate Islamophile, a Catholic suffering the ecclesial equivalent of that old Freudian canard, penis envy, when it came to the Muslim faith. For what could Muslims boast of now, to an extent the Vatican could only dream about? A higher birth rate than Catholics (well, except in Latin America). A much greater geographical landmass subject to theocratic rule (with which to accommodate that mushrooming birth rate). A far better track record of obedience among the flock, both to scripture and to clerical authority. A higher proportion of both subjugated women and women who identify as "liberated" but willingly embrace their religion. "The rebirth of Islam is not merely the product of the new material wealth of Islamic nations," said Ratzinger. "It is, in fact, also the result of an understanding that Islam can provide a strong spiritual foundation for the everyday lives of its people, a spiritual foundation that seems to elude the grasp of the European old world. And so that world, despite its continuing political and economic power, is increasingly viewed as condemned to decline and fall." By taking a cue from Muslims' rediscovery of their historic pride, the CDF prefect was suggesting that a "creative minority" of believers just might be capable of re-Christianizing Europe. Even in the Regensburg address, Benedict's respect for Islamic emphasis on the divine was apparent. "The world's profoundly religious cultures," he said, see the "exclusion of the divine from the universality of reason as an attack on their most profound convictions. A reason which is deaf to the divine and which relegates religion into the realm of subcultures is incapable of entering into the dialogue of cultures." This was a matter of opinion, to which His Holiness was entitled. But in how much "dialogue" had he truly engaged, between cultures and religions? And, more to the point, what was his record on supporting bishops and priests in this work?

One "True" Religion

On the question of interfaith dialogue, there were several instances in which Ratzinger's Roman Catholic supremacism put him in direct opposition with his pope. Indeed, as CDF prefect he often found it necessary to "correct" or otherwise educate John Paul II on his understanding of interfaith matters. The first inkling of this personal schism between the two men occurred with the gathering of world church leaders in Assisi in October 1986. At John Paul II's invitation, some 200 religious leaders convened in the birthplace of Saint Francis to "be together and pray" on behalf of peace. The gathering, says Vatican observer John Allen, "included rabbis wearing yarmulkes and Sikhs in turbans, Muslims praying on thick carpets and a Zoroastrian kindling a sacred fire. Robert Runcie, the Anglican archbishop of Canterbury, exchanged pleasantries with the Dalai Lama...Buddhists chanted and beat drums, and Shintoists played haunting melodies on thin bamboo reed instruments. Afterward they all assembled with the pope and formed a circle to offer their own prayers for peace."

All that was missing, it seemed, was the group hug. Ratzinger was clearly not amused, and said so in an interview with an Austrian newspaper. "This cannot be the model!" he sniffed, his thumbs-down on the gathering implying that the pope should have sought his advice before planning the event. At a press conference months later, Ratzinger's rejection of interfaith "truth"—even on a symbolic level—seemed harsh. Accepting the notion that all religions have a valid set of beliefs, he said, was "the definitive rejection of truth." The Assisi gathering had clearly delivered a serious blow to monolithic Roman Catholicism, the CDF prefect declared, with some exasperation. "The debate on religions has to be begun all over," he argued. "The category of truth and the dynamism of truth are put aside. The attitude that says that we all have values and nobody possesses the truth expresses a static position and is opposed to true progress. To accept that historical identity is to imprison oneself in historicism."

By the time a second Assisi gathering was held thirteen years later, the celebrations were muted by comparison: no reporters allowed, no non-Catholic services in churches, no joint prayer. Ratzinger's aggressive denunciation of Assisi I had killed the momentum of interreligious harmony, ensuring that no movement as such would arise in its wake. In his mind, religious pluralism was to the 1990s what liberation theology had been to the '80s, and just as dangerous. Of course, once he became Pope Benedict, he had to keep up appearances. In 2011, it may have seemed to some observers that Ratzinger had softened a bit by announcing plans to celebrate the twenty-fifth anniversary of the first Assisi gathering—the same event that had so offended him at the time. But Benedict made sure that there would be none of the "syncretism" that marred the first event. The October 27, 2011 gathering, said the Vatican, in a carefully worded media advisory, would "not feature communal prayer as part of the agenda." And it didn't.

It may have been a loophole in Vatican II ecclesiology that allowed Ratzinger to attack religious pluralism with such vigor. *Lumen Gentium*, the conciliar document on the church, was ambiguous on the whole question of interfaith dialogue. For one thing, it left lots of room for interpretation in the notion that the church of Christ "subsists in" the Roman Catholic Church. Exploiting this loophole, Ratzinger used it to discredit ecumenism. While John Paul II envisioned the third millennium as a period of reunification of the separate branches of Christianity, a time for the church to once again "breathe with both lungs" of East and West, his CDF prefect did not share such enthusiasm.

In July 1998, John Paul II released the document *Ad Tuendam Fidem*, an apostolic letter adding penalties to canon law for dissent from infallible magisterial teaching not formally defined.

Ratzinger added his own commentary, offering examples of infallible teaching such as Leo XIII's *Apostolicae Curae*, which declared Anglican ordinations to be "absolutely null and utterly void." In other words: the illegitimacy of the Anglican priesthood is an infallible teaching of the Catholic Church. This did not exactly charm the Anglicans. "A stark statement," noted the archbishop of York, David Hope. "Astonishingly insensitive and provocative," added Notre Dame University theology professor Richard McBrien. "When Cardinal Ratzinger says this is definitive," concluded Archbishop Michael Peers, "it's as if nothing has happened in the last 102 years, whereas a lot has happened."[22]

Ratzinger didn't show much more interest in finding common ground with the other major religions. In a 1987 interview with Italian newspaper *Il Sabato*, he suggested that Jews could only be fully true to their heritage by becoming Christian. "The pope has offered respect [to Judaism], but also a theological line," he explained. "This always implies our union with the faith of Abraham, but also the reality of Jesus Christ, in which the faith of Abraham finds its fulfillment." To elaborate on this, Ratzinger raised the example of Edith Stein, a Jew who converted to Catholicism and became a Carmelite nun before being murdered by the Nazis: "Finding faith in Christ, she entered into the full inheritance of Abraham. She turned in her Jewish heritage to have a new and diverse heritage. But in entering into

---

22 As Pope Benedict in the fall of 2009, Ratzinger would announce the creation of a "church within a church" that invited Anglicans to join Catholics without giving up their rites and traditions. But this was a conservative, not a liberal, move: it was aimed at accommodating traditionalist Anglicans worldwide (and US Episcopalians) who were angry about the acceptance of openly gay clergy in North America and female bishops in the Church of England.

unity with Christ, she entered into the very heart of Judaism." As a result of these comments, a December 1987 summit between Jewish and Catholic officials in Washington, DC was canceled in protest.

On August 19, 1985, John Paul II became the first pope to visit an Islamic nation when he spoke to a gathering of 80,000 young people in Casablanca. "Your God and ours [are] the same, and we are brothers and sisters in the faith of Abraham," the pope told Morocco's King Hassan II. Belgian Jesuit and religious pluralism expert Jacques Dupuis (who, as we shall see, became yet another of Ratzinger's clerical victims), supported John Paul II's statement as "an implicit admission that Muslims are saved in their own way as heirs of the faith of Abraham." As Pope Benedict, Ratzinger would not concede as much. (Until the Regensburg aftermath, in fact, he said very little to encourage Muslims that their faith had inherent "truth.") As the twentieth century drew to a close, Ratzinger was more concerned that it was the fastest growing religion in Europe—especially in his native Germany. Islam, he said, was undemocratic and intolerant of cultural difference—an odd critique, coming from someone who had crushed democracy and shown no respect for indigenous culture in his own religion. He also added this cheerful thought: "Nor must we forget that Islam was at the head of the slave traffic and by no means displayed any great regard for the blacks."

Interestingly, it was Ratzinger's comments about Buddhism and Hinduism that revealed the most about his interfaith politics—even though he had said the least about these religions. Buddhism he described as "an auto-erotic spirituality" that was full of "seductions." He dismissed reincarnation as "morally cruel," called Hinduism a "negative theology" that lends support to relativism, and, in general, decried the sensuality of both: "The use of bodily postures in Eastern spiritual traditions... is dangerous: It can degenerate into a cult of the body and can lead surreptitiously to considering all bodily sensations as spiritual experiences."

For the physically awkward, adolescent Ratzinger who was always picked last in sports, as much as for the cloistered academic (or for the celibate cleric no doubt mystified by the physical force that was John Paul II), perhaps any spiritual experience that privileged the body would be seen as a threat. However—as with Ratzinger's other public pronouncements on non-Catholic religions—his opinions about Buddhism and Hinduism did not go down well. The head of Italy's small Buddhist community described his comments as "uninformed and provincial." An American bishop actually apologized on his behalf, to the world Buddhist community, in advance of the Vesak holiday celebrating the life of Gautama Buddha.

Meanwhile, Ratzinger continued to second-guess Pope John Paul II on interfaith issues. As the Jubilee year of 2000 approached, the pope was mulling over the exact wording of a public apology for Roman Catholic injustices over the centuries. For a mostly cynical public, a skeptical flock, and masses of "lapsed" Catholics, such an apology—however worded—would amount to little more than empty symbolism. At best, it was a publicity-seeking attempt by His Holiness to ingratiate the Vatican with the innumerable groups of people it had offended over the ages—including those of other faiths. But in Ratzinger's litigation-phobic mind, the apology was fraught with danger: in his view, such a gesture was a potentially self-damning, self-destructive exercise in restorative justice. The CDF prefect did not want to see any admission of guilt that would give strength to critics of the church or be used as ammunition for "accusations made by those who are prejudicially hostile" to it. And so, in 1998, he used the full powers of his office to pre-empt the pope's announcement.

Acting in his capacity as president of the International Theological Commission, Ratzinger established a sub-commission to examine the various issues identified as requiring a church apology. The resulting document, *Memory and Reconciliation: The Church and the Faults of the Past* (March 7, 2000), relied on a healthy dollop of moral relativism (his favorite vice to condemn in others) to water down the apology, lessen the Vatican's guilt, and—most importantly—reduce its obligations to zero. "In events of the past, one must always distinguish the responsibility of fault that can be attributed to members of the Church as believers from that which should be referred to society during the centuries of 'Christendom' or to power structures in which the temporal and spiritual were closely intertwined," Ratzinger wrote. "Can today's conscience be assigned 'guilt' for isolated historical phenomena like the Crusades or the Inquisition?"

It was Ratzinger's great fortune to be speaking on behalf of an ancient, patriarchal empire accountable only to God rather than on behalf of a democratic government accountable to voters. One wonders how the American or Canadian public, for example, might respond if their apologizing leader referred to Japanese internment camps or native residential schools as "isolated historical phenomena" for which "today's conscience" need be assigned no guilt. True, the Inquisition and Crusades occurred centuries and not decades ago, unlike these latter injustices. But the point remains: an apology devoid of atonement is meaningless.

In Ratzinger's June 2000 *Note on the Expression "Sister Churches,"* he found it necessary to clarify John Paul II's use of the term "Sister Churches" in his outreach efforts to the Eastern Christian churches. "It must always be clear, when the expression Sister Churches is used in this proper sense, that the one, holy, Catholic and apostolic Church is not sister but *mother* of all the particular Churches," he wrote. John Paul II let this one go. But His Holiness must have found it somewhat irritating when, two months later, Ratzinger took him to task again. This time, the CDF prefect was undermining the pontiff's teaching on interreligious dialogue between Christians and Jews. During his April 13, 1986 visit to the Great Synagogue of Rome, John Paul II had spoken of the Jews as *fratelli maggiori,* or "elder brothers." But Ratzinger refuted this notion in *Dominus Iesus,* with typical subtlety. "To justify the universality of Christian salvation as well as the fact of religious pluralism, it has been proposed that there is an economy of the eternal Word that is valid also outside the Church and is unrelated to her, in addition to an economy of the incarnate Word," he wrote. "This position also is contrary to the Catholic faith, which, on the contrary, considers the salvific incarnation of the Word as a Trinitarian event."

In other words, outside of faith in Jesus as understood by the Roman Catholic Church, there is no possibility of salvation— even for Jews. This was taking the church back a few popes before John XXIII.

Dominus Iesus, subtitled On the Unicity and Salvific Universality of Jesus Christ and the Church, was published on August 6, 2000. This document is generally considered the mission statement of Ratzinger's Jesus doctrine and his final word on the subject. It says that non-Catholic Christian ecclesial communities are not "churches" in the proper sense. Even worse, non-Christians are seriously deficient in terms of their access to the means of salvation, compared to actual church members who have full access to the means of salvation. Dominus Iesus was not well received, even among Catholic theologians. Stanford University religious studies professor Thomas Sheehan, in the September/October 2000 edition of The American Catholic, referred to Dominus Iesus as a "sunset document." More political than theological, he wrote, its intention was to signal the tone of the next papal administration. "As befits a sunset document, its theological shelf-life will be very short," wrote Sheehan. "Given the shoddiness of its theological reasoning, it has already begun imploding under the weight of its own contradictions." He did not stop there. "True, it is embarrassing for those of us who cherish the Catholic tradition to see this sloppy document run roughshod, and with such theological vulgarity, over intricate and complex topics that theologians like Karl Rahner long ago treated with supreme finesse and delicacy," he wrote, recalling one of the CDF prefect's erstwhile mentors. "But then again, Joseph Ratzinger is no Karl Rahner. The intellectual distance that separates this third-rate document from the brilliance of Rahner and other theologians of the Second Vatican Council is a sad measure of how far the Catholic Church has fallen from its glory days in the 1960s."

Meanwhile, Ratzinger's relentless game of one-upmanship with the pope was beginning to earn him some bad press. By this point, John Paul II was physically ailing and producing less theological work. Critics accused Ratzinger of intellectual arrogance, and of a degree of theological rigidity beyond even that of the pope. During a September 22, 2000 interview with the *Frankfurter Allgemeine Zeitung*, Ratzinger responded with bored, let-them-eat-cake derision. "I must confess that I am quite tired of this sort of declaration," he told his German interviewer. "I have long since learned by heart this lexicon, which never seems to lack the concepts of fundamentalism, Roman centralism, and absolutism. I could write certain of these statements on my own, without even having to wait to read them, because they are repeated word for word each time, independent of the subject they treat. I wonder why on earth they never come up with anything new."

Clearly, Ratzinger regarded his critics as an amorphous mass—their various objections to his work interchangeable and unworthy of consideration. However, the pope himself decided to rein in his CDF prefect. At least, as much as Ratzinger could be reined in. Early in 2002, John Paul used the word "collaboration" five times in a 1,000-word address to the CDF in which the pontiff encouraged Ratzinger's office to work more closely with bishops and bishops' conferences before releasing CDF documents. Apparently, Ratzinger hadn't been doing a very good job of this and needed a nudge from the boss. And what was the reason for this intervention? Recent doctrinal statements had run into "difficulties of reception" (Vaticanese for, "Joseph, this my-way-or-the-highway approach of yours is pissing off too many of our prelates").

In Ratzinger's remarks before the papal address, he tried to put a positive spin on things. He pointed to recent investigations of theologians Jacques Dupuis, Marcel Vidal, and Reinhard Messner as examples of "a fertile collaboration between the magisterium of the church and theologians." *Fertile collaboration?* In the case of Dupuis, it was well established that the only "collaborating" going on was by the fellow Jesuit who ratted him out to the CDF by denouncing his 1997 book, *Toward a Christian Theology of Religious Pluralism.* Dupuis had to give up his job and take early retirement while the CDF investigated him, during which time he spent two weeks in the hospital recovering from the stress of the witch hunt. As a closer look at the Dupuis case (and those of a few other theologians targeted by Ratzinger) would reveal, the CDF prefect had a unique idea of "collaboration."

Weeding out the Heretics

In 1997, the CDF informed Dupuis that *Toward a Christian Theology of Religious Pluralism* contained ambiguous statements and insufficient explanations that could lead readers to "erroneous or harmful conclusions" about Christ's role as the "unique and universal saviour." The investigation dragged on for four years before Ratzinger released his ruling on the book. He told Dupuis to remove "ambiguities" from future editions of the book that "could lead a reader to erroneous opinions" and raise doubts about Christ's saving power. "According to Catholic doctrine," said the German cardinal, "the followers of other faiths are oriented to the church and are all called to become part of her."

Dupuis was well known at the Vatican, having served as an advisor to the Pontifical Council for Interreligious Dialogueue. So his support of religious pluralism was no big surprise. As far back as Vatican II, he had embraced the view that divine revelation is not limited to the Judeo-Christian tradition but extends to other faiths. This put him in the same camp as Jesuit contemporaries Henri de Lubac, Hans Urs von Balthasar (a Ratzinger fellow traveler), and Karl Rahner. His own view was inclusivist: salvation is offered most completely through Jesus but allows room for other saving acts in other traditions. Drawing from the Gospel of John, he argued that because *logos* is eternal it existed prior to incarnation in Jesus and is thus active in other cultures.

Ratzinger's hounding of Dupuis appears to have been based on ignorance. At worst, it was inspired by envy. Before he went to Rome, Dupuis spent thirty-six years teaching theology in India. He would later describe the experience as formative, saying that he would never have developed his view of pluralism without the rich diversity of cultural interactions he had enjoyed on the subcontinent. Despite positive reviews of *Toward a Christian Theology of Religious Pluralism*, the CDF jumped on the book almost as soon as it came out and began a doctrinal probe. Dupuis agreed to give up his teaching position at the Pontifical Gregorian University in Rome for three months while the investigation unfolded. But he would never return to his position. "I think the reason I was targeted was because, through me, the Congregation was targeting Oriental theologians and Asian theology," Dupuis said later. This makes sense: the interfaith and intercultural lessons Dupuis would have learned from three-and-a-half decades of exposure to Indian life were not something a Eurocentric, ivory tower academic like Ratzinger—who had never lived anywhere but in the privileged embrace of the global North—would have easily comprehended. Nor, from all appearances, did Ratzinger have much interest in comprehending it.

In 1990, Sri Lankan oblate Tissa Balasuriya published *Mary and Human Liberation: The Story and the Text*. The book celebrates the mother of Jesus as a strong woman who, in remaining faithful to her son during his darkest hour, became "a great inspiration to Christian movements for social transformation throughout the world." The book sold only a few hundred copies in the four years before Ratzinger excommunicated Balasuriya. After that, it sold in the thousands. Thanks to the platform Ratzinger gave its author by attacking him, Balasuriya became a minor celebrity. And why was he excommunicated? Because he refused to sign the profession of faith the CDF had sent to him, which included the prohibition on women's ordination.

(Balasuriya believed that the Blessed Virgin was the first female priest.) But feminism was not the core issue here, said Ratzinger: the problem was that Balasuriya insisted that Asian religions are valid and true in their own right. In his 1,800-word excommunication notice, Ratzinger accused him three times of "relativizing" or "relativism" in relation to the faith, of placing "the supernatural, unique, and irrepeatable character of the revelation of Jesus Christ" on the same level as those of other religions.

The excommunication was lifted a year later, but not without major concessions by Balasuriya. Although he admitted to no doctrinal error and would not have to sign a customized profession of faith, he acknowledged "perceptions of error" and agreed to submit all future writings to his bishops for imprimatur. He also signed and published a statement in the national Catholic newspaper of Sri Lanka that included the phrase "serious ambiguities and doctrinal errors were perceived" in his writings, and that he regretted "the harm" such perceptions had caused. Thus was he cowed into silence.

Then there was Indian Jesuit Anthony de Mello. Once again, this was a case where Ratzinger's perception and John Paul II's were at odds. Here's Karol Wojtyla on de Mello, known for his best-selling books that bridge Eastern and Western spirituality: "His theological compassion for humanity, passion for faith and belief in Christian values are a forward light for our collective future." And here's Ratzinger, on the same person: "In certain passages in [his] early works and to a greater degree in his later publications, one notices a progressive distancing from the essential contents of the Christian faith." On July 23, 1998—eleven years after de Mello's death from a heart condition—Ratzinger asked the presidents of the world's bishops' conferences to either withdraw de Mello's books from circulation or ensure that they be printed with a disclaimer attached. The CDF prefect had concluded, from reading de Mello, that he advocated the notion that Jesus was not the son of God but one master among many; that the question of life after death is irrelevant; that there are no objective rules of morality; and that the church is an impediment in the search for truth. These positions, said Ratzinger, were "incompatible with the Catholic faith and can cause grave harm."

Colleagues who spoke up on the late theologian's behalf said that he would have defended himself by pointing out that Thomas Aquinas had said the same things. Not surprisingly, Doubleday—which published eight of de Mello's books—raised the objection that withdrawing the author's works was hardly a reasonable request of a secular publishing house. Jesuit provincials of Asia, in a damning indictment of Ratzinger's imperialist neocolonialism, also came to de Mello's defence. "He has helped thousands of people in South Asia and across the world in gaining freedom and in deepening their life of prayer, of which we have abundant testimonies and our own personal experiences," they said in a joint statement, adding an admonishment: "There is a lack of appreciation of difference and of proper procedures, when decisions are taken unilaterally without a dialogue with the Asian churches. We are afraid that such interventions are eventually detrimental to the life of the church, to the cause of the Gospel and to the task of interpreting the Word to those who do not belong to the Western cultural tradition."

Ratzinger's attacks on pluralist theologians are too numerous to list here. One more that should be noted, however, is that involving the Dominican Matthew Fox. One of Ratzinger's favorite whipping boys, Fox is a New Age Catholic—one of those touchy-feely, "holistic" theologians, a dissenter whose embrace not only of other mainline religious traditions but also of pagan, women-centered movements like the Wiccans is antithetical to Ratzinger's views on just about everything. Fox's promotion of "creation spirituality" was particularly trouble-some for the German cardinal. An alternative wisdom tradition in Christianity, creation-centered spirituality embraces a deeply mystical and prophetic experience of the gospels that celebrates the physical and the ecstatic, a notion that Ratzinger abhors.

Fox's most famous creation spirituality concept, "original blessing," rejects the fall–redemption tradition of Christianity, which, as he puts it, "begins with the idea of original sin and so readily feeds into imperial and ecclesial structures that control by way of guilt and shame." Furthermore, Fox's four paths to enlightenment are a direct challenge to the magisterium's three paths of purgation, illumination, and unity: *Via Positiva* (joy, delight, and awe), *Via Negativa* (silence, letting go, letting be, and suffering), *Via Creativa* (creativity), and *Via Transformativa* (justice-making and compassion and celebration). Creation spirituality is also feminist- and ecology-centered, and more accepting of homosexuality than the church is—facts that, in themselves, raised enough alarm bells at the CDF to condemn Fox as a heretic, a dangerous thinker who had to be stopped.[23]

---

23 For many years, my own book collection contained a much dog-eared, underlined and annotated copy of one of Fox's titles under CDF investigation. *Whee! We, Wee All the Way Home: Toward a Sensual, Prophetic Spirituality* (Bear and Co., 1981) talks

Ratzinger's investigation of Fox began in 1983, when he ordered a panel of three American Dominican theologians to perform a review of his writings. After eighteen months, the initial findings exonerated Fox of any theological heresy, concluding that "there should be no condemnation of Father Fox's work" and that, on the contrary, he should be commended for his "hard work and creativity." Ratzinger rejected these findings and ordered a second review, which was never undertaken. Then in 1988, Fox wrote a public letter to the CDF prefect that appeared in the *National Catholic Reporter*. The letter, headlined "Is the Catholic Church a Dysfunctional Family?", went beyond the particulars of Fox's own case to focus on the nature of dissent.[24] At one point in it, Fox referenced the Soviet poet Yevtushenko's notion that not all blame in Soviet history should be laid at the feet of the ruling Soviet clique. The people, he said, "allowed the clique to do whatever it wanted. Permitting crimes is a form of participating in them, and historically, we are used to permitting them. It is time to stop blaming everything on the bureaucracy.

---

about God as an ecstatic experience, God as artist rather than master, and the spiritual journey as a process of thinking and acting symbolically, or "how spiritual voyagers reject literal thinking for symbolic playing and how our symbolic thinking is our God-consciousness." After I walked away from the institution of the Church, the presence of this book in my library (or, at least, the earnest naïveté and enthusiasm of my scribblings within it) gradually became an embarrassment. However, my shift away from the sacred and toward more secular ways of thinking does not diminish my respect for the work Fox has done, over four decades, to help thousands of Catholics reclaim a healthier sense of spirituality—and, in many cases, recover from the religious battery of Ratzingerian thought.

24 Ratzinger's specific objections to Fox's work are dismissed easily enough. Fox's reference to God as "Mother" and "Child" could be no worse than Pope John Paul I's statement that "God is both Mother and Father," and there is no evidence that Fox denies, for example, the "validity" of infant baptism.

If we put up with it, then we deserve it."

Fox, following this theme, told Ratzinger it was time for Catholics to speak out about church injustices. "I believe that for years I have been protecting you from the consequences of your behavior by remaining silent," he said. "To continue to do so would be sinful, for your behavior is becoming increasingly scandalous with greater and greater repercussions for the future of our church."

Later in the letter, he argued that the church under Ratzinger's influence and leadership had become authoritarian in nature. The signs? First, the silencing of dissent: the CDF prefect dealt with diverse opinions by silencing people and cutting off real dialogue, thus arousing anti-intellectualism and promoting rabid ideological behavior. Second was judgmentalism, which required separating from and judging the other and was non-participatory. Third was scapegoating: saving one's most vicious attacks for the weak, the marginal, or the most alternative (i.e., Ratzinger's targeting of Starhawk, a Jewish feminist Wiccan who taught at Fox's institution), and justifying the assault as a defence of the faith. Fourth was the growing prominence of ultra-right-wing organizations such as Opus Dei. Fifth was the rewarding of authoritarian personalities. Those who questioned the magisterium or offered alternative views were shunted aside; those who recognized Rome's authority climbed the Vatican career ladder.

Given how thoroughly Fox's letter captured Ratzinger's theology and modus operandi, it seemed almost counterintuitive that he would then invite Ratzinger to visit and experience the Institute in Culture and Creation Spirituality for himself.

"Instead of trying to kill this joy, why don't you join us?" he concluded. "Why not take a year off and step down from your isolated and privileged life at the Vatican to do circle dances with women and men, some in their twenties, some in their seventies, who come from all over the world in search of an authentic spirituality? ... If you could but open your heart, I believe that you could understand and celebrate Creation Spirituality. As Meister Eckhart tells us, 'Compassion begins at home with one's own soul and body.'"

In fairness to Fox, one suspects that this invitation was not in earnest; that he was wrapping up his open letter with a sarcastic jab aimed at entertaining readers. (Imagine a suddenly liberated Ratzinger—perhaps as a result of LSD dropped into his coffee—fleeing the Vatican and running off to California, letting down his hair and doing circle dances with lithesome young men and middle-aged witches. Getting in touch with his "soul and body.") Needless to say, Ratzinger did not take him up on the offer. Instead, he issued an order forbidding Fox from teaching or lecturing for a year. By 1993, Fox's conflicts with the church ended with his expulsion from the Dominican order for "disobedience." He has since been embraced by the Anglicans, continues to teach and lecture outside the Roman Catholic bubble, and recently published a book with a title that's easier to comprehend than those of some of his earlier, more New Age books.[25]

---

25 *The Pope's War: Why Ratzinger's Secret Crusade has Imperiled the Church and How it Can be Saved* (Sterling Ethos, 2011).

VI

Mary, Mary, Quite Contrary

*Women have been seen to complete men the way a second coat of paint
completes a house, whereas men have been seen to complete women the
way a motor completes a car.*
—Sister Sandra M. Schneiders, summing up Vatican gender
politics under Pope John Paul II and Cardinal Ratzinger

In March 2009, a senior Vatican cleric defended the Roman
Catholic Church's decision to excommunicate the mother and
doctors of a nine-year-old rape victim in Brazil who had gone
through a life-saving abortion. Cardinal Giovanni Batista Re,
head of the Pontifical Commission for Latin America, displayed
the bizarre and skewed priorities of his pope, Benedict XVI,
when he addressed reporters about the case. The girl had been
impregnated by her abusive stepfather, who had allegedly raped
her repeatedly from the age of six. But that was not "the real
problem," he said. "The twins conceived here were two innocent
persons," Batista Re told the Italian newspaper *La Stampa*. "Life
must always be protected." Although the girl's mother and doctors were excommunicated for agreeing to the emergency abortion, the church took no action against the girl's stepfather. The
act of rape may have been "a heinous crime," said the regional
archbishop for Pernambuco, but "the abortion, the elimination

of an innocent life, was more serious."

What the cardinal and the regional archbishop were saying was nothing new. Such barbaric stupidity had been church policy for years. But it had accelerated under the papacies of John Paul II and Benedict XVI. The year before his death, John Paul II had made a saint of a woman who died after refusing an abortion—even though she had been warned that her pregnancy could kill her. And Benedict, in the months before his resignation, sat in silence as the people of Ireland raised their voices in outrage against doctors who had refused to save the life of Savita Halappanavar because of archaic abortion laws supported by the church. The Indian immigrant was allowed to miscarry and die of septicemia and ESBL E. coli, a strain of bacteria that resists penicillin, rather than be allowed a half-hour abortion procedure that would have helped her recover from the cervical dilation that had complicated her pregnancy. She could have been back to good health within weeks. Instead, her fate was sealed with these words from the hospital staff: "This is a Catholic country."

For most people, cases like Savita's and that of the nine-year-old rape victim in Brazil inspire strong feelings of moral outrage. But the man who became Pope Benedict, as we have seen, has a different moral framework from the average person. His views on abortion, as with all other issues involving women, are determined by a misogynistic theology and worldview based on historically developed doctrine that governed the church for centuries before Vatican II. From his very beginnings in rural Germany, Joseph Ratzinger had grown up to embrace a patriarchal and misogynistic church doctrine that saw women as second-class citizens at best and as a form of chattel, or private property, at worst. When that doctrine was challenged at Vatican II, Ratzinger began to develop a fear of independent women, and a hatred of feminism, that would govern all his decisions surrounding women's issues once he had power. This fear and loathing would lead him to resist, with every fiber of his being, a woman-friendly church.

By all accounts, his own mother, Mary Ratzinger, was a quiet woman—never a boat rocker—who accepted without question the Biblical understanding of women as servants to God and the Lord Jesus Christ, servants to the church, and servants to the social order and its preservation. According to the future Pope Benedict, Mrs Ratzinger extended this role to the raising of her two sons. Like Mary to Jesus, she embodied a pre-liberationist trope of mother as servant to the son: from their earliest childhood days to their mutual pursuit of the priesthood, Georg and Joseph learned from their mother that a woman's purpose was to serve God on this earth by serving the men who run it.

The 2009 Vatican publication *Maria: Pope Benedict XVI on the Mother of God* (Ignatius) offers telling insight into Ratzinger's view of women. In this lush, almost voluptuous coffee table book—replete with glossy color photos of His Holiness paying homage to the Virgin at Lourdes and various other Marian shrines—Benedict presented his vision of Mary as the great Servant of Jesus. All sourced to the Bible, of course, the essence of this vision was a concept of maternal devotion based on subservience that the pope believed all women should embrace. Good Catholics, he said, can learn from Mary "the right way to pray" and that her son Jesus is more than "a mere man on whose ability and helpfulness she can count." Mary, he said, citing Luke 1:38 in Nazareth, "leaves *everything* to the Lord's judgment."[26]

That would include thinking, one presumes. In *To Love Like Mary*, Benedict proposed a head-scratching non sequitur as an argument for Marian selflessness. "With complete availability," he said, "let us give our own bodies to the Lord" so that we can be "inwardly free." Later, he referred to Mary as "the Mother of all believers." It is hard to argue with this, since no one could possibly live up to the perfection with which the pope, like his predecessor John Paul II, had anointed the Blessed Virgin. Indeed, in *Maria*, Benedict frequently cited the Vatican II document *Lumen Gentium* (*Light of the Nations*) to demonstrate Mary's exemplary sacrifice. As the closest to God of all human creatures, he said, "she still had to walk day after day in a pilgrimage of faith," as if still needing to prove her worthiness in His eyes. Mary exemplified "the most important, the most central truth about God," the very idea expressed in the opening declaration of Benedict's first encyclical as pope: *Deus Caritas Est!* God Is Love!

Vatican II warned against making an "excessive, even idolatrous" cult of the Virgin Mary. The 1964 text on dogma that Benedict was fond of quoting, *Lumen Gentium*, urged "theologians and preachers to refrain as much from all false exaggeration as from too summary an attitude in considering the

---

26 Emphasis added.

special dignity of the Mother of God." In other words: go easy on the Mary worship. Clearly, this message of restraint was long forgotten by the time Karol Wojtyla ascended to the papacy. Throughout his time as CDF prefect, Ratzinger had John Paul II's full support for his idolatry of the Blessed Virgin. In *The Vatican's Women: Female Influence at the Holy See*, Paul Hofmann argues that the Madonna in heaven represented "a sacred surrogate for [the pontiff's] own mother, who died when he was a small boy and of whom he could have had only faint recollections. He appears to have always idealized virginity." In his first address as pope, John Paul II said he accepted his nomination "in the spirit of obedience to our Lord and in the total confidence of his mother, the Most Holy Madonna." His coat of arms featured a golden cross with the letter M (for Mary) on a blue field; his lifelong motto, *Totus Tuus* (all yours), signified total devotion to the Madonna. After the attempt on his life on May 13, 1981, John Paul II was convinced that Mary had saved him: in a case of Immaculate Deflection, the Blessed Virgin had repelled the bullets fired by his Turkish would-be assassin away from his heart.

As many theologians have noted, this idea of the Virgin Mary—which represents the feminine as faithful receptivity to God and moral perfection—only serves to highlight the huge gulf between an exceptional woman born without original sin and all actual women who are "daughters of Eve." Since real women cannot possibly live up to Mary's example, any pursuit of the ideal ends up in sexual repression and total submission to male authority. As Rosemary Radford Ruether put it, in a 1987 essay about the growing alienation of women from the church:

"Thus Mary does not become a model of woman as autonomous person, but rather appears as a fantasy by which celibate males sublimate their sexuality into an ideal relationship with a virgin mother, while projecting the hostility caused by this sexual repression into misogynist feelings toward real women. The present pope seems to be a particular example of this combination of Marian piety and misogyny." Ruether was talking about John Paul II when she wrote this, but she could just as easily have been referring to Pope Benedict.

This view of women stands in stark contrast to that of Pope John XXIII. On April 11, 1963, less than two months before his death, Pope John released *Pacem in Terris* (Peace on Earth). This encyclical endorsed a range of civil liberties in a manner that echoed the US Bill of Rights, as if anticipating the tumultuous events of the following decade. *Pacem in Terris* declared that each person is endowed with intelligence and free will, and that the full and equal rights of all persons—including the right to freely express and communicate opinions—flow from this. The encyclical affirmed various freedoms, including the freedom to choose one's state of life. It also endorsed women's equal inclusion in these rights by declaring: "Since women are becoming ever more conscious of their human dignity, they will not tolerate being treated as mere material instruments, but demand rights befitting a human person in both domestic and in public life."

With the world-changing vision of Vatican II having faded over the decades, it is hard to imagine such words being penned by an actual Roman Catholic pope, but they were. The impact of this groundbreaking encyclical was dramatic, compounding the tragic sense of loss when Pope John passed away before he could see it come to fruition. The pope sanctioned birth control. He knew there was a UN conference on population coming up in 1964, and he wanted the Catholic Church to present a position based on reality. Were his views heretical—or, at the very least, theologically unsound? That is, was Pope John a "feminist"? It would appear that Ratzinger believed so. The response of "God's Rottweiler" to issues like inclusive language, female ordination, and reproductive rights went some distance in the opposite direction from Pope John's vision.

Name of the Father—and Other Male-Only Metaphors
As far as God's gender was concerned, Cardinal Ratzinger had no doubt. So unequivocal was his position that he was known to discipline theologians who referred to God as "Mother," despite Pope John Paul I's famous declaration of September 10, 1978. ("We are the objects of undying love on the part of God...He is our father; even more he is our mother.")[27] However, like captains referring to their ships or generals to their conquered colonies, the CDF prefect was more than happy to refer to the church itself in the feminine. No doubt this gender-specific reference was intended as a nurturing metaphor, in keeping with Ratzinger's Marian view of "Mother Church": the healing,

27 In *The Vatican's Women*, Paul Hofmann reports that when friends later asked Luciani what he meant by this statement, he said "Oh, it's not an invention of mine; it's all in Isaiah." A likely reference, said Hofmann, to Isaiah 66: 9-13: "Shall not I that make others to bring forth children myself bring forth, saith the Lord...As one whom the mother caresseth so will I comfort you: and you shall be comforted in Jerusalem."

serving mother of God. But referring to inanimate objects or complex entities as "she" is part of a grand patriarchal tradition of romanticizing female subjugation. For both Ratzinger and Karol Wojtyla, the church was a woman to control and pacify.

The clampdown on inclusive language is a good example. On the question of whether it was good and right to demasculinize language in the church, the Canadian Conference of Catholic Bishops concluded early on in the John Paul II pontificate that inclusive language was less a "cultural question" than a spiritual imperative of Vatican II; a recognition that "the Church exists in the world" and that "Christians have a responsibility to read the 'signs of the times' and interpret them in light of the gospel." The Canadian bishops went on: "One of the signs of the times identified by Vatican II and recent popes [before Karol Wojtyla] is the changing role of women in society. There is, therefore, a special duty to listen to what women are saying about the need for inclusive language. Through listening and reflecting, it becomes apparent that there are significant theological reasons for using and promoting inclusive language." Pope John Paul II and Ratzinger begged to differ. Refusing to recognize "gender" as a social construction of masculinity and femininity, they targeted the Roman Catholic texts with the most power to influence the flock and proceeded to masculinize them.

In 1990, the US National Conference of Catholic Bishops began working on a new translation of the lectionary.[28] Their mandate was to produce translations that were "as inclusive as a faithful translation permits." A year later, the bishops approved a

---

28 The cycle of Biblical texts used as daily readings during the Eucharist.

new lectionary for Sundays that used inclusive language, as well as an inclusive language version of the Psalter.[29] The Vatican's Congregation for the Sacraments approved of the new Psalter in 1992, but withheld approval of the lectionary. In 1994, the CDF revoked the previous approval of the Psalter. A year later, Ratzinger issued new norms for Biblical translations, but kept them secret. In 1998, he issued a final veto of the new Psalter. Any praying of the Psalms in American churches would henceforth conform to the male-only version of the 1970 translation.

Most telling was Ratzinger's treatment of inclusive language in the universal catechism, first published in 1992. As Joanna Manning put it in her 1999 bestseller, *Is the Pope Catholic? A Woman Confronts Her Church*, the Vatican embraced the updated catechism "as a means to crack the whip of orthodoxy by issuing a compendium of the Catholic faith." The new catechism was first published in French. A year later, it had been translated into all other major languages except English. The problem? Apparently, an insidious feminism had infected the committee entrusted by Rome to complete the English translation. At a Vatican meeting in February 1993, Ratzinger scolded the translators for applying "too much inclusive language" in their work. Shortly afterward the American committee chair, Father Douglas Clark, was booted out. His replacement, the Australian archbishop Joseph D'Arcy, was charged with revising and reversing Clark's version of the catechism—which had updated the definition of the human race from normatively male to a species with two genders. Like Ratzinger and John Paul, Archbishop

---

29 A collection of Psalms for liturgical or devotional use.

D'Arcy was preoccupied with the "richness" of the relationship between God and man. He thought that by using inclusive language the church would be diluting this "rich" relationship and the "natural resemblance" that only men could have to God. So it came as no surprise when, in 1994, his English translation not only converted all references to *homme* as "man" but added extra male pronouns into the text (i.e., from Clark's "The Father created the human race to share in his blessed life" to D'Arcy's "God created *man* to make *him* share in *his* own blessed life").[30]

That same year, Ratzinger overturned an approval by the Congregation for Divine Worship for use of the inclusive-language text of the New Revised Standard Version (NRSV) of the Bible for Catholic worship and education. The issue, once again, was the use of "gender-sensitive" terms, a practice the German cardinal described as "the result of ideology." The US bishops, who had overwhelmingly approved the NRSV, spent the next three years challenging Ratzinger on this. But, like so many others who had defied the CDF prefect, they were forced to back down. Meanwhile, Ratzinger got busy composing the Vatican's secret norms for translation of all Biblical texts and liturgical prayers. These included:

+ "The grammatical gender of God, pagan deities, and angels and demons according to the original texts must not be changed" [so even the devil must be male]

---

30 Emphasis added.

✦ "The feminine and neuter pronouns are not to
be used to refer to the Holy Spirit"

✦ "The word 'man' in English should as a rule
translate *adam* and *anthropos* because this is so
important for the expression of Christian doctrine and anthropology"

Why were Ratzinger and Wojtyla so determined to cleanse
the faith of inclusive language? A major papal encyclical from
1988, the ironically titled *Mulieris Dignitatem* (*The Dignity of
Women*), offers a few clues. Apart from reaffirming the ban on
artificial birth control and abortion and defending the doctrine
of an all-male clergy, *Mulieris Dignitatem* distinguished itself by
declaring virginity to be a higher state of female existence than
marriage or motherhood. At the same time, it claimed to be
pro-woman in its advocacy of *complementarianism*, the idea that
that men and women have different but *complementary* roles
and responsibilities in marriage, family life, religious leadership,
and elsewhere. The Biblically prescribed complementarian view
assigns leadership roles to men and support roles to women—
this "support" precluding women from specific functions of
church ministry.

By 1995, John Paul II had developed the themes from
Mulieris Dignitatem in his *Letter to the Women of the World*, just
before the Fourth UN Conference on Women in Beijing. In the
letter, the pope deplored anti-female discrimination and hailed
the "liberation of women from any form of coercion and domi-
nation." John Paul II sounded almost like a Sensitive New Age

Guy in his support for equal opportunities for women in education, professional life, and politics; his condemnation of sexual exploitation of and violence against women; and his advocacy of more space for "the genius of women" in social life and in the church. Of course, his letter said nothing about birth control or abortion. And it firmly restated the Catholic Church's rejection of any female role in the ministry.

Infallibly Prohibited

On October 7, 1979, during his first papal visit to the United States, John Paul II visited the National Shrine of the Immaculate Conception in Washington, DC. One of the official greeters that day was Sister Theresa Kane, president of the Leadership Conference of Women Religious. When she stepped forward to welcome the pope, in front of several TV cameras and microphones, Sister Kane instantly burned herself into global Catholic consciousness with the following statement:

> As I share this privileged moment with you, Your Holiness, I urge you to be mindful of the intense suffering and pain, which is part of the life of many women in these United States. Your Holiness, as women we have heard the powerful messages of our church addressing the dignity and reverence for all persons. As women, we have pondered upon these words. Our contemplation leads us to state that the Church, in its struggle to be faithful to its call for reverence and dignity for all persons, must respond

by providing the possibility of women as persons being included in all ministries of our church. I urge you, Your Holiness, to be open and respond to the voices coming from the women of this country who are desirous of serving in and through the Church as fully participating members.

The days and weeks that followed saw much outrage over Sister Kane's brazen act of protest. Many sent her hate mail. But many others were inspired by what they saw as a courageous act: in the face of a church that had centuries of practice in the intimidation of women, Sister Kane had spoken for all women who feared the consequences of speaking out.

In some ways, Ratzinger and John Paul II's resistance to the idea of women priests was understandable. Devout Roman Catholic women have always kept pace with their male counterparts when it comes to theological vigor, pedagogical influence, and efficiency in church administration. They tend to get things done and they command respect, which only raises the question: why not make them priests, since they're clearly as good as men at everything else? The answer is obvious: making them priests would launch Rome on a slippery slope toward women bishops, archbishops, cardinals, and—ahem—popes. Perhaps Ratzinger and Wojtyla would never have reached such lofty heights had women's ordination ever been a possibility after Vatican II.

In the first few years following Vatican II, all the leading

Catholic theologians were men: Pierre Teilhard de Chardin, Henri de Lubac, Karl Rahner, Bernard Häring, Edward Schillebeeckx, Bernard Cooke, Charles Curran, Hans Küng, and Hans Urs von Balthazar among them.[31] Ten or fifteen years later, the Catholic discourse had expanded to include female theologians such as Mary Daly, Elizabeth Scheussler Fiorenza, Rosemary Radford Reuther, Elizabeth A. Johnson, and Sandra M. Schneiders. By the mid-1980s, the influence of these women was causing alarm in Rome. Ratzinger said that "a feminist mentality" had invaded women's orders, a phenomenon "particularly evident, even in its extreme forms, on the North American continent." As signs of this degenerate "mentality" he pointed to a creeping "professionalism," the absorption of secular values to replace religious ones, and the use of psychotherapy in the convent. Such alarmist rhetoric about feminism, one supposes, was strategically necessary: if Ratzinger was to succeed in closing the lid on women's ordination, he would first have to discredit its philosophical underpinnings.

Ratzinger would not begin his major offensive against female ordination until well into his tenure at the CDF. Deborah Halter captures it all in her exhaustive account of the debate, *The Papal No: A Comprehensive Guide to the Vatican's Rejection of Women's Ordination*. In this book, Halter recalls how the Jesuit theologian Joseph Fessio, a close associate of Ratzinger's, had written a "lucid if overblown" defence of male-only altar service: "He argued that the altar was a sacred place, the Eucharist a sacred

---

31 In the early post-Vatican II period, Ratzinger was still a few years removed from publishing fame—and even once he *was* getting noticed, not a lot of Catholic women were reading him.

act, and the priest a sacred person, and the altar boy became 'the hands of the priest.' If a girl were to take this role, she would cause a 'serious disharmony with the very nature and character of the whole order of grace and redemption' and would even confuse the 'symbolic character of men and women.'"

Fessio's objections to allowing girls to serve on the altar may be summed up as follows:

+ Serving beside altar boys would fill girls with the "false hope of ordination"

+ Priestly vocations would decline because "boys would no longer want to take a job that girls were allowed to do"

+ Girls would suffer "an identity problem" and "the faithful would be confused"

+ Faithful Catholics "would be demoralized"

+ Feminists would be "emboldened to seek even greater victories"

The first four explanations were pessimistic, to be sure. But Fessio turned out to be right on the final count. When John Paul announced in March 1994 that girls would be allowed to serve on the altar he "contributed to a climate in which his teaching on male priesthood would be increasingly rejected by Roman Catholics."

But the pope's decision on girls at the altar (which also confirmed that females could serve as lectors, Eucharistic ministers, and religious educators) was merely a pre-emptive breadcrumb. Just over two months later, on May 30, he released the apostolic letter *Ordinatio Sacerdotalis* (*On Reserving Priestly Ordination to Men Alone*), which closed the door forever on women's ordination. "I declare," he said, "that the Church has no authority whatsoever to confer priestly ordination on women and that this judgment is to be definitively held by all the Church's faithful." The document confirmed John Paul II's belief that a male priesthood was based on Christ's decision to choose only males as his twelve apostles.

The world's bishops knew little or nothing about the contents of *Ordinatio Sacerdotalis* before its release. Many were concerned that its main argument seemed based more on papal authority than on Christ's example. There was so much blowback in response to this document, in fact, that Ratzinger was compelled to write the *Responsum Ad Dubium* (*Response to a Question*) about *Ordinatio Sacerdotalis*, which the pope approved for publication on October 28, 1995. Here, the CDF prefect got into a great deal of trouble. Saying that the prohibition against women priests was based on the written word, he concluded that this teaching had been "set forth infallibly by the ordinary and universal magisterium [bishops in union with the pope]."

Ratzinger appeared to think he was being helpful. Instead, he created more confusion as theologians and clerics were sent scrambling to their canonical texts to get the goods on infallibility. The pope could have played the infallibility card on women's ordination if he had used his *ex cathedra* authority. But he didn't do that, and so—according to canon 749:3—any infallible doctrine would have to be "manifestly" established: proposed not only by the pope but by the whole body of Catholic bishops. However, the world's bishops had neither been consulted nor given a chance to review *Ordinatio Sacerdotalis* before its publication. So where did this put the question of women's ordination—or, for that matter, infallibility?

Because the claim of infallibility had appeared nowhere in *Ordinatio Sacerdotalis*, the question became: could an administrative curial congregation (the CDF) declare a teaching "infallible" when the pope had not? Or, as Benedictine Sister Joan Chittister put it, in an interview with the *National Catholic Reporter*: "Has there been a palace coup and someone forgot to tell us about it? Is the pope's name John Paul II or Joseph Ratzinger?" By this point, Wojtyla was getting frustrated. A week after the *Responsum*'s publication, he warned the CDF that dissenters were challenging the "authentic concept of authority" and threatening to form a "countermagisterium." Edward Schillebeeckx of the Netherlands said it was "totally impossible, dogmatically" for a male-only priesthood to be a matter of infallibility. The National Coalition of American Nuns said that the Vatican's teaching against women's ordination could not be infallible because it was "unjust and, therefore, in error." And the Catholic Theological Society of America established a task force to examine the issue. Among its conclusions:

+ The CDF had failed to establish any basis in Biblical history, or an unbroken tradition, for the refusal to ordain women

+ Many women were active in the ministry in the early church

+ Jesus's naming of the twelve apostles did not constitute ordination

+ The Catholic Church's "traditional" exclusion of women from the priesthood did not make it a "legitimate" tradition

+ Even *Humanae Vitae* was not declared "infallible" by Pope Paul VI

Still, the CDF prefect was undeterred. "In his zeal to defend the male priesthood," wrote Halter, "Ratzinger used selective history, internal contradiction, and remarkably pejorative language; but, as always, he made his point." In a most obfuscatory fashion, yes, he did. In 1997, Ratzinger confounded the *National Catholic Reporter* by telling a news conference that claiming women could be ordained was not "heresy" but just plain wrong. His reasoning? The male-only priesthood rule did not belong to the "deposit of faith" (the entire collection of revealed teachings and church tradition) but was a "second-order truth" connected to (but not required for) the deposit of faith. The NCR referred to this mumbo-jumbo as a shift from "revealed, primary truth" toward "the more murky, more imponderable and probably more impenetrable fortress of 'secondary truth.'" Others called it bullshit: a self-justifying form of sophistry on par with Bill Clinton's moral hair-splitting during the impeachment hearings ("It all depends on what the definition of 'is' is"), or Donald Rumsfeld's equally infamous riddle about "knowns" and "unknowns" regarding weapons of mass destruction in Iraq. When obfuscation didn't work, Ratzinger pointed out that women weren't the only ones prohibited from celebrating Holy Mass. So were priests who were allergic or alcoholic (and thus could not ingest the host or the wine of the Eucharist). Of course, this would be of little consolation to most women, who did not take kindly to having their very existence equated with vice (alcoholism) or constitutional intolerance (food allergies). Compounding the insult, Ratzinger included women's ordination among four actions condemned by the church—the others being fornication, prostitution, and euthanasia. Not content to win the argument about infallibility, he couldn't resist rubbing salt into the wound. "In the future," he said in 1998, "the consciousness of the church might progress to the point where this teaching could be defined as a doctrine to be believed as divinely revealed."

Over the years, in defence of this "infallible" law, he would discipline several people who challenged the CDF's view of female ordination. In 1985, there was Edward Schillebeeckx, his former colleague. Ratzinger sent the Belgian theologian "notification" for holding a number of unacceptable views, among them his support for women priests. In 1994, there was Lavinia Byrne. The English theologian's book, *Women at the Altar*, was prohibited for circulation and ordered for destruction because of Byrne's advocacy of priesthood for women. Byrne had actually worked with the publisher to include the pope's apostolic letter in the back of the book just before its publication. But

1,300 copies were incinerated anyway. "You can go to a rape therapist or a grief counselor," a shaken Byrne told the BBC, "but there aren't too many book-burning counselors around."

In 2002, Ratzinger excommunicated the Argentinian priest Romulo Antonio Braschi—along with the several Catholic women he ordained on the banks of the Danube River. In May 2005—a month after the ascension of Pope Benedict— the American priest and journalist Thomas J. Reese became Ratzinger's final victim as CDF prefect when he was forced to resign after seven years as editor-in-chief of *America*, a weekly Catholic magazine. This followed five years of pressure from Ratzinger's office regarding various editorial decisions made by Reese on certain issues covered in the magazine—including the ordination of women.

As Pope Benedict, Ratzinger ramped up his war on women priests. In July 2010, he declared the ordination of women a "crime against the faith" subject to discipline by the CDF. Women attempting to be priests, and those who ordained them, already faced automatic excommunication. But the new decree put attempts at ordaining women among the "most serious crimes," equating a female clergy with pedophilia. Ratzinger had once said that "being taken into the sacrament of [orders] is a renunciation of oneself in order to serve Jesus Christ." But this was hard to square with his adamant assertion that priests must be male, particularly in light of his theology of the Virgin Mary as passive and receptive to God's word. In the Ratzingerian universe, there was no contradiction between God's choice of a woman to physically give birth to Jesus and the church's refusal to allow women to represent God. In *Catholic (Does*

Not Equal) the Vatican: A Vision for Progressive Catholicism, Rosemary Radford Ruether examines the patriarchal nature of this clericalist approach to doctrine. In Ratzinger's view, she writes, the Eucharist is "transformed into a tool of clerical power over the people and is the sacrament most rigidly guarded as a clerical privilege, a sacred act that no layperson can perform. Ordination is the hierarchically transmitted power to 'confect' the Eucharist … Thus the simple act of blessing and distributing food and drink as a symbol of giving and nurturing life is turned into a power tool to control access to God."

Whose Body Is It, Anyway?

In 1962, the infallible teaching on contraception was challenged by leading reformers in Europe such as Dutch bishop William Bekkers and Belgian bishop Cardinal Leo Joseph Suenens. When Vatican II opened that autumn, Bekkers and Suenens were there. It was Suenens who convinced Pope John XXIII to form a small commission to study the issue of birth control in depth. After the pope's death in June 1963, his successor Pope Paul VI inherited the commission. He expanded it to fifty-eight members, including five women, a majority of lay people, and representatives from every continent. By 1964, no fewer than four books dissenting from the Vatican's position on birth control had been rushed into print and circulated at the Council. On June 28, 1966, when the commission delivered its final report, *Responsible Parenthood*, the vote was fifty-two to four in favor of the church developing a more progressive view of contraception.

That should have ended the issue. However, the conservative

head of the Holy Office and the leader of the four who had voted against the report were determined to get a second chance by appealing to the pope. As history records, *Humanae Vitae* (1968) was their reward. Less than two decades later, the momentous and possibly groundbreaking dialogue about birth control at Vatican II would be a fading memory. In 1981, Pope John Paul II established the Pontifical Council for the Family and charged it with promoting "responsible procreation" (i.e., the rhythm method of abstinence limited to the period of ovulation, as dictated by *Humanae Vitae*). The agency also toed the Vatican line on sex education, biogenetics (including artificial insemination), homosexuality, AIDS, pornography, prostitution, and drug abuse. In 1994, the pope created the Pontifical Academy for Life to boost his campaign against abortion and birth control. The Academy consisted of seventy scientists named by the pope, including a few women, who pledged to uphold the church's teachings on bioethics. "The chief purpose of this body," noted Vatican observer Paul Hofmann, "appears to be to give academic prestige and credibility to the papacy's positions on issues involving human biology."

The Academy's policing of orthodoxy would certainly come in handy at the United Nations' International Conference on Population and Development in Cairo in 1994, where the Roman Catholic Church proved the biggest obstacle to having women's reproductive rights declared an integral part of human rights. The Vatican game plan had become all too familiar by this point. Appealing to the lowest common denominator had been the default strategy since the beginning of the 1980s— about the same time that Ratzinger showed up at the CDF. At

Cairo, this took the form of exploiting Islamic hostility toward Western imperialism and feminism by trying to sway certain Third World nations against women's reproductive rights. At the conference, Vatican officials did everything possible to, as Rosemary Radford Ruether put it, "prevent advocacy for any element of sex education, accessible contraception, family planning, and legal and safe abortion, in alliance with some of the most reactionary Islamic countries, as well as a handful of conservative representatives of Catholic states, such as Nicaragua and Malta." The "no" campaign had Ratzinger's fingerprints all over it.

In 1987, Ratzinger published *Donum Vitae*, his instruction on medical ethics concerning human reproduction. In it, the CDF prefect declared that the church's teaching on marriage and human procreation affirmed *Humanae Vitae*'s "inseparable connection, willed by God and unable to be broken by man on his own initiative, between the two meanings of the conjugal act: the unitive meaning and the procreative meaning." Because homologous in vitro fertilization and embryo transfer occur outside the body—a process requiring "actions of third parties whose competence and technical activity determine the success of the procedure"—this form of birthing was deemed immoral. "Moral" procreation required the conjugal act of married spouses united as "one flesh." Sterile couples were out of luck.

There were special exceptions, of course. According to Enrico Chiavacci, professor of moral theology at the University of Florence and one of the Vatican's leading experts on the topic, the church accepts only two methods of homologous artificial fertilization. "The first method, which is practiced but not officially recognized, consists of removing sperm directly from the testicles with a hypodermic needle," he wrote in *Lezioni brevi di bioetica* (*Short Lessons in Bioethics*). "It is extremely painful, but it has the advantage of avoiding the sin of masturbation; it also has the shortcoming—no pun intended—of taking place outside of physical intercourse. The second method calls for the sexual act to be performed in a clinic, with a doctor just outside the door, ready to hurry in immediately after ejaculation to remove semen directly from the woman's vagina."

Needless to say, the perspectives of women were completely absent from the German cardinal's deliberations on all matters of human reproduction. In many a Ratzingerian observation, the leaps of logic are comical in their impact. Here, for example, is a statement he made about the birth control pill, in 1991: "If sexuality can be safely disconnected from procreation, in an increasingly pure technical development, then sex will have the same relationship to morality as having a cup of coffee."

In 1993, the CDF published *Responses to Questions Proposed Concerning 'Uterine Isolation' and Related Matters.* To the question, "When the uterus (e.g., as a result of previous Caesarian sections) is in a state such that while not constituting in itself a present risk to the life or health of the woman, nevertheless is forseeably incapable of carrying a future pregnancy to term without danger to the mother, danger which in some cases could be serious, is it licit to remove the uterus (hysterectomy) in order to prevent a possible future danger deriving from conception?", his response was a flat "No." To the question, "Is it licit to substitute tubal ligation, also called 'uterine isolation'?", his answer was "No" again. But he elaborated: "The uterus in and of itself does not pose a pathological problem for the woman ... The end of avoiding risks to the mother, deriving from a possible pregnancy, is thus pursued by a means of a direct sterilization, in itself always morally illicit, while other ways, which are morally licit, remain open to free choice. The contrary opinion, which considers the interventions described ... [above] as indirect sterilizations, licit under certain conditions, cannot be regarded as valid and may not be followed in Catholic hospitals."

There was something oddly off-putting in the clinical, bureaucratic tone of this clerical declaration, which implies an understanding of women's health issues. It's the priority Ratzinger places on religious law over all other considerations that leaves one cold. As the anonymous author of *Against Ratzinger* put it: "The sacrifice of reality (a woman's health) to an ideal (a future potential pregnancy) could not have been expressed with any greater clarity or inhumanity."

Then there was the "rubber." On November 19, 2010, it was revealed that Pope Benedict had opened the door to allowing the use of condoms, in limited cases, as a way to fight HIV. He did not mention married couples where one spouse is infected, but he did say that male prostitutes could use condoms as a first step in assuming moral responsibility "in the intention of reducing the risk of infection." This was in conversation with the German journalist Peter Seewald for his book, *Light of the World: The Pope, the Church and the Signs of the Times*. Elsewhere in the book, Benedict reaffirmed the church's teaching against artificial contraception with his usual rhetorical flourish: "How many children are killed who might one day have been geniuses, who could have given humanity something new, who could have given us a new Mozart or some new technical discovery?" The rhythm method, he said, was "not just a method but a way of life. And that is something fundamentally different from when I take the pill without binding myself interiorly to another person, so that I can jump into bed with a random acquaintance."

The comment about male prostitutes was in response to a general question about Africa, where heterosexual HIV spread was rampant. On March 17, 2009, Pope Benedict drew the wrath of the United Nations, European governments, and AIDS activists everywhere when he said that the AIDS crisis on the continent could not be resolved by distributing condoms. "On the contrary, it increases the problem," he told reporters on a flight to Cameroon for the first leg of a six-day trip that would also take him to Angola. This was a stunning assertion, given that an estimated twenty-two million people were HIV-positive in sub-Saharan Africa. The region accounted for more than two-thirds of the global total, and three-quarters of all the world's AIDS deaths in 2007. According to the World Health Organization, AIDS in Africa produced at least 2.5 million deaths in 2006.

While the pope's comment inspired predictable outrage ("Religious dogma is more important to him than the lives of Africans," remarked Rebecca Hodes of the Treatment Action Campaign in South Africa), it should not have come as a surprise. Shortly after becoming Pope Benedict in 2005, Ratzinger held an official audience with bishops who had flown in from South Africa, Botswana, Swaziland, Namibia, and Lesotho, just to see him. In remarks quoted for public consumption, Benedict told the bishops that the "cruel epidemic" of African AIDS could not be cured by using condoms and that, on the contrary, condoms were threatening African life itself. "It is of great concern," he said, "that the fabric of African life, its very source of hope and stability, is threatened by divorce, abortion, prostitution, human trafficking, and a contraception mentality."

In the pope's view, the African AIDS catastrophe was not the result of an insufficient distribution of condoms and encouragement of their use, but the dictatorship of Western relativism. Ratzinger had explained all this in 2004, the year before he became pope, in a public conversation with the philosopher Jurgen Habermas: "Here the West imported its vision of the world, it permanently armed Africa and destroyed *mores maiorum*, the moral rules upon which the tribe was built. Naturally, before the colonization Africa was a paradise ... there was a fundamental force: life in common, the sharing of liberty, the definition of being human in the various tribes. The [E]nlightenment destroyed this moral force." Today, Ratzinger concluded, the effects of the West's interference could be seen in the increase in violence and the higher death rate from AIDS.

What was missing from Ratzinger's tidy, post-colonial analysis of AIDS in Africa was some recognition that the moral rules upon which most African tribes were built incorporated polygamy into the mix. Polygamous sexuality, a traditional aspect of African societies, should not be excluded from any discussion of the continent's *mores maiorum*. True, Africa *is* the fastest-growing region for the Roman Catholic faith: the church is more than holding its own with Islam and the evangelical churches. So Pope Benedict's response might be that this signifies acceptance of church teachings on the continent. But thanks

to its vast cultural distance from Europe, the African phenomenon of "pick-and-choose" Catholics—people who embrace some
aspects of the faith, but not others—puts the lie to this notion.
Preaching fidelity in polygamous societies is a losing proposition. So if the pope was going to allow male prostitutes to use
condoms to exercise responsibility, then why not female prostitutes? Why not the infected husband or wife?

Abortion and the Ratzingerian "Life" Ethic

One of Ratzinger's more celebrated targets on the abortion issue
was Ivone Gebara, a Brazilian theologian he disciplined because
of her blending of liberation theology with ecology and feminism. Gebara—who had a PhD in philosophy and religion from
Louvain University in Belgium—returned to her native land in
the 1970s and spent sixteen years teaching at the Theological
Institute in Recife. During the 1980s, she fell afoul of male colleagues when she began reading feminist theory and theology
from Europe and North America. They didn't like the fact that
she embraced feminism's challenge of classical Christian theology's hierarchical dualisms (spirit over body; male over female).
In 1990, the new conservative bishop closed the seminary in
Recife and fired its faculty. Gebara moved to a slum neighbor-
hood in northern Brazil, where she worked with poor women
and children. It was this experience that ultimately got her into
trouble with CDF.

In 1993, Gebara gave an interview with a popular magazine in
which she expressed support for legalized abortion based on her
experiences with the poor women of Camaragible. She did not

explicitly endorse abortion but said it could be a "lesser of evils in many cases." The following year, she fell into a conflict with the Vatican and the Brazilian church hierarchy over the interview, in which she traced the development of Latin American feminist theology over the previous two decades. Gebara had recounted how feminist theologians discovered their oppression as historical subjects ("in the Bible, in theology, in our churches") and advocated female role models in the Bible, including "prophetesses and matriarchs, and female disciples of Jesus, such as Mary Magdalene." Gebara survived several meetings with the president of the Brazilian conference of bishops concerned about the interview, but the Vatican wasn't so easily mollified.

On June 3, 1995, Ratzinger instructed Gebara to refrain from speaking, teaching, and writing for two years. He also ordered her to return to Europe for "re-education" in Catholic teaching during this period. (A rather Maoist touch, for a cleric so appalled by Communist excess.) Gebara dutifully returned to her alma mater at the University of Louvain, where she did a second PhD in theology. But Ratzinger's punishment seemed to backfire. For Gebara also began writing a book about the nature of evil from a woman's perspective. When she returned to Brazil in 1997, she continued working with an eco-feminist network based in Chile and helped organize theological workshops on ecofeminist thought in Santiago, Recife, and Washington, DC.[32]

---

32 Ratzinger had better luck punishing Marciano Vidal, the Spanish theologian to whom the CDF prefect delivered notification regarding his book *Moral de Actitudes* (2001). Following Ratzinger's citation of "errors" on the subjects of abortion (including therapeutic abortion), artificial fertilization, contraception, and masturbation, Vidal corrected his book in compliance with instructions.

Examining Gebara's brand of radical feminism, it's not hard to see why Ratzinger would find her such a threat. "If a theology does not emerge from and relate to our human experience, and assist us in moving towards freedom," she wrote in the *Catholic New Times*, "then it should be abandoned." Gebara, an educated, white, middle-class Brazilian woman, acknowledged her privilege as an academic who chose to work in "a region of violent contrasts of wealth and poverty shaped by centuries of colonialism, feudalism, and capitalism." The fact that she chose to identify with the poorest Brazilians—doing theology, as she put it, surrounded by "noise and garbage"—stands in stark contrast to the monastic tranquility of the traditional Christian apprenticeship. It's a long way from the ivory tower where Ratzinger spent so many years shielded from the kind of harsh realities that create the circumstances for abortion.

In 2003, John Paul II issued new guidelines for Catholic politicians, demanding their opposition to abortion. During the primary season in advance of the 2004 US presidential elections, Democratic candidate John Kerry went on the record as pro-choice. This drew a response from Cardinal Francis Arinze, prefect of the Congregation for Divine Worship and the Discipline of Sacraments. Cardinal Arinze said that unambiguously pro-abortion politicians such as Senator Kerry were "not fit" to receive Communion. Ratzinger publicly agreed, blasting any Catholic who supported abortion and suggesting that they avoid Communion. He also authorized priests to withhold Communion from politicians who pledged support for abortion laws but then reneged on the promise once elected. To voters, he demurred somewhat. It was okay to vote for pro-choice

politicians, he said—as long as they had something else to recommend them and the pro-choice stance was not the reason for
voting for them.

Many have pointed out a contradiction in the Vatican's claim
to a consistent "life" ethic with regard to abortion. In 1988, the
Catholic ethicist Christine Gudorf said that the Vatican applies
"an absolutist version of natural law ethics when it speaks
of abortion, asserting one value above all others. It allows no
debate, applies coercive sanctions and excommunication, and
demands criminalization. Yet, when the Vatican speaks of war,
it shifts to a consequence-based ethic that carefully balances
conflicting values." In these contrasting approaches, the Vatican
demonstrates a form of moral relativism known as situational
ethics. Gudorf rightly points out that the Vatican is disproportionately concerned with "life" before birth; at the same time,
it displays a seeming indifference to unjust death after birth.
"Where is the bishop who would say that soldiers who directly
massacre noncombatant civilians are to be excommunicated?"
she asked in 1988. "Where are bishops who would suggest that
those who manufacture nuclear weapons are excommunicated
and should repent by leaving such forms of employment?"
Before 2005, Joseph Ratzinger was silent on this question; for
his entire papacy, so was Pope Benedict.

On April 18, 2012—the day before the seventh anniversary
of his pontificate—Pope Benedict declared war on US nuns.
Cardinal William Levada, Ratzinger's successor as prefect for

the Congregation for the Doctrine of the Faith, blasted the umbrella group representing most of the country's 55,000 nuns because they had not spoken out strongly enough against gay marriage, abortion, and women's ordination. The Leadership Conference of Women Religious (LCWR) was also guilty of sponsoring conferences with "a prevalence of certain radical feminist themes incompatible with the Catholic faith" and supporting President Obama's health care reform (including the provision of insurance coverage for birth control for employees at religious institutions) over the objections of US bishops. The CDF's eight-page statement described the nuns' "doctrinal and pastoral situation" as "a matter of serious concern" because "the church's Biblical view of family life and human sexuality" was "not part of the LCWR agenda in a way that promotes church teaching." The nuns' biggest sin was their failure to obey their bishops, who—as the CDF statement made clear—"are the church's authentic teachers of faith and morals."

Cardinal Levada announced that the Vatican had appointed three American bishops, led by Seattle archbishop Peter Sartain, to clean house at LCWR. The bishops would be charged with overhauling the organization's governance and reviewing its plans and programs—including its relationship with certain groups condemned by the Vatican. Sister Simone Campbell, the LCWR's executive director, said she was "stunned" by the news, which came just as the Vatican was preparing to welcome back a controversial right-wing splinter group of ultra-traditionalists. The notion that a leading US nun would be "stunned" by such an announcement, seven years into Benedict's pontificate, was hard to fathom. For most informed observers of this pope, the real surprise was that he had taken so long to declare war.[33]

On May 31, 2004, Cardinal Ratzinger wrote a letter to Catholic Bishops on the collaboration between men and women in the church and in the world. In this letter, he described women's liberation as "the antechamber to disaster." What could he possibly have meant by that? "The obscuring of the difference or duality of the sexes has enormous consequences on a variety of levels," he continued. "This theory of the human person, intended to promote prospects for equality of women through liberation from biological determinism, has in reality inspired ideologies which, for example, call into question the family, in its natural two-parent structure of mother and father, and make homosexuality and heterosexuality virtually equivalent, in a new model of polymorphous sexuality."

Here, Ratzinger was crediting feminism with a spirit of permissiveness that presumably allowed the gay and lesbian liberation movement to flourish. In this he would be absolutely right—although his moral response to the consequences departs significantly from human rights discourse. In any case,

---

33 Notwithstanding Sister Campbell's apparent shock, the nuns did not passively accept this latest form of theological bullying. Instead, after six weeks of virtual silence and reflection, they launched a counter-offensive: condemning the Vatican's "unsubstantiated accusations" and "flawed process," they sent a delegation to Rome to speak with Vatican officials, held vigils in more than fifty US cities, and gathered a petition with 52,000 signatures urging Roman Catholics to redirect their church donations from Peter's Pence, a special collection sent to the Vatican, to nuns' groups instead.

Pope Benedict understood that women and homosexuals have a great deal in common as Catholics. First, to be true to their natures, they make choices independent of "God's will" as the pope would define it. Second, the kinds of institutional misogyny and homophobia they experience in the church as a result of these choices—private intimidation, public humiliation, character assassination, shunning, and even violence—are, in many ways, identical. Finally, they are the two groups of people whose critiques of the church Pope Benedict had the least interest in hearing.

VII

"Objectively Disordered"

*He found sex disgusting and he was profoundly hostile to it. He suffered
from a pathological lack of emotional maturity and was psychologically
unstable, and was therefore too apt to confuse his instinctive reactions
and capricious value judgments with rules emanating from on high.*
—Andrew Priest on Saint Paul, "Can a Homosexual be a
Christian?" in *Arcadie* 160 (April 1967)

What do we know of Emeritus Pope Benedict's personal life?
What are his passions and his interests? What does "beauty"
mean to him? One of the most frequently cited facts about
Joseph Ratzinger is his love of music. Throughout his career,
the man who became Pope Benedict was always effusive with
journalists about his adoration of Bach, Beethoven, Mozart,
and the other classical composers. As a youth in Traunstein,
his memoirs tell us, he learned to play the piano. Today, hagi-
ographers call him "a virtuoso." Music and art, it seems, might
be the only things in this world—apart from faith itself—for
which Ratzinger has ever been willing to suspend the rational.
In *Salt of the Earth*, he accounted for the intractable gulf between
art and reason. "Music, after all, has the power to bring people
together," he told Peter Seewald. "Art is elemental. Reason alone
as it's expressed in the sciences, can't be man's complete answer

to reality, and it can't express everything that man can, wants to, and has to express. I think God built this into man."

Three years before he became pope, in an address to a meeting of Communion and Liberation in Rimini, he illustrated the importance of listening to the heart when in the presence of beauty—the clear implication being that stirrings of the heart produce valid "truths" that must not be ignored. "To disdain or reject the impact produced by the response of the heart in the encounter with beauty as a true form of knowledge would impoverish us and dry up our faith and our theology," he said. "We must rediscover this form of knowledge; it is a pressing need of our time."

With these words, the German cardinal captured the essence of a perfectly sensible, humanistic idea: that human beings cannot be reduced to the mechanistic any more than music can be reduced to mathematics. Ergo: an encounter with beauty, to the beholder, cannot be dismissed if it comes from the heart.

In the 1980s, Cardinal Ratzinger attended a concert performance of Bach dedicated to the late conductor Karl Richter. For this tribute performance, the conductor was Leonard Bernstein. At one point, carried away by the beauty of the strings, Ratzinger turned to a Lutheran bishop sitting next to him and declared: "Anyone who has heard this knows that faith is true." Apparently, Ratzinger found the concert in no way tainted by the fact that the man conducting it was a homosexual—this despite the German cardinal's having said, many times on the record, that homosexuality does not represent "a significant or positive contribution to the development of the human person in society," but that it does represent an "intrinsic moral evil."

Was Ratzinger even aware that Bernstein was gay? Perhaps not: the legendary American composer, conductor, pianist, author, and lecturer was married and in the closet for most of his life. But it is hard to fathom that Ratzinger would be unaware that Michelangelo, da Vinci, Tchaikovsky, Maynard Keynes, Wittgenstein, and sundry other titans of his beloved Western civilization were also gay. Would he have boycotted the Bach performance had he known of Bernstein's extra-marital gay life, to maintain consistency between his aesthetics and his theology? Probably not. Would he argue that Bernstein's and Tchaikovsky's "positive contribution[s] to society" were nullified by their sodomitical ways? If the answer were yes, then that would make Ratzinger a brutish philistine and a vulgarian. Not a serious thinker. He would not wish to be regarded in this way.

All of which naturally raises the question: how can a man who loves music so dearly, a man who accepts the "truth" of the heart in recognizing beauty, find homosexuality so completely beyond the pale? Ratzy is not a Nazi, after all, in the Hannah Arendt sense: he cannot be compared to the Auschwitz camp guard who coldly shoots Jews in the head before going home and weeping over his Beethoven. Or to Hitler himself, who loved his Germanic operas. Hitler was an insane mass murderer; Ratzinger is a rational man of the cloth. So how does a Mozart-loving, cat-stroking, Sistine Chapel-admiring cleric condemn homosexuality to the extent that he has, knowing—as he must—how many fabulous pieces of music and art have been produced by gay men? Can it really all be reduced to scripture?

Pedagogy of a Prejudice

Ratzinger's views on homosexuality were hardly a secret when he arrived at the CDF in 1981. But five years later, his *Letter to the Bishops of the Catholic Church on the Pastoral Care of Homosexual Persons* (October 1, 1986) spelled out the Vatican's position in terms that left no room for ambiguity. Quite apart from its historically atrocious timing—it arrived during the height of the AIDS crisis in North America, adding fuel to the fires of anti-gay hatred, further devastating a community already reeling from the plague—this instruction was significant in its claim of a "more global vision" than science could provide. Repeatedly referring to homosexuality as a "problem," Ratzinger went much further than his predecessor's *Declaration on Certain Questions Concerning Sexual Ethics* (1975), which made a distinction between the homosexual condition, or tendency, and homosexual actions or behavior (the condescending "hate the sin, love the sinner" approach).

The 1986 instruction said that the church's doctrine on homosexuality was based "not on isolated phrases for facile theological argument, but on the solid foundation of a constant Biblical testimony." In fact, the isolated phrases Ratzinger pulled from Genesis, Leviticus, 1 Corinthians, Romans, and 1 Timothy made for pretty facile theological argument. Leviticus is a good example. "In Leviticus 18:22 and 20:13, in the course of describing the conditions necessary for belonging to the Chosen People," Ratzinger said, "the author excludes from the People of God those who behave in a homosexual fashion." Of course, the same "author," in Leviticus 25:44, says it's okay to possess slaves; in Lev. 24: 10–16, that those who curse and blaspheme should be stoned to death; and, in Lev. 20:14, that those who sleep with their in-laws should be burned to death.[34] Was this the stuff from which to build a "solid foundation" for "pastoral care" in the twentieth century and beyond? The five most significant statements from the 1986 instruction, in terms of their contemporary relevance, are:

1. To choose someone of the same sex for one's sexual activity is to annul the rich symbolism and meaning, not to mention the goals, of the Creator's sexual design.

Ratzinger may have intended nothing more here than the predictable "Adam and Eve, not Adam and Steve" gender argument. As for "rich symbolism and meaning," the CDF prefect was unlikely to acknowledge the fireplace wrestling scene from D.H. Lawrence's *Women in Love*, Alexander the Great's tortured love life, or any number of other explicitly gay representations in history and art. But in light of Ratzinger's standard for such things, it seems more than a little hypocritical that the Vatican Museum would continue to display, under his authority as Pope Benedict, a bust of Hadrian's strapping young lover Antinous, described as the gay emperor's "young favorite," along with countless other works of homoerotic art infused with "rich

---

34 Plus a number of other minor, but stupid, rules regarding conduct such as men avoiding women while they menstruate, burning bulls on the altar to leave a "pleasing odour for the Lord" (but prohibiting the blind from approaching the altar), as well as forbidding men from trimming the hair around their temples and women from wearing garments made of two different kinds of thread.

symbolism and meaning."

> 2. Homosexual activity is not a complementary union, able to transmit life…When [homosexual persons] engage in homosexual activity they confirm within themselves a disordered sexual inclination which is essentially self-indulgent.

By "complementary," Ratzinger was referring here to Pope John Paul II's idea of *complementarity* as described in *Mulieris Dignitatem*: the idea that men and women complement each other by virtue of their sexual difference and a host of gender role stereotypes approved by the church. Obviously, a homosexual union is "not complementary" on this basis. But one wonders why Ratzinger and John Paul would exclude all other aspects of *complementarity* that loving couples may possess: skills and abilities, talents, interests, family backgrounds, cultural traditions, emotional dispositions, physical attributes, and so on. With so facile an understanding of this concept, there is no basis for Ratzinger to argue that homosexuality is any more "essentially self-indulgent" than heterosexuality. To do so is to suggest that mutual intimacy between two people is only possible between heterosexuals.

> 3. (A) As in every moral disorder, homosexual activity prevents one's own fulfillment and happiness by acting contrary to the creative wisdom of God. (B) The Church, in rejecting erroneous opinions regarding homosexuality, does not limit but rather defends

personal freedom and dignity realistically and authentically understood.

As with most of Ratzinger's statements on homosexuality, the opposite of (A) is true. Every gay and lesbian person who does not subscribe to Ratzinger's program of self-loathing closetry (but rather wishes only to be true to his or her nature) would bear witness that true happiness and fulfillment arrive only with the full embrace and expression of one's true nature, including one's sexuality. Ratzinger does not explain how the so-called "creative wisdom of God" could possibly be violated by a particular individual's decision to be true to him or herself. As for the nonsensical doublethink he expresses in (B), that statement is itself an "erroneous opinion," and one of exceeding Orwellian creepiness. By 1986, the Catholic Church had never defended the "personal freedom and dignity" of homosexuals. Nor has it ever done so, to this day. Just the opposite.

> 4. [Gay rights activists outside the church] are guided by a vision opposed to the truth about the human person, which is fully disclosed in the mystery of Christ. They reflect, even if not entirely consciously, a materialistic ideology which denies the transcendent nature of the human person as well as the supernatural vocation of every individual.

Leaving aside the oxymoronic idea of truths being "fully disclosed" in mysteries, there's the whole problem here of ideology. Ideology has long been Ratzinger's default critique for every social movement with which he disagrees (feminism being the most prominent example). Again, his statement is hypocritical, given the importance of ideology to his own intellectual arsenal. The materialist/transcendent dichotomy doesn't work here, either: human beings are not by "nature" "transcendent" but must choose whether or not to embrace the mystery of "transcendence."

> 5. The proper reaction to crimes committed against homosexual persons should not be to claim that the homosexual condition is not disordered. When such a claim is made and when homosexual activity is consequently condoned, or when civil legislation is introduced to protect behavior to which no one has any conceivable right, neither the Church nor society at large should be surprised when other distorted notions and practices gain ground, and irrational and violent reactions increase.

In logic, intelligence, and compassion for the people concerned, this statement is equivalent to blaming rape victims for wearing provocative clothing. But it is more than that: it is an incitement to hatred against an entire group of people. How *is* an orthodox conservative, masculine male to react, for example, when his church brands homosexuals as somehow less than human? When it rejects civil legislation to protect them? When it says they have "no conceivable right" to their own behavior? Ratzinger might as well have instructed his bishops to hand out baseball bats to the gay-bashers. This was the most reckless statement ever produced by the Vatican on homosexuality. There is no way of knowing how many deaths it caused—either through homophobic violence, self-loathing-induced unsafe sex, or suicide. But then, the word of the doctrine has always mattered more to Ratzinger than its human consequences.

The *Letter to the Bishops on the Pastoral Care of Homosexuals* was a clear signal from the CDF that denigrating an entire population was preferable to dealing with the pastoral care needs of, say, people suffering from AIDS. Six years later, Ratzinger issued a four-page document reconfirming homosexuality as an "objective disorder" not subject to human rights. Titled *Some Considerations Concerning the Response to Legislative Proposals on the Non-Discrimination of Homosexual Persons* (July 22, 1992), the document was a desperate attempt to discredit the gay rights movement, which the AIDS crisis—far from stamping out, as he might have hoped—only strengthened. Three of its statements deserve comment:

> 1. An individual's sexual orientation is not generally known to others unless he publicly identifies himself as having this orientation or unless some overt behavior manifests it.

Ratzinger's advice for all homosexuals to remain in the closet, invisible and voiceless (so as not to trouble others with their frivolous claims to human rights) depends on a fallacy revealed in this statement. How could there be discrimination, the CDF prefect wondered, if sexual orientation is invisible; that is, if there is no declaration, disclosure, or obvious behavior? This ignores the fact that homophobic discrimination, including gay-bashing, occurs on a daily basis regardless of visible signs. Landlords and employers respond to rumors, as well as to non-overt behavior or appearances. Even straight people who "look gay" are gay-bashed or shunned because of a suspiciously astute fashion choice or physical appearance. But Ratzinger as Pope Benedict empowered Canadian clerics, for example, to oppose gay-straight alliances in high schools, arguing that such programs at Catholic schools constitute "an intrusion or limiting of religious freedom."

> 2. The passage from the recognition of homosexuality as a factor on which basis it is illegal to discriminate can easily lead, if not automatically, to the legislative protection and promotion of homosexuality.

This was the first of two "slippery slope" arguments. In this one, Ratzinger dismissed sexual orientation as a legitimate category for human rights comparable to sex, race, ethnic background, able-bodiedness, etc., because an "objective" or "intrinsic" "disorder" was not deemed worthy of protection. And why not? Because human rights legislation would only validate the "disorder" of homosexuality. Therefore, governments should keep firing gay teachers and lesbian athletic coaches, prohibiting homosexuals from adopting children or serving as foster parents, and barring them from military service.

3. There is a danger that legislation which would make homosexuality a basis for entitlements could actually encourage a person with a homosexual orientation to declare his homosexuality or even to seek a partner in order to exploit the provisions of the law.

This second "slippery slope" argument revealed the depth of Ratzingerian cynicism. It proposed that the only reason gays and lesbians come out of the closet—and are willing to subject themselves to endless harassment, gay-bashing, and all forms of discrimination—is so they can get on the gravy train. You know: they're all just gold diggers, intent on making the state complicit in their sick, evil plot to find rich lovers and get on their same-sex medical, dental, and pension plans.

There was *some* progress in the 1992 document. Ratzinger did concede that gays and lesbians were, in fact, human beings who deserved at least some rights, like employment and housing. But the CDF prefect recommended withdrawing these rights in instances where "objectively disordered external conduct" (gay sex) has occurred. In the meantime, Ratzinger wielded his power to marginalize Catholic clerics who ignored church teaching and supported gay and lesbian rights. The following is but a small selection from his anti-gay "hit list" between 1986 and 2005:

+ Charles Curran: Professor of moral theology at the Catholic University of America is censured by the Vatican and subsequently suspended from his teaching duties for his positions on divorce, masturbation, euthanasia, and homosexuality (1986).

+ Raymond Hunthausen: The archbishop of Seattle is ousted from his diocese for his pacifist beliefs and his spiritual aid to the homosexual community (1986).

+ Andre Guindon: Ratzinger demands that the Canadian theologian retract his essay defending the moral legitimacy of contraception, pre-marital sexual relations, and homosexual relations. It also asks him how his book, *The Sexual Creators: An Ethical Proposal for Concerned Christians* is faithful to Catholic teaching. Guindon dies while the investigation is underway (1992–93).

+ Jacques Gaillot: Bishop of Evreux, France, is deposed because of his acceptance of the use of contraception to prevent the spread of HIV and his open avowal that homosexuals and people who remarry are still members of the church (1995).

+ Sister Jeanine Gramick and Father Robert
  Nugent: Found guilty of providing aid to gay
  and lesbian Catholics through their ministry
  and their published writings, Gramick and
  Nugent are summoned to the Vatican, ordered
  to renew their profession of faith, and issued
  notifications. Later ordered into silence, Nugent
  complies but Gramick does not (1999).

+ Don Franco Barbero: Because of his support
  for gay marriage, the pastor of Pinorolo, Torino,
  is defrocked by Ratzinger, prevented from
  instructing theology in Catholic institutions,
  and subjected to monitoring by his bishop to
  prevent him from "giving scandal to the faithful"
  (2003).

+ Don Fabrizio Longhi: The Italian pastor is
  removed from his parish church in Rignano
  Garganico because of his decision to allow a
  twenty-one-year-old gay man from Salerno,
  Pasquale Quaranta, to deliver the homily at
  Christmas. Quaranta's message? "Please do not
  judge us badly—we only want the right to live
  our lives fully, including emotionally and sexually" (2004).

+ Don Aitor Urresti: The pastor of Deusto-
  San Ignacio in Bilbao, Spain, is removed and

deposed from the diocese for his affiliation with the We Are Church movement, which is tolerant of homosexuality (2005).

Fear and Loathing

So, apart from the historical bigotry of Roman Catholic doctrine, what is the basis for Pope Benedict's fear and loathing of homosexuality? Alas, there appears to be little support for any it-takes-one-to-know-one theories that might expose him as a self-loathing closet case. No clues from his early life that might provide fodder for speculation or psychoanalysis. No abuse at the hands of a priest in Traunstein. No secret male lovers in the seminary. Nothing like that. There are a few theories, based on Ratzinger's life since becoming pope, which we will address shortly. But for the most part, his bigotry appears to be based on personal conviction in his embrace of church doctrine, which historically has supported the persecution of homosexuals in all kinds of ways. This is not helped by his disproportionately cerebral approach to life, honed by decades spent in perpetually cloistered academic and clerical environments. Some years ago, when he was still CDF prefect, Ratzinger was accosted on a plane by Jeannine Gramick, the Philadelphia nun he had defrocked because of her ministry and writings on behalf of gay and lesbian Catholics. Sister Gramick asked him if he had ever met any gay people. His response, she said, was: "Oh yes, the pope and I witnessed a protest in Berlin." Apparently, he was being serious. So the hundreds of homosexual priests and bishops he had met since the early 1950s, and the countless other queer seminarians, curial aides, and Swiss guards who served him every day at the Vatican, didn't count. They couldn't be gay, apparently, because they hadn't told him they were.

Clearly, Ratzinger's homophobia is theoretical, rather than experience-based. It all starts with a document written by his predecessor at the CDF, Franjo Seper. The *Declaration on Certain Questions Concerning Sexual Ethics* (December 29, 1975) contained the following gem, which Ratzinger has frequently quoted: "According to the objective moral order, homosexual relations are acts which lack an essential and indispensable finality." As in all subsequent Vatican documents on this subject, including Ratzinger's, there was no attempt here to account for the CDF prefect's linguistics. Never mind "objective moral order," which was probably a silent reference to the "word of God" (whose "objectivity" we were to take for granted). By "essential and indispensable finality," Seper was echoing the Freudian notion of normative psychosexual development, in which "genital finality" is represented by heterosexual coitis as the goal and the basis for mature sexuality. (This is supposed to lead to mature sociality, denoted by the recognition of and compassion for the binary opposite in the gender difference.) The fact that this theory had been deconstructed and consigned to the dust bin by feminist and queer theory was all the more reason for Ratzinger and his ultra-conservative intellectual circle to embrace it. For all the Biblical references he relied on to justify his homophobia, the CDF prefect was more than happy to mingle with the secular "science" of Freud to "prove" the wrongness of homosexuality.

As married heterosexual couples have demonstrated

throughout history, the "gift" of life can often be anything but "essential and indispensable." Too many fetuses not aborted are brought into the world as an afterthought and then abused, neglected, abandoned, or worse. Babies among this group who survive and grow up often turn to crime or become monsters, their unfortunate childhoods turning them into cauldrons of hatred that poison everyone around them. Of course, one thing that may not have occurred to Cardinal Seper in 1975 was the importance, for a lonely gay man or lesbian, of finally experiencing love or companionship after a long time in the desert of the heart. As a presumably celibate cleric, Seper—like Ratzinger—could not have understood how that first orgasm with a long-desired partner would be absolutely "essential" and "indispensable" to the homosexual person's self-confidence, his or her well-being, his or her empathic abilities, and his or her profound recognition of the beauty and grace of shared intimacy with another. It must not have occurred to Seper or Ratzinger that when people are sexually satisfied and happy, they tend to be easier to be around. Perhaps they lacked the moral imagination to see how an increase in queer visibility and acceptance might improve the conditions for world peace.

As with his views on women, Ratzinger always had an ally in Pope John Paul II when it came to the pink menace. Karol Wojtyla had made his feelings known in one of his first encyclicals as pontiff, *The Theology of the Body: Human Love in the Divine Plan* (1979). For John Paul, homosexuality was all about lust. The only acceptable gay man, in his eyes, was a celibate one who had achieved "self-mastery." As he put it, "The man of lust does not control his own body. Self-mastery [is] essential for the formation of the human person … man is ashamed of his body because of lust."[35]

During his inaugural visit to the United States in October 1979, the pope congratulated a group of clerics for toeing the Vatican line on the "condition" versus "behavior" split. "As compassionate pastors," he told them, "you also rightly stated that homosexual activity, as distinguished from homosexual orientation, is morally wrong."

None of this changed for the remainder of John Paul's pontificate. Toward the end, however, as he began to lose his grip and care less about public relations (or maintaining the mask of ambiguity that was his hallmark), Wojtyla did have one undignified moment; an instance of bad optics that exposed his conservative, Polish machismo. It happened during the summer of 2000, at the height of the Vatican's "Jubilee" celebrations. Some time earlier, the Italian gay and lesbian movement had decided—and received civic approval—to hold its largest pride parade in Rome, near the Vatican. Until this moment, gays and lesbians around the world had been blissfully spared any significant public record of the pope's actual views about them. But

---

35 In fairness to Pope John Paul II, he would apply the same principle of "self-mastery" to heterosexuals. In his view of adultery, for example, he went even further than US president Jimmy Carter, who once famously said that he felt he had committed "adultery in his heart" just by looking with lust at a woman other than his wife. Because John Paul regarded the morality of a sexual act as being determined by the underlying intention, rather than by the act itself, even a married man could commit adultery with his own wife just by thinking lustfully about someone else during intercourse with her.

that ended with the "Jubilee" showdown. "I consider it my duty to mention the demonstrations in Rome over the last few days," he told the thousands gathered in Saint Peter's Square. "In the name of the Church of Rome I cannot not express the bitterness following the affront to the Jubilee 2000 celebrations and the offence to the Christian values of a city dear to Catholics world-wide. Homosexual acts are against nature's laws. The church cannot silence the truth, because this … would not help discern what is good from what is evil."

What was the reason for John Paul's outburst, in which he dredged up the old "objective disorder" argument? Why did he tell gays and lesbians that they should be pitied and prayed for like murderers, thieves, rapists, and drug dealers? Why the sudden outrage, which seemed so personal? The simple answer was that gays and lesbians had ruined his party. It was not just that 200,000 homosexuals had invaded the Italian capital, coming too close for comfort to the "Jubilee" celebrations: it was that the "Jubilee" events had included a special visit to Rome by tens of thousands of the Pope's Polish compatriots. It was that drag queens in stiletto heels, S/M fetishists in handcuffs, and muscle-bound gym queens wearing nothing but leather thongs were shaking their buns on the same streets where pious Poles were trying to pray.

Perhaps another reason for the pope's outrage was that the queer movement was winning the public relations war, trumping the Vatican in every department at which it usually excelled: visible pageantry, shameless self-promotion, maximum media coverage, and conversion of souls. The Pride event had reclaimed space that was previously forbidden. It had outshone the "Jubilee" event by placing gays and lesbians historically in the context of church evils. (One banner read "1943: The Vatican says nothing about the deportation of Gays and Jews.") Finally, it had embarrassed the church with the drag-festooned vision of Nuns On The Run, one man dressed up as His Holiness, and another carrying a banner that read, "God is Gay."

A few years later, as Karol Wojtyla's time on earth was drawing to a close, the international gay marriage movement was picking up steam. In his final year as CDF prefect, Ratzinger began to ramp up the Vatican's anti-gay messaging. On May 13, 2004, during a speech in the Senate library in front of Italian politicians, he attacked the idea of legal status for cohabiting homosexuals. "With this move," he said, "we are abandoning the whole of the moral history of humanity … [and] facing the destruction of the very image of mankind, the consequences of which can only be extremely serious." Alarmist and apocalyptic as this was, Ratzinger did not settle for mere hyperbole. Insisting that marriage be limited to men and women, he threw in a non sequitur for good measure: "This is not discrimination, but rather concerns what the human person is, man or woman, and how the coming together of a man and a woman can be granted legal status." Reacting to the legalization of gay marriage in Spain, he said that homosexual unions were "a danger to the proper development of human society, especially if their influence on the fabric of society were to increase." None of this would change during the Benedict pontificate. In January

2012 he ramped up the rhetoric, calling gay marriage a threat "to humanity itself."

Of course, such a starkly pessimistic view, if sincerely held, depended on a belief that homosexuality—rather than being a natural, biological reality for ten percent of the world population—was really a choice, a choice subject to the influence of others, like deciding what movie to watch or how to cut one's hair. But even if every homosexual on the planet was paired off—unlikely, since large numbers of gays and lesbians have no interest in marriage—wedded queer couples would still max out at around ten percent of the population. Where was the apocalypse in that? On the contrary: if all homosexuals married, then—just like their straight majority counterparts—they could soon be having a lot less of the sex that Joseph Ratzinger apparently finds so repugnant. There might be more monogamy and fewer casual encounters. Would that not have been more palatable to His Holiness? Apparently not. For Benedict's rejection of homosexual relationships was based not only on the lack of procreation involved; it was based, perhaps more importantly, on his belief that gay relations are trapped in *eros*; that they are constitutionally incapable of making the transition into *agape*, which the pope described as "the experience of a love which involves a real discovery of the other, moving beyond the selfish character that prevailed earlier. Love now becomes concern and care for the other. No longer is it self-seeking, a sinking in the intoxication of happiness."

In his first encyclical as Pope Benedict XVI, *Deus Caritas Est* (*God Is Love*), released on Christmas Day in 2005, the pontiff distinguished between two types of love. *Eros* he defined as selfish love, or sex, which attempts to capture the object of its desire; *agape* as love that "seeks the good of the beloved: it becomes renunciation and it is ready, and even willing, for sacrifice." Translated from the Greek as "love," and referred to in the New Testament as the fatherly love of God for humans (and human reciprocal love for God), *agape* naturally extends to the love of one's fellow human beings. Since Vatican II, it has become one of the great Catholic concepts. Jean Vanier, founder of the L'Arche movement, often cited *agape* as one reason that people with developmental disabilities can accept others as they really are. *Agape* is a kind of unconditional, self-sacrificing, thoughtful love. A form of wisdom in itself.

In keeping with his dualistic manner of thinking, which has a tendency toward simplistic dichotomies (chaos and cosmos, anarchy and order), Benedict set out in *Deus Caritas Est* to re-inscribe *eros* and *agape* as polar opposites. He demonized the former, so that avoiding it becomes a higher purpose that requires discipline: "The contemporary way of exalting the body is deceptive. Eros, reduced to pure 'sex,' has become a commodity, a mere 'thing' to be bought and sold, or rather, man himself becomes a commodity...Man is truly himself when his body and soul are intimately united; the challenge of eros can be said to be truly overcome when this unification is achieved."

Given that sex addiction can be a problem for people of all sexual orientations, there is some validity to the above passage. These ideas have long been associated with Buddhist precepts regarding balance and harmony, a harnessing of the appetites to achieve spiritual calm, or a mind/body "Zen" state. Although there's a virtual cottage industry of gay men who subscribe to this philosophy as almost a religion in itself, there is no evidence in any of Ratzinger's writings or public statements as CDF prefect or pope that he sees homosexuals as constitutionally capable of embracing and demonstrating *agape* in their lives. In 1992, he acknowledged that homosexuals are human beings. Perhaps, before he dies, the former Pope Benedict will acknowledge the *agape* of an "out" gay person he happens to know. But despite all his opportunities for doing so—despite all the gay men that surround him on a daily basis, heeding his words, following his directives, and doing nice things for him he does not particularly deserve—he has yet to extend such a gesture.

The Ballad of Ratzy and Georg

Certain Vatican observers, angry at Benedict's homophobia, have attempted to paint the pope as a closeted homosexual himself: a self-loathing, right-wing gay man like the odious Roy Cohn[36], who enjoyed all manner of homosexual revelries in private while railing against gay rights in public. They think that, after he became pope and gained a global public profile in old age, he revealed enough telltale signs to mark him as a nancy boy. But this author is not a proponent of such theories. Although he could be self-loathing in the sexual sense, I do not think he is actually gay—despite the many delicious ironies that

---

36 Notorious US Republican lawyer who was chief counsel on Senator Joe McCarthy's Permanent Subcommittee on Investigations during the anti-Communist witch hunts of the early 1950s. Cohn, the vilest of history's closet cases, opposed anti-discrimination legislation for gays and lesbians throughout the 1970s and 1980s—even as he was dying of AIDS, the diagnosis of which he refused to acknowledge until the bitter end.

surround him. But since there are so many of these ironies, one cannot help but comment on them.

The first that comes to mind, a YouTube video that received more than a million hits when it surfaced, has enjoyed much circulation in social media as: "Pope Benedict—It's Raining Men." Recorded at the Vatican during the pontiff's weekly general audience on December 14, 2010, the rather sumptuous, one-minute-and-forty-five-second clip begins with four strapping young hunks dressed in white suits—trapeze artists from the Italian circus troupe Fratelli Pellegrini—ascending the marble staircase in unison. Stopping at a Persian rug about twenty feet from the papal throne, the young men take off their jackets and proudly display their perfectly chiseled, naked torsos. Then they perform an acrobatic routine for His Holiness.

Does Benedict stop this gratuitous display of titillating homoerotica? Not at all: as the men hoist each other into the air, one on top of the other, three high—their tight pants flexing to accentuate their attributes as they spread their legs wide open—he doesn't take his eyes off them for an instant. In fact, he is visibly on the edge of his seat—as is a gallery full of nuns, who wave their hankies in enthusiastic approval. When the performance is over, Benedict rises from the Papal throne and applauds them before waving them off—making it clear that, while this may not have been the entertainment he was expecting, it was not an altogether unpleasant surprise requiring that heads roll.

Then there's Benedict's flair for dress, which some have heralded as a return to the papal fashion of the dawn of modernity itself, to the last of the pope-kings. When Ratzinger was CDF prefect, he was rarely seen in anything but clerical black. But in the transition from cardinal to pope, he revealed a surprising fetish for the dandyesque that spoke to why so many gay men have been attracted to the priesthood. Apart from the red shoes[37], there were the wraparound Ray-Ban and Bushnell sunglasses (which seemed an odd accessory for a man in his eighties), a fabulous pink chasuble, and a fancy red camauro hat—the likes of which hadn't adorned a pope's head in centuries. Indeed, to some papal observers, Benedict's exquisite vestments were reminiscent of Raphael's portraits of Popes Julius II and Leo X, or Velazquez's of Innocent X. But Benedict's sudden taste for flamboyant finery, his delight in surrounding himself with glittery accoutrements,[38] suggested something else. Papal observers with long memories might wonder, for example, what Albino Luciani would say if he could see Ratzinger now. "Could this be a 'simple and humble laborer in the vineyard of the Lord'?," Pope John Paul I might well have asked. Or: "When's the last time 'preferential option for the poor' passed your lips?" Or: "What's with the padded shoulders?"[39]

Finally, there is Monsignor Georg Gänswein, Pope Benedict's personal secretary. In the first few years of his pontificate, there was no end to online rumor-mongering that the Pope and Georg had a thing going because Georg was a hunk,

37 It had been rumored that the shoes were Prada, but they were, in fact, made by the papal shoemaker who has a storefront near the Vatican.

38 During his pontificate, Benedict acquired gold cuff links, an iPod Nano, a four-wheel drive BMW X5, and two 2010 Ducati Multistrada motorcycles (gifted by the company—for His Holiness's security motorcade, of course), all possessions he showed no interest in acquiring while CDF prefect.

39 Padded shoulders hardly convey meekness or humility in a pope, as L'Espresso has astutely observed. Doctrinal rigidity and flamboyant dress do go hand in hand.

three decades younger than his boss, and in the pope's company day and night. This author will not descend to such prurient voyeurism as wondering what the pope emeritus and Georg talked about over intimate dinners at the Vatican. On the other hand, if Ratzinger was in fact gay, then Georg would have to be considered a nice "catch": ruggedly handsome and athletic, he really does have that windswept, George Clooney thing down pat. So handsome is Ratzinger's personal assistant that by 2009 there were four Facebook fan pages dedicated to him, as well as a counterfeit page claiming to be his. Known by his swooning fans as "gorgeous George," the Monsignor inspired an Italian play on words which could mean either that he should leave the priesthood or take off his priestly clothes.

Some Vatican observers were all too eager to connect the dots between appearance and reality. Angelo Quattrocchi, late author of the ironically titled *The Pope Is Not Gay!*, saw conspiracy in Benedict's relationship with Gänswein. In November 2004, less than six months before becoming pope, Ratzinger suddenly promoted Msgr. Josef Clemens, who had been his private secretary for nineteen years, to the position of secretary to the Pontifical Council for the Laity. Quattrocchi saw "a sort of Peter Principle" at work here: "promoting someone to get rid of them." In this case, Clemens was shoved aside in favor of Gänswein, Ratzinger's new "golden boy" and "adoring batman" in his perfectly ironed cassock with its eighty-six buttons.

Using Georg as his muse, Quattrocchi applies more than a little nudge-nudge, wink-wink analysis in pondering Pope Benedict's homophobic theology. "The secularist will inevitably wonder, not particularly maliciously," he says, "whether such fury isn't the fruit of a deeply repressed desire for what he condemns. Of an unconscious desire which manifests itself as its opposite." Tempting as it is, this author does not share Quattrocchi's psychoanalytical perspective. So what if Ratzinger *is* gay? That would hardly have made him the first "queen" on Saint Peter's throne.[40] More to the point, few would have begrudged Benedict and Georg a bit of happiness if what the two men shared was deeper than fraternal love. The problem would be that, over the decades, Ratzinger has caused so much unhappiness for millions of people with his words and his deeds about homosexuality.

The Biggest Gay Club in the World

For the longest time, it was the Vatican's biggest elephant in the room: the church railed against homosexual acts while a large number of its priests and bishops were gay and, presumably, getting plenty of "action." Among the clergy, the number of gays is far greater than for the general population: in the United States, conservative estimates put the gay priesthood at thirty-three percent; others say it's more like fifty. And, from the mid-1980s to 2000, Catholic priests in the US died from AIDS-related illnesses at a rate four times higher than the general population. Most of these men contacted the virus through same-sex relations, and the exact nature of their illness was often concealed on their death certificates. Similar stories have surfaced in other parts of the world.

---

40 According to the historical record, there is enough information to suggest that Popes Paul II (1464–1471), Sixtus IV (1471–84), Julius II (1503–1513), Leo X (1513–1521), and Julius III (1550–1555) were homosexual. It was a busy century, sodomitically speaking.

Why were so many gay men attracted to the Catholic priest-hood? Colm Tóibín, one of Ireland's best novelists-who-happen-to-be-gay, offered a few clues in a 2010 article that appeared in the *London Review of Books*. In 1971, at the age of sixteen, Tóibín himself had considered entering the seminary. What was he thinking? First of all, that the priestly calling would provide a great cover. Until the 1980s, becoming a priest "seemed to solve the problem of not wanting others to know that you were queer," he wrote. "As a priest, you could be celibate, or unmarried, and everyone would understand the reasons. It was because you had a vocation; you had been called by God, had been specially chosen by him. For other boys, the idea of never having sex with a woman was something they could not even entertain. For you, such sex was problematic; thus you had no blueprint for an easy future. The prospect, on the other hand, of making a vow in holiness never to have sex with a woman offered you relief." Since the church considered homosexuality beyond the pale and never talked about it, Tóibín added, the notion of scrutinizing priests for sodomitical tendencies was never considered.

Of course, if you're hiding your sexuality from others, chances are you might also be hiding it from yourself. And it's easy to lose perspective with the boost in self-esteem that occurs when your arrival in the priesthood immediately makes you a role model. "As a priest, you would be admired and looked up to, you would spend your life...being seen to be good, being needed by the sick and the dying, being wanted to officiate at weddings and baptisms and funerals, saying the sacred words which would mean so much to the congregation, all this would offer you a fulfilled and fulfilling life," argued Tóibín. "Becoming a priest solved not only the outward problem of forbidden and unmentionable sexual urges, but, perhaps more important, offered a solution to the problem of having a shameful identity that lurked in the deepest recesses of the self."

Most gay priests recognize the responsibility that such power represents and are more interested in the introspective value of the priesthood. For all the disapproval of the outside world, most of these men grow into the healthy awareness that their sexuality is indeed a natural state. "While the world's view often ate into the self," continues Tóibín, "there was another part of the self which remained intact, confident, sure." Such a conflict, within certain introspective gay Catholic men, could lead to a desire to nurture a spiritual part of themselves: "something private, wounded, solitary and self-aware," said Tóibín, that "had reason to come to the fore and seek nourishment in a close relationship to God." Hence the desire to enter the priesthood.

There is another, much rarer, kind of gay man who seeks the priesthood; a more confident soul who enters the seminary in good faith and makes no attempt to hide himself or even his sexuality. On the contrary, he enjoys "self-knowledge and more good faith" among other out gay seminarians, whom Tóibín refers to as "flutterers" for their unabashed flamboyance. "They are either celibate as a conscious, thought-out choice, or they use the gay scene when it suits them," said Tóibín. "Many of them are open to themselves and, to some extent, to their congregations about their sexuality, which is no longer a poison, but a gift, a way of understanding others, including Christ himself and his apostles, whom the world wished to victimise and marginalise." But the "flutterers" were a distinct minority. Most gay clerics—including those in the Vatican—were in the closet and susceptible to blackmail because of their desperate behavioral choices.

In 2007, a senior official was suspended from the Congregation for the Priesthood after being filmed in a "sting" organized by an Italian TV program while allegedly making sexual overtures to a younger man. Three years later, a twenty-nine-year-old chorister in the Vatican was fired for allegedly procuring male prostitutes, one of them a seminarian, for a papal gentleman-in-waiting who, according to Vatican observer John Cornwell, "was also a senior adviser in the curial department that oversees the Church's worldwide missionary activities." Shortly afterward, a weekly newsmagazine used hidden cameras to record priests visiting gay clubs and bars and having sex. By 2013, the notion of the priesthood as "the biggest gay club in the world" would take on literal significance when it was revealed that a building in Rome purchased by Vatican officials housed the biggest gay bathhouse in Europe. There appeared to be a vast underground network of gay priests operating with impunity behind Vatican walls—a story that, as we shall see in Chapter IX, would blow up in Pope Benedict's face.

Four months into his papacy, on August 31, 2005, Pope Benedict approved for publication the Congregation for Catholic Education's *Instruction Concerning the Criteria for the Discernment of Vocations with Regard to Persons with Homosexual Tendencies in View of Their Admission to the Seminary and to Holy Orders.* Apparently unconcerned with the priesthood's rapidly depleting ranks, the *Instruction's* authors made no distinction between homosexual "orientation" and "behavior." As they put it: "The Church, while profoundly respecting the persons in question, cannot admit to the seminary or to holy orders those who practice homosexuality, present deep-seated homosexual tendencies or support the so-called 'gay culture.'"

The implicit assumption was that, simply by declaring it would not accept homosexuals, the church would attract only heterosexual candidates. Of course, such a directive would stop some men from seeking the priesthood: men for whom sexual honesty is important. Meanwhile, it would encourage men who are closeted and emotionally immature to step forward.

Within a few years, it would become apparent why Pope Benedict had approved such wording; why he was willing to slam the door shut on good men while opening it wide for potentially more damaged ones. He was covering his tracks, building up his defence for the day that lawyers would begin knocking on his door. He was preparing to blame homosexuality for a problem the church had willingly enabled for hundreds of years. He was creating a climate to scapegoat gay men for a scandal that had less to do with sexual orientation than with medieval taboos on all forms of sexuality. Above all, he was maintaining a cult of secrecy that, for as long as anyone could recall, had placed church power and control over all other considerations.

VIII

Bewitched, Buggered, and Bewildered

It is surely worth asking, at a time when Benedict XVI has set his face against essential reform, whether the Pope should be the one man left in the world who is above the law.

—International human rights lawyer and
judge Geoffrey Robertson

On September 13, 2011, Pope Benedict XVI achieved yet another dubious milestone: on that day, he became the first pope in history to be formally cited for crimes against humanity. In an eighty-four-page complaint filed with the International Criminal Court (ICC), a survivor-led support group for victims of clerical sex abuse charged Vatican officials—specifically the pope, Cardinal Tarcisio Bertone, Cardinal Angelo Sodano, and Cardinal William Levada—with actively encouraging the systematic and widespread concealing of violent rape and child sex crimes by Roman Catholic priests and other clergy throughout the world. The complaint, filed by attorneys from a New York-based human rights organization, urged the ICC's chief prosecutor to recognize the court's jurisdiction over the case and proceed, based on its mandate to prosecute crimes against humanity.

It was an explosive accusation—the kind that lends itself to sensational media coverage. And the plaintiffs, members of the

Survivors Network of those Abused by Priests (SNAP), knew how to maximize the coverage. At high noon on September 13, just before Benedict left Rome on his first state visit to Germany, eight adult members of SNAP who had been sexually abused by priests as children held a news conference in The Hague with two human rights lawyers from the Center for Constitutional Rights (CCR). Before the cameras, the survivors held large photos of themselves at the ages at which they were violated. After the press conference, they joined the lawyers in delivering boxes filled with more than 20,000 pages of supporting documents to the ICC offices.

The lead lawyer argued that the case fell under the ICC's jurisdiction because the Court includes rape, sexual assault, and torture as crimes against humanity that occur in peacetime. The ICC also recognizes individual criminal liability for those with "command" responsibility over the people who directly commit such crimes. "National jurisdiction can't really get their arms around this," CCR lawyer Pamela Spees told the *New York Times*. "Prosecuting individual instances of child molestation or sexual assault has not gotten at the larger systemic problem here. Accountability is the goal, and the ICC makes the most sense, given that it's a global problem."

Response from the legal community did not give the case much hope for prosecution. International Bar Association executive director Mark Ellis said he thought the court would open a preliminary investigation to determine whether it had jurisdiction—but would likely conclude it did not. British attorney Neil Addison, author of *Religious Discrimination and Hatred Law*, dismissed the SNAP case as nothing more than "a publicity stunt."

Child abuse crimes, he told the *Christian Science Monitor*, should be prosecuted nationally, not globally, as the ICC was "supposed to exist for situations of war crime" and was "not designed for dealing with normal criminality." And David Akerson, writing for the *Denver Journal of International Law and Policy*, said that while there is precedent for criminal trials of clergy for commission of mass atrocities (i.e., Rwanda), there were several reasons that prosecuting the pope for the church's sex abuse crimes would be "a legal non-starter." As for the Vatican's response? A statement to the Associated Press described the court action, to no one's great surprise, as "ludicrous" and "a misuse of international judicial processes."

Despite the daunting legal obstacles that the SNAP victims faced, the mere fact that they filed their case with the ICC—i.e., that the Center for Constitutional Rights found it worthy of representation—was significant. If the prosecutor decided to proceed, it would mark the first time that an international court had asserted jurisdiction over the Vatican for crimes committed by its agents worldwide. Even if the case was rejected, admitted the International Bar Association's Ellis, "the filing does something that's important. It raises awareness." The sexual abuse of minors by Roman Catholic priests was sufficiently repugnant and widespread to be taken to the court. "For the safety of children and the prevention of yet more heinous wrongdoing, the International Criminal Court may be the only real hope," SNAP member and clerical abuse victim Barbara Blaine wrote in the *Guardian*. "What other institution could possibly bring prosecutorial scrutiny to bear on the largest private institution on the planet?"

It may well have been that no other court on the planet could do what Ms Blaine suggested. And it may well have been that the ICC would not do it, either. If this case never saw the light of day, millions of angry Catholics hungry for justice would be deprived of their dream of seeing their pope in the dock—forced, like Slobodan Milošević, to justify his existence. However, the mere fact that this case was out there did raise an intriguing question: after such a long career of dedication to the church—including a successful campaign to redefine it on his own ideological terms—why was it that Pope Benedict now found himself in this deplorable situation? How was it that, under his own watch, the office of supreme pontiff had been reduced to such an indignity that its holder was being regarded as a mere mortal, no less subject to the whims of international jurisprudence than any other human being?

In the early days of the church's sexual abuse crisis in the United States, Cardinal Ratzinger tried to shut down discussion of the issue by reducing clerical abuse to a minor problem involving a few isolated cases. When that didn't work, he blamed the US media for sensational coverage. When that didn't work, he called it a recent phenomenon. And when that didn't work either, he blamed it all on "the gay culture" of the 1980s and '90s, which he said had caused a homosexual "take over" of the seminaries. Perhaps a bit of perspective is in order.

The church's first sex abuse scandal occurred in 153 CE. It passed its first law against the clerical sex abuse of boys at the

Council of Elvira in 306 CE. By the fourteenth century, lusty clerics and their sodomitical ways were the stuff of ribald satire in Chaucer's *The Canterbury Tales*. England's first anti-buggery laws, passed by Henry VIII in the sixteenth century, were directed at Catholic priests. But the church did not regard the priestly sex abuse of children as requiring formal censure until canon law was codified in 1917. At that time, the abuse of children under age sixteen (the limit is now eighteen) was outlawed as a "sin." In 1922, the church issued its first instruction on the canon law procedures and penalties for child sex abuse, and would update it forty years later. In the meantime, the issue would find a town crier of sorts in the Reverend Gerald Fitzgerald.

The first Roman Catholic priest to alert church authorities about pedophilic sex abuse by the clergy, Fitzgerald (1894–1969) was best known as the founder in 1947 of the Servants of the Paraclete. The group operated centers to assist "fallen" priests who were dealing with alcoholism and substance abuse issues; eventually these centers became the place to send priests who had sexually offended. At first, Fitzgerald used the same spiritual methods of intense prayer with pedophile priests that he used with the other "guests" at the centers. But he soon reconsidered. Convinced that these priests could not be cured, he began writing to their bishops, recommending that they be laicized immediately. In 1952, he told Bishop Robert Dwyer of Reno: "I myself would be inclined to favor laicization for any priest, upon objective evidence, for tampering with the virtue of the young, my argument being, from this point onward the charity to the Mystical Body should take precedence over charity to the individual ... Moreover, in practice, real conversions will be found to be extremely rare ... Hence, leaving them on duty or wandering from diocese to diocese is contributing to scandal or at least to the approximate danger of scandal."

On August 26, 1963, Fitzgerald met with newly elected Pope Paul VI and told him that sex abuse in the clergy was on the increase and that several seminaries were affected. Because pedophilia was incurable, allowing such priests to continue in their ministries would have a devastating impact on the reputation of the priesthood, he said. The next day, at His Holiness's request, Fitzgerald wrote the pope a letter advising a course of action. "Personally, I am not sanguine of the return of priests to active duty who have been addicted to abnormal practices, especially sins with the young," he wrote. "Where there is indication of incorrigibility, because of the tremendous scandal given, I would most earnestly recommend total laicisation. I say 'total' ... because when these men are taken before civil authority, the non-Catholic world definitely blames the discipline of celibacy for the perversion of these men." Fitzgerald's entreaty to the pontiff seemed all the more urgent in light of Rome's most recent response to the issue: about a year and a half before this exchange, Pope Paul's predecessor had approved an updated version of canon law dealing with pedophile priests.

For liberal, pro-Vatican II Catholics who tend to idealize Pope John XXIII as a kindly old sage and lover of all humanity (as this author once did), belated disclosure of the 1962 document *Crimen Sollicitationis* came as both a shock and a letdown.[41]

---

41 Apparently produced only for bishops' eyes, *Crimen Sollicitationis* (March 16, 1962) was unknown to the faithful until 2003, when it was leaked to lawyers for US victims hoping to bring action against the Vatican.

Written by Holy Office chair Cardinal Alfredo Ottaviani, approved by Pope John, and released seven months before the opening of Vatican II, the language in *Crimen* offers persuasive evidence that, for all his progressive views about women, the "Good Pope" may have been just as homophobic as the average eighty-one-year-old Italian male in the early 1960s. More damningly, it reveals him as willing to countenance a form of damage control or cover-up that would lead to the biggest scandal in Roman Catholic history.

One of the more bizarre documents ever to come out of the Vatican, the *Crimen's* purpose was to instruct bishops on how to proceed in cases of "the unspeakable crime": sexual solicitations by priests of their penitents in the confession box, or in circumstances closely related to the sacraments. It applied to "any external obscene act, gravely sinful, perpetrated or attempted by a cleric in any way with pre-adolescent children of either sex or with brute animals."

It also incorporated "the foulest crime," which was any obscene act committed by a cleric "in any manner whatsoever with a person of his own sex." The *Crimen* was obsessed with pontifical secrecy: the penalty for revealing its existence was excommunication. It imposed "utmost confidentiality" and "permanent silence" on all persons involved in the complaint process, including even the victims and their witnesses, who were bound "under pain of incurring automatic excommunication." The *Crimen* contained virtually no investigation process, no acknowledgement of child abuse as a serious crime, and thus, no suggestion that the police should be involved.

Finally, the *Crimen* provided no consequences of note for

priests found guilty of molesting children. A first offense might get you "chiefly spiritual exercises to be made for a certain number of days in some religious house, with suspensions from the celebration of mass during that period." A relapse might get you "special supervision" such as suspension from saying mass or working with children. Only for "more grievous cases," like sexual seduction in the confessional, might "the extreme penalty," defrocking, be applied. But that was only if you were one of those priests whose ministry had caused such "great scandal to the faithful...that there seem[ed] to be no hope, humanly speaking, or almost no hope, of [your] amendment." As distinguished human rights lawyer and judge Geoffrey Robertson wryly puts it, the terms of *Crimen* may have been "no substitute for police investigation and criminal punishment," but they seemed appropriate "for a small Masonic society that needs rules to discipline members and, as a last resort, to remove them from the club." Robertson compares the "pontifical silence" order of the *Crimen* as similar in tone and intention—if not in consequences—to the honor code of *omerta* that governs the mafia: no cooperation with authorities in the event of a crime, and total silence on pain of death.

The mere existence of the *Crimen* is damning evidence that the Vatican's official culture of denial, cover-up, and shaming goes back more than half a century.[42] Some would argue that fifty-plus years should be plenty of time for the world's largest organization to fix a bad policy, proceed on a path of social justice for

---

42 More than sixty years, if one includes Father Fitzgerald's earliest warning to US bishops in 1952.

victims of priestly sexual abuse, and begin to foster an environment in which children are safe—rather than subjecting them to
a nightmare. As both CDF prefect and Supreme pontiff, Joseph
Ratzinger was in a position of authority for more than thirty of
those fifty years to actually do something about this. But when
he did act, his responses were unconvincing, overly defensive, or
too little and too late. He seemed to act only at the last minute,
when the bad publicity could get no worse, and only in damage
control mode. In his mind, there must have been a larger principle at stake that prevented him from taking a proactive stance
to seek justice. Perhaps it was a venerated tradition that, for the
sake of the Old Boys' Club, was not to be meddled with.

Mandatory Celibacy and the "Service" Myth

Vatican apologists, including the pope emeritus, have argued
for years that the vow of celibacy—the priestly commitment
to refrain from marriage or sexual relations with women—has
nothing to do with the sex abuse crisis that had, at last count,
cost the church nearly $2 billion in US lawsuits[43] and untold
millions elsewhere, as well as destroying the credibility of the
church's pastoral mission throughout the world. Nor, said Pope
Benedict, does it have anything to do with the rapidly declining
ranks of the priesthood since Vatican II. On this, as with most
issues that challenged his authority, His Holiness appeared—at
best—to be in deep denial.

---

43 *Forbes* magazine has predicted that the total bill for sex abuse in the US could top
$5 billion.

For one thing, there is *no* Biblical justification for celibacy. "Do we not have the right to be accompanied by a wife, as the other apostles and the brothers of the Lord and Cephas?" wonders Paul, in 1 Corinthians 9:5. "Let deacons be the husband of one wife, and let them manage their children and their households well," say the authors of 1 Timothy 3:12. Even the Gospels' supporters of celibacy tempered their esteem "with a kind of hedged earthy realism," theologian Daniel C. Maguire has noted. "Being a 'eunuch' for the Kingdom of Heaven was all right, but 'not all can receive this word, but only those to whom it is given' (Matthew 19: 10–12). Paul, too, preferred celibacy but saw it as a 'special gift from God' (1 Corinthians 7)." Yes: Saint Paul, whom Benedict has been all too fond of quoting to justify his austerity on such matters. Pope Felix (483–92) was the son of a priest, as was Pope Agapitus in the sixth century. Pope Hadrianus II (867–72) was married.

It was thanks in large part to the church's anti-woman, sexphobic biases that the pendulum began to shift toward celibacy. Pope Gregory VII (1073–85), who regarded priestly marriage as a form of concubinage, called upon the flock to boycott married priests.[44] But it was only at the Second Lateran Council in 1139 that priests were formally prohibited from marriage. Four hundred years later, with the Protestant Reformation snapping at its heels, the church added muscle to this law at the Council of Trent, (1545–63).[45] Another four hundred years later, at Vatican

---

44 Part of the problem was the politics of property inheritance: priests' wives were passing on property to their heirs, taking it away from the Church. Mandatory celibacy protected church property while limiting the influence of women.

45 Mandatory celibacy, from the very beginning, engendered a kind of cynicism as it

II, the church was once again in a reformist mood. The conciliary buzz was that bishops wanted mandatory celibacy on the council agenda: Pope John boasted that he could end it with the stroke of a pen. But he died before the issue came up. His successor, Pope Paul VI, forbade the council from discussing it. In 1967, Pope Paul effectively ended the debate when he released the encyclical *Sacerdotalis Caelibatus (On the Sacredness of Celibacy)*, which reaffirmed the church's celibacy requirement.

Removing the optional element of celibacy pretty much destroys its spiritual impact. For what value is there in forcing someone to embrace a model of behavior for which only the freedom to choose it would demonstrate true commitment? Perhaps the biggest myth about celibacy is that it represents some kind of heroic sacrifice: the assumption is that, because marriage is so highly valued, the sacrifice of it is noble. Again: what validity can there be to a "sacrifice" that is assumed as a condition of employment? "Sacrifice is good if it is conducive to something positive. Otherwise it is an idol," argues Daniel C. Maguire.

For a Daniel Berrigan[46], celibacy was good for the freedom it gave him to pursue justice in a special way. He would not have been morally free to leave young

---

was all too often breached. When the Council of Constance (1414–18) met to discuss celibacy, among other things, more than 1,000 prostitutes showed up to provide extracurricular assistance.

46 The American Jesuit priest, peace activist, and poet who, along with his brother Philip, was for a time on the FBI Ten Most Wanted Fugitives list and received multiple prison sentences because of his involvement in antiwar protests during the Vietnam war.

children or an unwilling spouse to go to jail for many years. Celibacy might give mobility or, for some, it might be, at least for a time, a useful discipline. A group of celibates might form an enriching kind of community of a sort that could not exist with families. But celibacy is only one of many ministerial and religious options. It is good or bad according to the circumstances that give it meaning.

Joseph Ratzinger would call such reasoning "relativist." A large number of priests, who have either broken their celibacy vows or walked away from the church, would call it "reality." The simple truth Ratzinger refused to acknowledge was that optional celibacy could have prevented the post-1960s exodus of priests from Holy Orders.[47] Having married priests, and female priests, would eventually produce a healthier and more balanced Catholic theology of sexuality. For that matter, ending the demonization of homosexuality would allow gay men (and lesbians, once women were admitted to the priesthood) to pursue both their pastoral missions and personal relationships free of self-loathing and guilt. Optional celibacy would allow *all* priests to lead transparent lives, drastically reducing the risk of unhealthy behavior that can ultimately manifest itself in criminal acts.

During the mid-1980s, the US bishops commissioned a research project on the causes of the priest shortage. Conducted

---

47 Between 1970 and 1995, in the United States alone, it is estimated that 20,000 priests left the priesthood. The global estimate for that period was 100,000.

by sociologists Richard A. Schoenherr of the University of Wisconsin and Lawrence A. Young of Brigham Young University, the project took several years to complete. When the results came in, the US bishops were so disturbed by what they found that a shoot-the-messenger mentality took over: the bishops cut the project's funding after the third private interim report. Schoenherr and Young scrambled to find other funding, and in 1993 they published their final results. In their conclusion, the sociologists offered the church some unsolicited advice on how to respond to the priest shortage. "We believe the church is being confronted with a choice between its sacramental tradition and its commitment to an exclusively male celibate priesthood," they wrote. "We speculate further that, to preserve the more essential elements of Roman Catholicism, the nonessentials—first compulsory celibacy and later male exclusivity—will need to be eliminated as defining characteristics of priesthood."

As noted in the previous chapter, there are many things that attract gay men to the priesthood. But gay priests have a paradoxical relationship to the vow of celibacy: it does not strictly apply to them, as they have no inclination toward marriage or sex with a woman. So it is easy to be celibate, but not so easy to be chaste. At the same time, gay pride is a relatively new phenomenon. The gay liberation movement began less than half a century ago, and it is only recently that gay and lesbian teenagers in the West have been able to embrace their sexuality at puberty—the same time as their heterosexual brothers and sisters. This means that most gay men who became priests or entered the seminary between the 1950s and '70s grew up with a pre-liberationist view of their own sexuality. So Cardinal Ratzinger's declaration that homosexuality was an "intrinsic moral evil" was hardly an invitation to transparency for incoming pastors. And thus, gay Roman Catholic priests who had come to terms with their sexuality, who were out of the closet to themselves, each other, and their parishioners, who had either opened their hearts to healthy, loving relationships or embraced chastity (secure in the knowledge that they were accepted for who they were and had nothing to hide), and who were unafraid of addressing issues of sexuality in their Sunday homilies, would be few and far between.

For the final half of the twentieth century, a large number of priests with homosexual feelings were closeted and wallowed in self-loathing from the cloister. Too afraid to pursue secret sex lives outside the church, they were otherwise incapable of enjoying intimate adult relationships within it. Many heterosexual priests, for that matter, struggled with their commitment to celibacy and were no more capable of enjoying intimate adult relationships than were their gay brothers. Many others didn't know which way they swung, but they suffered, too. Andrew Sullivan, in a column for *The Atlantic*, described the bulk of these priests as "tortured" men suffering from arrested sexual and emotional development, men who had never had a sexual or intimate relationship with any other human being:

> Sex for them is an abstraction, a sin, not an interaction with an equal. And their sexuality has been frozen at the first real moment of internal terror: their

early teens. So they tend to be attracted still to those who are in their own stage of development: teenage boys. And in their new positions, they are given total access to these kids who revere them for their power. So they use these children to express themselves sexually. They barely see these children as young and vulnerable human beings, incapable of true consent. Because they have never had a real sexual relationship, have never had to deal with the core issue of human equality and dignity in sex, they don't see the children as victims. Like the tortured gay man, Michael Jackson, they see them as friends ... As emotionally developed as your average fourteen-year-old wanting to be loved, they sublimate a lot of their lives into clerical service. But they also act out sexually all the time.

Being human, such men struggled not only with loneliness but with resentment: all that service, and no reward until the afterlife? That didn't seem fair. All those selfless acts—the late-night phone calls or knocks on the door, the counseling sessions over coffee, the weddings, the funerals, the first communions, the court testimonials, the character references—and at the end of the day? Nothing. Back home to the rectory, alone. No kisses, no caresses, no "How was your day, Honey?" Despite all those sacrifices, these priests were denied the one thing most adults take for granted: intimacy with another. And in that yawning vortex of emotional deprivation lay a recipe for disaster.

At this point, it is helpful to define some terms. First, most pedophilia involves an adult male and a female child. But in the Catholic Church, where all but a few environments are exclusively male, the pattern has mostly involved an adult male and a male child. So Cardinal Tarcisio Bertone resorted to an easy cop-out in 2010, when he claimed that child sex abuse in the church is homosexuality's fault: in fact, child sex abuse, regardless of sexuality, was the church's fault. Bertone's comment was also misleading. "Child abuse" refers to pedophilia, a sexual disorder not equivalent to sexual orientation; homosexuality is the opposite.

There is also a distinction between pedophilia, which refers to sex with pre-adolescent children, and ephebophilia, which refers to sex with post-pubescent teens of up to seventeen years of age. When gay priests are guilty of ephebophilic acts, they are more likely to be tarred by the media as "child abusers" or "pedophiles" than are their heterosexual counterparts guilty of similar acts with post-pubescent girls. (Thus is homosexuality further demonized, and the Vatican's homophobic agenda reinforced. Hence Cardinal Bertone's sneaky game of scapegoating.) In any case, there was lots of pedophilia going on, and by the late 1980s the time bomb was ready to explode.

Red Flags Everywhere

The outbreak of child rape and sexual violence in the Roman Catholic Church unfolded a bit like the AIDS epidemic: after simmering under the surface a while, the first revelations were followed by a slow trickle of cases in various parts of the world, followed then by a full-scale outbreak of "recovered memory." In one of the earliest cases, Father Gilbert Gauthe from Lafayette, Louisiana, in 1985 became the first Catholic priest in the US to be convicted of sexual abuse of young boys. He was sentenced to twenty years in prison. After his story was picked up by the *National Catholic Reporter*, the freelance journalist covering it went on to reveal dozens of other cases throughout the US, most involving multiple victims. In 1989, the Mount Cashel orphanage in Newfoundland, Canada, was exposed as a house of horrors where more than 300 children had been sexually abused by the Christian Brothers. Over the next few years, similar horror stories began to emerge from Catholic parishes in the rest of Canada, the US, Australia, Ireland, and the European continent.

In October 1992, a group of sex abuse survivors and their families from the Chicago suburb of Arlington Heights held the first national meeting about sex abuse in the clergy. Before long, a deeply disturbing pattern emerged from their stories. Each victim had been sexually abused at puberty or pre-adolescence by a priest or other member of the clergy, each had tried to go public, and each was greeted by denial and cover-up when their case was brought to the attention of a bishop or other senior church official. This was what the *National Catholic Reporter* had found in its coverage of different cases throughout the country: "the almost invariable pattern of church response: first a denial by the local bishop, then the reshuffling of the accused priest to another assignment and the discrediting of the accuser by church officials, and finally, the lawsuit."

One of the speakers at the Arlington Heights conference was Richard Sipe, a former Benedictine monk and priest who had moved into clinical mental health counseling and was now a consultant specializing in the mental health problems of Catholic priests.[48] Sipe told delegates that sex abuse by priests was partly a result of mandatory celibacy. The celibate male priesthood was a man's world where the ideal women are mothers or virgins (i.e., forbidden objects of sexual fantasy), men have the power and boys are the precious future. "It is clear that the institutional church is in a preadolescent state of psychosexual development," argued Sipe. "This is a period, typically prior to eleven years of age in which boys prefer association with their own sex; girls are avoided and held in disdain, often as a guise for fear of women as well as of their own as yet unsolidified sexuality." Sipe's conclusion was rather prescient. "When the whole story of sexual abuse by presumed celibate clergy is told," he said, "it will lead to the highest corridors of Vatican City."[49]

Sipe's research into the psychology of sex abuse in the clergy has led him to some more recent conclusions that give one pause. By his estimates, between six and nine percent of all priests are sexually active with children. While this number includes a few devious perverts attracted to the priesthood for its easy access to children and its power to protect abusers from scrutiny, most offenders are of the psychosexually immature variety referred to earlier: in denial about their condition and hoping that the

---

48 The author of several books on priestly sexual behavior, Sipe conducted a twenty-five-year ethnographic study of the celibate/sexual behavior of priests and has participated in documentaries on celibacy and priest sexual abuse aired by HBO, BBC, and other major networks in several countries, as well as being widely interviewed on the subject.

49 This and the previous two citations from Fox, Thomas C., *Sexuality and Catholicism* (New York: George Braziller, 1995).

demands of pastoral work will protect them from themselves. In this they find a brotherhood among fellow priests, a fraternity that—in its interest to protect the good name of the church—leads to a culture of ready forgiveness in which "even sex with minors becomes just another sin to be forgiven."

A decade after the Arlington Heights conference, the US Catholic Bishops Conference commissioned a study of clerical sex abuse that would confirm the worst of Sipe's fears. According to the group of criminologists from New York City's John Jay College of Criminal Justice who conducted the two-year study, no fewer than 10,667 individuals had made plausible allegations against 4,392 priests in the US between 1950 and 2002. That was 4.3 percent of active priests during the period. This figure was considered a lowball estimate for the actual number of offenders, since the study had no confidential access to parish records and relied on information voluntarily provided by church authorities. The church itself accepted a figure closer to 5.3 percent, and others claimed the true figure was closer to Sipe's six to nine percent. In any case, the hard numbers easily dismissed Ratzinger's claim in 2002, the year the study began, that "less than one percent of priests are guilty of acts of this type." (A large percentage of those "acts" included penile penetration or attempted penile penetration or oral sex—acts which, in the context, constituted rape, attempted rape, or sexual violence.) The John Jay study, released in 2004, also revealed that the vast majority of abusive priests were ordained before the late-1970s—thus dismissing Ratzinger's oft-quoted claim that "the gay culture" of the 1980s and '90s was to blame.

Eighteen years before the John Jay study's release, Robert

Nugent offered the Vatican some good advice on how *not* to deal with the sex abuse crisis. Nugent was the Catholic priest who, along with Sister Jeannine Gramick, Ratzinger had silenced because of his support for gay and lesbian Catholics. In his mind, the worst thing a bishop could do upon learning of a sex abuse case in his diocese was to "deny, repress or sidestep actual cases involving peoples' lives and ministerial careers hoping that the 'problem' will either disappear, resolve itself naturally, or, at the very least, not reach the public's attention." Nugent described the typical senior cleric who adopts this approach as one who: "simply continues to reassign individuals struggling with obvious sexual issues (including arrests, blackmail, complaints from parents or other clergy); who provides no supportive counseling or direction for individuals involved in affective/genital sexual relationships; or who refuses even to address the situation when it has been called to his attention with substantial evidence... [and] those who view sexuality and celibacy issues solely in terms of confession, spiritual direction, or therapy with little or no appreciation of the social and political implications, let alone the need for open, honest discussion."

Father Nugent did not know it at the time, but these words could have served as fair warning to the Vatican official who would one day convict him for Thoughtcrime because of his ministry to gay and lesbian Catholics (see Chapter VII).

The People vs. Joseph Ratzinger

The case filed with the International Criminal Court at The Hague in 2011 did not accuse Pope Benedict of ordering priests to go out and bugger young boys. Rather, it accused him of maintaining a church policy, *Crimen Sollicitationis*, that was itself criminal (despite the ironic reference to "crime" in its title), and then updating and refining that policy so that the cover-up of sexual abuse of children would continue without the knowledge of, or interference from, state criminal authorities. It also alleged that Benedict's primary concern, as a cleric with "command responsibility" over the conduct of the priests, was not the welfare of children under their care but the reputation of the "universal" church. Among the supporting documents the plaintiffs produced was evidence that—in his capacity as archbishop of Munich, as prefect of the CDF, and as Pope Benedict XVI— Ratzinger had aided and abetted the continuing rape of children through his decisions. Collectively and over decades, the filing argued, the incumbent pope's handling of the issue—and that of the three cardinals named along with him—constituted crimes against humanity.

The following is a selection of clerical child sex abuse cases, and decisions involving them, that bear Ratzinger's fingerprints:[50]

Stephen Kiesle: In 1981, the bishop of Oakland, John S. Cummins, wrote to Ratzinger's predecessor at the CDF with an urgent recommendation to defrock Kiesle, who had been convicted in a criminal court the previous year for tying up and

---

50 With the exception of the German priest Peter Hullermann, whose case is referenced in the Prologue and Epilogue.

molesting two young boys in a San Francisco monastery. Kiesle himself had agreed to be defrocked. Before turning his office over to Ratzinger, Cardinal Seper asked Cummins for more information. The bishop provided it on February 1, 1982, along with some advice. "It is my conviction," wrote Cummins, "that there would be no scandal if this petition were granted and that as a matter of fact, given the nature of the case, there might be greater scandal to the community if Father Kiesle were allowed to return to the active ministry."

Father Kiesle, it turned out, had first been convicted for child molesting in 1978, six years after he was ordained. (He pleaded no contest to a misdemeanor charge of lewd conduct while he was a pastor at Our Lady of the Rosary in Union City, California.) In any event, Ratzinger sat on Bishop Cummins' letter for three years, despite anxious and repeated requests, for fear of provoking what the CDF prefect would call "detriment within the community of Christ's faithful." Meanwhile, the diocese withdrew permission for Kiesle to work as a minister. While Ratzinger was dithering, Father Kiesle was able to serve the full three years' probation for his misdemeanor and undergo treatment, enabling him to wipe his record clean. In his 1985 response to Cummins, written in Latin, Ratzinger said that the case needed more time and that "the good of the Universal Church" had to be considered in the final decision. His letter mentioned Kiesle's relative youth—he was thirty-eight at the time—as one reason for delaying his defrocking: the "faithful," Ratzinger said, would be scandalized if a priest under forty were laicized.

Ratzinger waited until the day before Father Kiesle's fortieth birthday before finally defrocking him. In 1987, the priest was volunteering in the youth ministry at one of his former parishes, Saint Joseph's in Pinole, California. It is not known whether he abused anyone there before his record was discovered, and he was forced to leave the position a year later. But in 2002, Kiesle was charged with several cases of molestation, including abusing at least a half-dozen young girls while at his former parishes in the 1960s and '70s. Those charges were dropped when the US Supreme Court struck down a California law that extended the statute of limitations on child molestation cases. Eventually, he pleaded no contest to a separate felony charge of molesting a child at his vacation home in Truckee, California, in 1995 and was sentenced to six years in prison.

Lawrence Murphy: Branded by SNAP as "one of the worst pedophiles in US history," Murphy was headmaster of Saint John's School for the Deaf in Milwaukee, Wisconsin. Between 1950 and 1974, he raped and sexually abused as many as 200 deaf boys. The vulnerability of these children is perhaps best exemplified by victim Terry Kohut, who had recently lost his brother to electrocution by accident when he arrived at the school in 1960 at age ten. His father committed suicide a year later, and his favorite dog died a year after that. Kohut put his trust in Father Murphy as a second father—and was repeatedly raped for it. In 1995, finally prepared, as an adult, to confront his abuser, Kohut wrote a letter to Murphy, telling him how devastating the experience had been. He sent a copy to Ratzinger at the CDF but got no reply.

On July 17, 1996, Milwaukee Archbishop Rembert Weakland wrote to Ratzinger about Murphy, describing not only the abuse but the twisted priest's opportunistic use of the confessional to solicit "sinful actions." He asked the CDF prefect what should be done. But Ratzinger did not reply to this letter, nor to a second inquiry from Weakland. Eight months later, Archbishop Tarcisio Bertone finally replied, advising Weakland to hold a secret church trial. Weakland took that advice, and commenced proceedings. Then Murphy himself wrote to Ratzinger, asking for leniency because he was seventy-two and in poor health. "I have repented of any of my past transgressions," he wrote, "and I simply want to live out the time that I have left in the dignity of my priesthood." The tone of Vatican correspondence changed after that.

In his next letter to Weakland, Bertone asked him to consider pastoral measures—counseling and supervision—instead of a trial. Weakland disagreed, and in May 1998, flew from Wisconsin to Rome to meet with Ratzinger and his staff. At that meeting, Weakland later wrote, "it became clear that the Congregation was not encouraging us to proceed with any formal dismissal." On August 19, 1998, Weakland agreed to a pastoral plan and stopped the trial. But it was all too late: Murphy was gravely ill, died two days later, and was buried with the full dignity and honors of a Roman Catholic priest in good standing. Kohut proceeded to sue the Vatican, and Ratzinger specifically, for the injustice. Posthumous discipline though it may have been, he wanted nothing less than for Father Murphy to lose his title and good standing as a priest. His question to Ratzinger, broadcast in a CNN investigative report in September 2010, was straightforward: "Why? Why did you stop that trial? Why did you give pity to Father Murphy? I mean, what about me? What about the 200 other boys?"

Marcial Maciel Degollado: The Mexican founder of the Legionaries of Christ surely ranks as one of the biggest hypocrites and slimeballs in modern Roman Catholic history. A favorite of John Paul II, who blessed him at the Vatican in 2004, Maciel was a good fundraiser, a dedicated right-winger, and a virulent anti-feminist—just like his pope. But unlike John Paul, he was also a bigamist who fathered six children, a pederast, and a child sex addict who raped two of his sons from the ages of eight to fourteen. The Caligulan gluttony of this treacly psychopath apparently knew no bounds: Maciel, who kept several wives and mistresses, insisted on being masturbated by young boys whenever he visited the seminaries of the Legionaries of Christ. In 1998, eight ex-Legionaries filed a canon law case to prosecute him through Ratzinger's CDF tribunal. But the prefect himself had been stalling the process—even as Mexican newspapers were beginning to expose Maciel's sordid, hypocritical life.

In fact, it would take Ratzinger another seven years to act on the case. (This may have had something to do with Maciel's support from Cardinal Angelo Sodano[51]; Cardinal Eduardo Martínez Somalo, prefect of the Congregation for Institutes of Consecrated Life and Societies of Apostolic Life; and Msgr. Stanislaw Dziwisz, John Paul II's Polish secretary.) In 2005, after John Paul had died, Ratzinger, as the new pope, did banish Maciel to a monastery, inviting him to lead "a reserved life of

---

51 Sodano, a big supporter of Maciel, reportedly received cash payments from the Mexican fundraiser and his organization. (For a talk at Christmas, Sodano would get $10,000 USD.) It was Sodano who is said to have intervened in 1998 to halt Ratzinger's investigation into Maciel. If this is true, the Vatican's then-Secretary of State was—to say the very least, and among other things—in a conflict of interest.

prayer and penance." But that was no more a defrocking than it was a criminal penalty. In addition to Sodano, another of Benedict's three co-accused in the ICC filing, Cardinal Tarcisio Bertone, shows up in the Maciel case. It was Bertone, in his former capacity as a canon lawyer, who sheltered Maciel by creating "professional secrecy" for clergy regarding the case. Maciel died in 2008. A couple of years later, Benedict accepted a report confirming the horrors of Maciel's reign and appointed an overseer for the Legionaries of Christ. To the Pope's credit, he then put the organization under Vatican administration.[52]

Cardinal Hans Hermann Groer: Here was one example where Ratzinger may have done some good but was stymied in his efforts to do more. Groer, the leader of Austria's Catholics, was estimated to have molested 2,000 boys in his twenty-year passage to the bishopric. When abuse allegations against Groer first surfaced, Ratzinger pushed for an investigative commission. However, according to Vienna Cardinal Christoph Schoenborn, Cardinal Sodano, and Pope John Paul II's personal secretary, Stanislaw Dziwisz,[53] blocked the attempts. In 1995, Ratzinger managed to force Groer's removal as archbishop of Vienna. (He was replaced by Schoenborn, Ratzinger's old student and friend.) But the abuser was allowed to fade into the background while some of his victims were paid compensation in return for keeping quiet. At Pope John Paul II's request in 1998, Groer

---

52 For a detailed account of Maciel's crimes and Legionaries officials' attempts to cover them up, see Chapter III, "Nuestro Padre," of John Thavis's *The Vatican Diaries* (New York: Viking, 2013, pp. 69–116).

53 After Pope John Paul II's death, Ratzinger appointed Dziwisz as archbishop of Krakow, John Paul's former position, and later elevated him to cardinal.

relinquished his remaining ecclesiastical duties and privileges as an archbishop and cardinal. But he never admitted his guilt. In the end, he retired without punishment and spent his final years protected in a nunnery once his criminal behavior was public knowledge. He died in 2003.

Cardinal Bernard Law: Considered a poster boy for the US pedophile priest scandal, Cardinal Law was revealed to have sheltered 250 priests and church workers accused of acts of rape and sexual assault of children. According to Massachusetts Attorney General Thomas Reilly, "Law had direct knowledge of the scope, duration and severity of the crisis experienced by children in the Archdiocese; he participated directly in the crucial decisions concerning the assignment of abusive priests, decisions that typically increased the risk to children." (In one of the worst cases, Father John Geoghan was accused of having molested 150 youths. Law kept reassigning him—including an eight-year stay in one parish where Geoghan was said to have abused at least thirty boys.) When the horror stories emerged in 2000, Law stubbornly remained as archbishop for another two-and-a-half years. It was only after a petition signed by fifty-eight priests, and pressure from the attorney general, plus relentless media coverage and complaints from lay groups, that he resigned in December 2002.

With cloak-and-dagger intrigue reminiscent of *The Godfather*, Cardinal Law fled Boston a few hours before state troopers arrived with a subpoena seeking his grand jury testimony. He flew to Rome where, in May 2004, John Paul II rewarded him with a plum assignment: the majestic, fourth-century basilica of Santa Maria Maggiore. A cathedral under direct

Vatican jurisdiction and considered one of the four most important basilicas in Rome, it was also the largest church in the city
dedicated to the Blessed Virgin Mary. At a monthly salary of
$12,000, Cardinal Law was put in charge of the administration
of the priests and anything related to the basilica. A year later
he presided, on behalf of those four main basilicas in Rome,
over one of the major funeral masses for John Paul. (Ten days
later, he voted in the conclave that elected Ratzinger as Benedict
XVI.) "By sheltering such a salient offender at its very heart, the
Vatican had invited the metastasis of the horror into its bosom
and thence to its very head," Christopher Hitchens wrote in
Newsweek in May 2010. "It is obvious that Cardinal Law could
not have made his escape or been given asylum without the
approval of the then-pontiff and of his most trusted deputy in
the matter of child-rape damage control, then-cardinal Joseph
Ratzinger." During the 1960s, "Vatican Roulette" was an earnest
reference to the rhythm method. Thanks to Cardinal Law and
his ilk, it has since become a cynical reference to "priest shifting."

Father Michael Teta and Monsignor Robert Trupia: In the
early 1990s, two bishops pleaded with Ratzinger to take action
regarding these two child-abusing priests in Tuscon, Arizona.
In a letter signed by Ratzinger on June 8, 1992, the CDF prefect told the bishops that he would take care of it. But five years
later, Ratzinger still had done nothing. Father Teta had been
molesting children since the 1970s. A church tribunal set up in
the 1990s described an "almost satanic quality in his mode of
acting toward young men and boys," including the molestation
of boys aged seven and nine in the confessional as they prepared
for their First Communion. Bishop Manuel Moreno wrote to

Ratzinger repeatedly over the years, never receiving a response. By 2003 Moreno was sick with cancer and retired early. But before he did, he wrote to Ratzinger once more. His replacement also sent requests that went unanswered. "There's no doubt that Ratzinger delayed the defrocking process of dangerous priests who were deemed 'satanic' by their own bishop," an attorney of one of the victims said. Ultimately, it took Ratzinger twelve years to remove Teta and Trupia from the priesthood.

Alvin Campbell: The Springfield, Illinois, priest was convicted of the sexual abuse of seven boys and sentenced to fourteen years in prison in 1985. This was after workers at a rape crisis center alerted authorities that they were treating one of Campbell's victims: police found that the priest had been plying boys with video games, bicycles, watches, and other gifts in order to coax them to the waterbed in his second-floor rectory bedroom. After his conviction, Campbell's bishop, Daniel Ryan, visited him in jail and tried to convince him to give up the priesthood, but he refused. Ryan petitioned Ratzinger to defrock him, rather than putting the victims through a church trial. But Ratzinger denied the request. The reason? Campbell's refusal to go along with it. "The petition in question cannot be admitted in as much as it lacks the request of Father Campbell himself," Ratzinger wrote in a July 3, 1989, letter to Bishop Ryan. Released after serving half his sentence in 1992, Campbell was convinced by priests in his diocese to accept defrocking without a church trial.

René Bissey: The French priest was sentenced to eighteen years in jail for repeatedly raping a boy and sexually assaulting ten other children. Bishop Pierre Pican of Bayeux-Lisieux kept the priest in parish work despite the fact that he admitted committing pedophilic acts. The bishop received a three-month suspended sentence for not reporting the abuse, contrary to French law. Despite all this, the Vatican actually congratulated Bishop Pican for refusing to call the police about Bissey: Cardinal Darío Castrillón Hojos of Colombia, acting in his capacity as the Vatican official in charge of priests worldwide, wrote Pican with the personal approval of Pope John Paul II and other senior cardinals—including Ratzinger.

Juan Carlos Patino-Arango: In 1996, while studying for the priesthood at Saint Mary's Seminary in Houston, Texas, Patino-Arango allegedly sexually molested three children, ages eleven, twelve, and thirteen, during counseling sessions at Saint Francis de Sales Church. In May 2004, Patino-Arango was indicted with criminal charges by a Harris County grand jury. According to the Archdiocese of Galveston-Houston, the seminarian was removed from his parish as soon as the accusations against him surfaced; he was returned to Colombia with the full knowledge of the police. In June 2004, a lawsuit filed in a southern district of Texas accused three defendants—the Archdiocese of Galveston-Houston, its Archbishop Joseph Fiorenza, and Cardinal Ratzinger—of conspiracy to prevent Patino-Arango from facing the music.

According to the prosecution, the archdiocese and Fiorenza covered up Patino-Arango's crimes and moved him out of the country so he could avoid civil courts. Ratzinger was considered an accomplice in the cover-up because of the official order in his May 2001 letter for bishops to take such action. The lawyer for one of the plaintiffs, Daniel Shea of Houston, accused Ratzinger of obstruction of justice—a charge carrying a maximum statutory sentence of twenty years in prison. In the spring of 2005, Ratzinger was scheduled to face charges of abetting the archdiocese in its efforts to obstruct justice when he became Pope Benedict XVI and was suddenly unavailable. On May 20 of that year, the Apostolic Nunciature of the Holy See in Washington, DC sent a note to the US State Department asking for assurances of the pope's diplomatic immunity as a foreign head of "state." In December 2005, a federal district judge in Houston accepted the request for immunity.

So far, there has been no mention of Pope Benedict's third co-accused in the ICC filing, Cardinal William Levada. Named Ratzinger's replacement as CDF prefect when the former became pope, Levada was bishop of Portland, Oregon, when sex abuse cases in the archdiocese were first brought to his attention. He did nothing, and his archdiocese was forced to raise $75 million for legal settlements to get out of bankruptcy. Meanwhile, he defended his priests to the point of parody. In one instance, a priest witnessed a colleague "straddling a kneeling fifteen-year-old altar boy in a dark rectory room." Archbishop Levada accepted that this was "horseplay and wrestling" and suspended the witness instead of the "wrestler"—whose later confession cost the archdiocese $750,000 in damages. In April 2010, Cardinal Levada appeared on PBS's *Newshour* program to blame "unfair" reporters from the *New York Times*, fed with information from plaintiffs' attorneys, for the crisis.

Levada is named in the ICC filing because of his role, as then-CDF prefect, in maintaining a church policy that "will continue to result in the sexual assault of children and vulnerable adults by members of the Catholic clergy." There are two particular cases cited in the filing of relevance to Levada, one of which names him as a person of interest. In that case, Father Joseph Palanivel Jeyapaul was accused of molesting two girls while he was a priest in Minnesota. One of them, a twenty-one-year-old artist and college student named Megan Meterson, was fourteen when Jeyapaul allegedly repeatedly raped and sexually assaulted her. Her case was reported to law enforcement authorities by a counselor. An arrest warrant was issued—as was an extradition warrant, as Jeyapaul had fled the country. Cardinal Levada was notified about Jeyapaul's case shortly after the complaint was first filed. Although the priest's whereabouts were later confirmed (by 2010, Jeyapaul was known to be head of approximately forty Catholic schools in the diocese of Ootacamund in Tamil Nadu, India), Levada did nothing to facilitate his return or ensure that he would not have future access to children. Instead, after seven years on the run, Jeyapaul was finally arrested in the southern Indian town of Erode on March 16, 2012 after Interpol issued an alert. The US then began extradition proceedings.

The other case involving Levada concerned a victim in Africa. On September 13, 2011, when the SNAP filed its case with the ICC, one sex abuse victim addressed the press conference via Skype connection from the Democratic Republic of Congo. Benjamin Kitobo told journalists that he was abused from the age of thirteen by a Belgian priest at the Junior Seminary in Kanzenze, Komwezi in the DRC. The priest, Kitobo said, was never punished and still worked with children at a school near Kigali in neighboring Rwanda. (The priest would not have had the opportunity to rape Kitobo had he not been transferred from Belgium after getting into trouble for sex abuse in his own country.)

On May 18, 2001, at Pope John Paul II's request, Cardinal Ratzinger updated *Crimen Sollicitationis* with an apostolic letter to all bishops that, unlike its predecessor, was widely published. The letter, *Sacramentorum Sanctitatus Tutela*, declared definitively that all cases of sexual abuse must be referred to the CDF. Ratzinger's office would then decide, case by case, whether or not a diocesan trial was necessary. Such referrals would still be governed by "pontifical secret," meaning that once the allegation was dealt with internally, every detail of it was "to be completely suppressed by perpetual silence." In other words, no snitching to civil authorities. Complaints of a "delict," or crime "against morals with a minor below the age of eighteen years," would be subject to a ten-year statute of limitations, a period commencing after the minor had reached eighteen years of age. Anyone wishing to complain after turning twenty-nine would be out of luck.

Missing from *Sacramentorum* was any explanation as to why child sex abuse or rape—considered a serious offence under every national criminal law—was placed as a "delict" beside such priestly misbehavior as using the consecrated host (the "body of Christ") for sacrilegious reasons or sharing Eucharistic celebrations with non-Catholic ministers. But no matter: the apostolic letter had the full blessing of Ratzinger's curial colleagues, including Archbishop Tarcisio Bertone, then his secretary at the CDF. In February 2002, Bertone praised the spirit of *Sacramentorum*, particularly its rejection of the applicability of civil laws. "The demand that a bishop be obligated to contact the police in order to denounce a priest who has admitted the offense of paedophilia is unfounded," said the future Secretary of State. "Naturally civil society has the obligation to defend its citizens. But it must also respect the 'professional secrecy' of priests, as it respects the professional secrecy of other categories, a respect that cannot be reduced simply to the inviolable seal of the confessional. If a priest cannot confide in his bishop for fear of being denounced, then it would mean that there is no more liberty of conscience."

Ireland: The Ultimate Betrayal

Every leader has an *annus horribilis*. Pope Benedict's was 2010. That was the year the sex abuse scandals broke open in Europe, throwing the Vatican into what the Associated Press called "full damage control mode." It was the year that five of the pope's European bishops resigned, and tens of thousands of lay Catholics left the church in disgust. It was the year that the US Supreme Court rejected Benedict's request to review and overrule a judicial decision that left the Vatican open to questioning and disclosure duties in negligence actions in US courts. Finally, it was the year that the people of Ireland—a country whose hearts Roman Catholicism had virtually owned for hundreds of years before its official statehood—collectively gave up on Mother Church. In Ireland, Roman Catholics left the pews in droves, sending one archdiocese after another into lawsuit-driven bankruptcy. In 2010, the cumulative impact of three successive, major commissions on clerical sex abuse—all of which concluded that violent exploitation of Irish children was widespread and the church's cover-up of the crimes systematic—boiled over into national rage.

The anger of Ireland was the anger of a people betrayed by their church. Roman Catholicism had infiltrated virtually every area of life for as long as anyone could remember. But—after the Ferns Commission addressed 100 allegations against twenty-one priests in a single county between 1962 and 2002, its final report (2005) revealing that molestation in Catholic boys' institutions, reformatories, and orphanages had been "endemic"; after the Ryan Commission's ten-year inquiry and its massive, five-volume report (2009) revealing that tens of thousands of children had suffered systematic sexual, physical, and mental abuse in Irish schools run by the church; and finally, after the Murphy Commission's report on the Dublin Archdiocese, which featured 320 cases against 172 priests, its conclusion identical to that of Ferns and Ryan, that "the sole concern of the church was to protect against scandal" and that the church "placed children and others at risk of rape and other forms of sexual violence"— the church had worn out its welcome.[54]

The papal nuncio who had presided over much of the outrage

---

54 *Victims' Communication: Pursuant to Article 15 of the Rome Statute Requesting Investigation and Prosecution of High-level Vatican Officials for Rape and Other Forms of Sexual Violence as Crimes Against Humanity and Torture as a Crime Against Humanity,* Center for Constitutional Rights, September 13, 2011, p. 13.

wasn't talking. Giuseppe Lazzarotto had not only refused to speak to the Murphy Commission, but chose not to extend the courtesy of a reply. (He was pilloried in the report, and later in the Irish press and parliament, but by then had moved on to become the papal nuncio to Australia.) Cardinal Desmond Connell spoke to the Murphy Commission but quoted an oath of secrecy when asked if the problems in Ireland were discussed at the CDF under Ratzinger. He also confirmed that "mental reservation," the notion of allowing bishops to lie without consequence, was common practice. This did not help the national mood. People needed to know the answers to questions like: why was it that, under canon law, the fact that an accused priest might be a pedophile actually amounted to a defence, since pedophilia can produce "uncontrollable impulses" not subject to accountability?

On March 19, 2010, Pope Benedict wrote an open letter to all Irish Catholic abuse victims. "You have suffered grievously and I am truly sorry," it read. "I know that nothing can undo the wrong you have endured. Your trust has been betrayed and your dignity has been violated. Many of you found that, when you were courageous enough to speak of what happened to you, no one would listen … It is understandable that you find it hard to forgive or be reconciled with the Church. In her name, I openly express the shame and remorse that we all feel." The apology was unprecedented, in terms of its source. But it still rang hollow for many Irish, who saw no serious consequences for most of the abusers. "Jesus may have said that those who make children suffer are to be drowned in the depths of the sea," commented Geoffrey Robertson in *The Case of the Pope*, quoting a famous passage from Matthew 18:6[55], "but Pope Benedict XVI told his pedophile priests in Ireland that penitence offered them a life after death-jacket."[56]

The media optics got worse in January 2011, when it was revealed that a Vatican department had advised Ireland's Catholic bishops in 1997 not to report priests suspected of child abuse. In a letter obtained by the Irish broadcaster RTE, the late Archbishop Luciano Storero, Pope John Paul II's chief representative to Ireland, told the bishops that the Congregation for the Clergy had studied their new policy and found it wanting. (The previous year, an advisory committee of Irish bishops had drawn up a policy advising "mandatory reporting" of suspected abusers to the police.) Storero said that such policy needed "to conform to canonical norms presently in force ... The situation of 'mandatory reporting' gives rise to serious reservations of both a moral and a canonical nature."

Things reached rock bottom on July 20, 2011, when Irish Prime Minister (Taoiseach) Enda Kenny launched a blistering

---

55 The full quote reads: "But if anyone causes one of these little ones who believe in me to sin, it would be better for him to have a large millstone hung around his neck and be drowned in the depths of the sea."

56 Two years later, on June 17, 2012, His Holiness made matters worse with a classic foot-in-mouth attempt to empathize with the Irish public. In a video address from the Vatican to an outdoor mass in Dublin attended by 75,000 Catholics for the church's quadrennial Eucharistic Congress, Benedict told the faithful that it was a "mystery" that priests and other church officials would abuse children entrusted in their care. "How are we to explain the fact that people who regularly received the Lord's body and confessed their sins in the sacrament of penance have offended in this way?" he said. "It remains a mystery. Yet evidently their Christianity was no longer nourished by joyful encounter with Jesus Christ. It had become merely a matter of habit." This statement was shocking for a number of reasons, not least of them Benedict's documented role in having covered up the abuse.

attack on the Holy See. Kenny lambasted the "dysfunction, dis-
connection and elitism" and the "culture of narcissism" in the
church's failure to properly address clerical child sex abuse. He
was speaking during a parliamentary debate after yet another
report—from the two-year Cloyne Commission, which investigated allegations against nineteen clerics in one diocese—found
that "inadequate and inappropriate" responses by the church
had compounded the victims' pain. A practicing Catholic, the
Taoiseach was unhinged by what he had read. "For the first time
in Ireland," a trembling Kenny told the Dáil (Irish parliament),
"a report into child sexual abuse exposes an attempt by the Holy
See to frustrate an inquiry into a sovereign, democratic republic
as little as three years ago, not three decades ago."

The Vatican's response to Kenny's outburst was typical of
its defensiveness from the moment the sex abuse scandals went
global the previous spring. A few days after his speech, the Holy
See briefly recalled its ambassador. One Vatican official lamented
the Irish leader's "excessive reaction" to the Cloyne report. Another
accused Kenny of using the report to divert attention away from
the Irish euro crisis. In any case, Kenny's speech seemed a declaration of war on the Vatican, which to this point was unaccustomed to acts of resistance from one of its most loyal countries.
"This is the Republic of Ireland in 2011," he had said: "A republic
of laws, of rights and responsibilities, of proper civic order, where
the delinquency and arrogance of a particular version, of a particular kind of 'morality,' will no longer be tolerated or ignored."
Kenny backed up his words with legislation: a new Irish law
would make it a crime not to report child sex abuse—even if the
act was revealed in the privacy of the confessional.

Quite apart from the Irish controversy, the Vatican had its hands full in 2010–11 with new scandals in Norway and other European countries. By Palm Sunday 2010, the Twittersphere was abuzz with fresh revelations. Deciding he had had enough, Pope Benedict urged the faithful not to be intimidated by the "petty gossip of dominant opinions." Despite the defiant tone, however, the crisis was etched on his face. "Some in the Vatican called it sorrow, like unto Jesus' sorrow on the Cross," a report in *Time* magazine read. "Benedict appeared worn and gloomy even when framed by the glories of St. Peter's Basilica and the liturgies that typically infuse him with vigor." Meanwhile, papal apologists were not behaving well. Cardinal Sodano interrupted Benedict's Easter mass to defend him with a sycophantic rant: "Holy Father, the people of God are with you and will not let themselves be influenced by the petty gossip of the moment, by the trials that sometimes assail the community of believers." Cardinal Bertone, pathetically, linked the scandal to homosexuality. It would not be his last outrage of the season: in June, when Belgian police detained for a day the country's nine Catholic bishops and its papal nuncio while looking for evidence of child sex abuse[57], he declared: "There are no precedents for this, even under Communist regimes."[58]

On July 15, 2010, the Vatican released *De Gravioribus Delictis*, the new rules governing "most serious" crimes. This latest update

---

57 The police seized some church computers and took 475 case files from a church-appointed commission no longer in operation.

58 The hyperbole seemed a bit much, given that "the cardinals had suffered no more than a brief confiscation of their episcopal cell phones," notes Geoffrey Robertson in *The Case of the Pope*.

of the *Crimen* doubled the length of time after the eighteenth birthday of the victim that clerics can be tried in a church court—from age twenty-nine to thirty-nine. For the first time, a priest could be defrocked through an "extra-judicial decree"— effectively without a hearing. But the rules still made no reference to handing abusers over to civil criminal authorities (which Benedict referred to as "collaboration"), and all details of sex abuse crimes were still subject to the "pontifical secret." As well, a new "more grave delict" was added: the attempted ordination of women to the priesthood was now considered a "grave" offense on par with pedophilic priestly sex abuse. On May 16, 2011, there was one more update of the sex abuse guidelines, drawn up by Cardinal Levada: bishops and the heads of Catholic religious orders were given one year to develop "clear and coordinated" procedures for dealing with sexual abuse allegations. On one hand, bishops were to cooperate with the police and respect relevant local laws in investigating and reporting allegations of sexual abuse by the clergy to the civic authorities. On the other, such reporting would not be mandatory. The guidelines also reinforced bishops' exclusive authority to deal with abuse cases.

During a 2008 trip to the US, Pope Benedict met with five sex abuse victims at the Holy See's embassy in Washington. Later that year, he met with victims in Australia. In April 2010, he met with victims in Malta. But none of these gestures, or the pope's administrative changes, would be enough to grant him the forgiveness he so clearly desired. But then, as Geoffrey

Robertson has noted, the real work of penance involves concrete actions of the bolder variety. His advice to the pope? Establish a Commission of Inquiry to examine the CDF archives and give a full account of what was done—or left undone—during his prefecture. It was a period, after all, in which "tens of thousands of children were bewitched, buggered and bewildered by Catholic priests whilst [Ratzinger's] attention was fixated on 'evil' homosexuals, sinful divorcees, deviate liberation theologians, planners of families and wearers of condoms," wrote the esteemed international human rights lawyer and judge. "Until this fallible man admits his errors and abjures Canon Law as a substitute for criminal law, there can be no guarantee that he— or his successor—will learn from his mistakes."

Of course, Robertson was not holding his breath waiting for His Holiness to follow this advice. One major obstacle, as he knew, was the Vatican statehood that shielded Benedict from accountability.

IX

State of Disgrace

*The times called for a man such as he whom Providence has ordained
that We should meet ... It is with profound satisfaction that We express
the belief that We have given God to Italy and Italy to God.*

—Pope Pius XI, on signing the Lateran Treaty with Mussolini
that established Vatican statehood

On February 8, 2005, US Secretary of State Condoleeza Rice
paid a diplomatic visit to the Vatican to meet with her "coun-
terpart," Vatican Secretary of State Cardinal Angelo Sodano.
"Alongside predictable exchanges on Iraq, the Middle East and
religious liberty," noted John Allen Jr in the *National Catholic
Reporter*, Rice "also received an unexpected request—to intervene in a US lawsuit naming the Holy See as the defendant in a
sex abuse case." Sodano wanted to know whether the US government could stop a class-action lawsuit that was then before a US
District Court in Louisville, Kentucky, that sought to hold the
Vatican financially responsible for the sexual abuse of minors.
Rice informed Sodano that, under American law, foreign states
are required to assert claims of sovereign immunity themselves
before US courts. While most legal experts considered any lawsuit against the Vatican in an American court a "long shot" (at
least two dozen previous attempts had gone nowhere, partly due

to Vatican "sovereignty" but also because of First Amendment issues around prosecuting on religious matters), this exchange was intriguing. The mere fact that Sodano had raised the issue with Rice, noted Allen, suggested "concern in Rome that sooner or later its immunity may give way, exposing the Vatican to potentially crippling verdicts."

Five years later, with the Kentucky case still before the courts, the Vatican filed a motion to dismiss based on the lawsuit's attempt to blame clerical sex abuse on the pope and the Holy See. The suit claimed that bishops are employees or officials of the Holy See, which was found to have orchestrated the decades-long cover-up of priestly sexual abuse. In a legal sleight of hand that appeared to throw its US bishops under the bus, the Vatican's May 2010 appeal argued that bishops are neither employees nor officials of Rome; that their relationship to the pope was merely a "religious" one. "The pope and the bishops constitute ... a group of people who received from Jesus Christ the mission to announce the Gospel and administer sacraments," explained one canon lawyer, in flawless ecclesial bureaucratese. A bishop therefore represents Christ in his diocese—not the pope.

The Vatican lawyers needn't have bothered appealing. Two months later, on August 10, 2010, the attorneys leading the class-action lawsuit against the Vatican announced that they were dropping it. This was stunning news: a case described by some observers as the most serious civil challenge of the Holy See in US courts was bound for the dust bin. Apart from the practical difficulty of finding enough additional victims to come forward who hadn't already sued the church, Louisville-based attorney William McMurry cited a legal problem: the Vatican's sovereign immunity under American law set the bar too high. Score one for the church: a rare victory on the child sex abuse front. Vatican spokesman Federico Lombardi tempered his celebratory reaction so as not to "minimize the horror and condemnation" of child sex abuse—or, presumably, the compassion due to its victims.

On the other hand, *Doe v. Holy See* was still looming on the horizon in Oregon. The US Supreme Court had recently allowed that case to proceed, and lead attorney Jeffrey Anderson was talking tough. America's best known and most successful litigator against the Catholic Church, with more than 2,000 claimants in sex abuse cases, Anderson told Italian newspapers that he planned to go to Rome and depose not only senior Vatican personnel such as Secretary of State Tarcisio Bertone, but also Pope Benedict himself. However, the legality of this case once again hung on sovereign immunity: the threshold question was whether the Foreign Sovereign Immunities Act could allow the Vatican, a sovereign state in international law, to be sued for acts of local Catholic clergy. Given the power that the Holy See has enjoyed through statehood since 1929, Benedict's odds were looking pretty good.

Palm Greasing with Il Duce

One of the more impressive aspects of Joseph Ratzinger's career—and his most critical survival skill—was his knack for deflecting criticism. He was especially adept at dismissing controversy over his Nazi youth, particularly the kind of facile critique that saw equivalence between the Third Reich and his own modus operandi as both CDF prefect and pope. But still, the political ironies abounded. They certainly haunted Benedict throughout his papacy. How must it have felt, knowing that the Vatican "statehood" and "sovereignty" he so took for granted in his dealings with the outside world—indeed, the very foundation of his status as a head of "state"—was based entirely on a deal with the devil, a bit of Machiavellian realpolitik that was fascist to the core?

The Holy See bases its claim to Vatican statehood on the February 11, 1929 concordat that Vatican Secretary of State Pietro Cardinale Gasparri signed with Italian Fascist leader (and soon-to-be-dictator) Benito Mussolini. With the Lateran Treaty, the Fascists were paying off the Vatican for a historic grievance that had been festering for six decades. Prior to 1870, the pope was a virtual monarch who ruled a defined territory known as the Papal States, which consisted of 17,218 square miles in central Italy. Pope Pius IX was a megalomaniac, an authoritarian, and a reactionary. He hated liberal democracy and freedom of speech, deeply resenting their advance in Europe. While his wish for papal infallibility was granted with a proclamation at Vatican I (1869–70), he would not be satisfied until the Catholic Church was established as the only religion in every state. Meanwhile, he proved to be the biggest obstacle to Italian statehood.

In 1870, the Italian army annexed the Papal States, claiming all of the pope's territory except for the Vatican and Lateran Palaces and the Villa of Castel Gandolfo. Pius IX was defiant: "This corner of earth is mine. Christ has given it to me." (It was this pope that Lord Acton had in mind when he uttered his famous quote about power, corruption, and the absolute of both.) From this point on, Pius IX ordered the faithful to treat the new democratic state of Italy as illegitimate. Catholics were not to vote or stand in national elections. It would be half a century before Rome softened its stance, and the Vatican proved most adept at political opportunism during this period, thriving on the chaos. During the 1920s, the Holy See tried to join the League of Nations, but was turned down because of its lack of state status and concerns that its membership would unduly influence the votes of Catholic member states. This is where Mussolini comes in.

After World War I, the church began supporting the Popular party, a Catholic political organization that opposed votes for women. But the church was nervous about the rise of Godless Italian Communism, so in 1921 the Bishop of Milan came out in support of Mussolini. Only the Fascist leader, he said, "has a proper understanding of what is necessary in this country." That bishop became Pope Pius XI, who shortly afterward advised the king to appoint Mussolini as prime minister. Mussolini returned the favor by saving the Vatican Bank from collapse. In 1924, when the new PM was implicated in the murder of Socialist leader Giacomo Matteotti, the pope gave him a glowing character reference. Crisis averted. Mussolini rewarded Pius XI by increasing state payments to priests and ordering that crucifixes be displayed in all schools and courtrooms.

So by 1926, when secret negotiations began for what would become the Lateran Treaty, the palm greasing between Pius XI and Mussolini had already begun. The 1929 concordat would, on one hand, win Mussolini the church's endorsement of his future dictatorship in a one-party state (and silence for his crimes); on the other, it would guarantee Mussolini's support for the church's position against socialism and women's rights—as well as its campaign to promote procreation. Under the Lateran Treaty, the government of Italy created Vatican City as compensation for the lost Papal States. The Vatican was granted independent statehood and placed under church law—rather than Italian law—and the Holy See (referred to in the collective as "Rome" ever afterward) thus became its "government" as well as that of the entire church.

Thanks to the Lateran Treaty, Catholicism would be recognized as Italy's state religion and taught in all secondary schools. The church also regained authority over marriage and the power to ban birth control. The clergy continued to receive subsidies from the state and was exempted from taxation. The Lateran Treaty and concordat were announced with a grand ceremony in Rome. Two months later during the election, Pius XI called Mussolini "a man sent by Providence." And what do you know? *Il Duce* won the election. All this is clear. But what the Lateran Treaty does not explain is how Vatican City—108 acres of land, in the middle of Rome, that would barely fill a large golf course—went from enjoying privileges conferred by Italy to being recognized as a "state" outside of Italy.

How did this medieval hamlet and its leader gain sovereign immunity in the event of any legal action? How did the Holy See gain direct access to the United Nations and its agencies, conferences, and conventions, with the ability to promote its "apostolic mission" (moral agenda) worldwide, a privilege enjoyed by no other religion on the face of the earth? How could a tiny enclave within the Italian capital establish diplomatic relations with 178 actual states, receiving ambassadors from all of them and sending papal nuncios in return? This did not happen overnight. Vatican statehood was a work in progress, requiring both persistence and the fine art of diplomatic persuasion—or, rather, the more subtle and passive-aggressive form of bullying at which the Vatican has always excelled.

A "Santa Claus" State

The notion of a Vatican "statehood" based on the Lateran Treaty has always been bogus. For one thing, the Treaty was not a "treaty" according to international law. The Vienna Convention defines "treaty" as an "international agreement concluded between states in written form and governed by international law." Since Italy was the only "state" involved in the Lateran Treaty, as Geoffrey Robertson and others have noted, then it was never a treaty but an agreement between a state and a non-state entity. Then there are the requirements for actual "statehood." According to the Montevideo Convention,[59] the essentials are possession of a defined territory, a permanent population of citizens or subjects, an ability to exercise territorial power over those citizens (i.e., government), and a capacity to enter into relations with other states.

---

59 The Montevideo Convention on the Rights and Duties of States was a treaty signed at Montevideo, Uruguay, on December 26, 1933, during the Seventh International Conference of American States. The Convention codified the declarative theory of statehood as accepted as part of customary international law. Church apologists would argue that the Montevideo standard did not apply to the Vatican, whose statehood was entrenched four years before the convention.

As to the first, "Vatican City" cannot be regarded as a "territory" in the sense that an actual nation-state has territory. The Vatican, Robertson has said, amounts to nothing more than

> a large palace built on top of land that was once Caligula's private circus where Christians were thrown to the lions. It has a few attached buildings, but gardens take up two-thirds of its 108.7 acres. The Palace—the basilica opens on to St. Peter's Square—has buildings to the side that house a radio station, a bank and the official newspaper (*L'Osservatore Romano*) and various museums, whilst its secret archives (which may contain the CDF files relating to sex abuse) are flush against the Sistine Chapel... [The] Vatican is not even a city, let alone a city state: it is a palace entirely within an Italian city (Rome) which city is itself within a state, i.e., Italy.

This is not "defined territory." This is Disneyland-on-the-Tiber, a religious amusement park and heritage site with a few offices. Nor does it have citizens. The full-time population of the Vatican is no more than a few hundred, mostly celibate male clerics. It has Italian workers who maintain the site daily before going home to Italy (across the street in Rome) every night, plus a few thousand curial employees who work in Rome (i.e., Italy, not "Vatican City") and are mainly Italians subject to Italian law. Giving birth in this "state" is not a good idea, since there are no health care facilities or health insurance, and any instances of human birth on Vatican "soil" are no doubt of the scandalous variety.

As for "government"? The Holy See does not govern a national people; it exists to govern the church throughout the world, increase the ranks of the faithful, and control the sex lives of all Catholics. It has no interest in any of the other functions normally assumed by a state government. Vatican City has no elected officials, but is governed by the Holy See with the pope as its sovereign, and its day-to-day operations overseen by a "president" who functions as a chief executive (as of this writing, Italian cardinal Guiseppe Bertello). It has the Swiss Guards but no strategic defence. Even as a "city state," the Vatican does not measure up: there is no municipal infrastructure, and the pope most assuredly is not its "mayor." Italy carries out most of its municipal functions, providing its police force and punishing crimes committed within its property. The federal Italian government also maintains the Vatican's water and railway systems. Finally, since there is no income or property tax in Vatican City, the main source of income is tourism.

In terms of its capacity to establish consular relations with other states, the Holy See has papal nuncios. But the relationships are largely ceremonial and completely concerned with the Catholic religion; they are not ordinary diplomatic relations. Furthermore, most countries that have consular relations with the Holy See locate their embassies outside the Vatican, in Rome—in addition to their embassies to Italy. "It would save money to house them within the premises of their embassies to Italy," notes Robertson, "but this prospect enrages Cardinal Sodano, who has been prepared to make an exception only in the case of Israel, for security reasons." Then, of course, there's the Institute for Works of Religion (IOR), otherwise known as the

Vatican Bank. We have seen, with the slippery Paul Marcinkus, how hard it can be to hold a "state" bank accountable when its financial operations are shrouded in secrecy. It's rather difficult to get to the bottom of insurance fraud, or the Vatican stash of Nazi gold, when there's no transparency.

However, despite the fact that the Holy See fails every relevant test for statehood (Robertson likens it to a "Santa Claus" state: "no matter how many believe in it, it does not really exist"), the Roman Catholic Church managed to fool the international community. Today, most states recognize it as "sovereign," and thus a sort of quasi "state." And, as Robertson woefully admits, "state practice, however politically skewed, is a powerful formative influence on international law." So, since the middle of the twentieth century, Roman Catholicism has had a leg up on all other religions when it comes to influencing global political policy—and the Holy See has taken full advantage of its bogus statehood.

Under the UN Radar

Oddly enough, no one saw it coming. Having failed in its bid for acceptance as a member of the League of Nations in the 1920s, the Vatican in the 1940s began targeting the United Nations but was rebuffed when it sought full membership. In 1944, UN co-founder Cordell Hull, the US Secretary of State, emphatically declared that the Vatican could never attain statehood. But in many ways, full membership was not necessary: there were other ways to join the club, and for the church to get its priorities on the UN agenda. Ultimately, the Holy See would attain the

UN status of non-member state and permanent observer—a rarely used designation that was shared only by Switzerland until that famously neutral country finally assumed full membership in 2002.

The Holy See achieved its permanent observer status by an accident of history that proved fortunate for the church—not so fortunate for everyone else. On June 1, 1929, a few months after the Lateran Treaty, Vatican City was admitted to the World Telegraph Union. Five years earlier, it had joined the Universal Postal Union by becoming a State Party of the Stockholm Postal Convention. Being an owner of both postal and radio services, the Holy See thought it made sense to join these unions. In 1931, Vatican City joined the Radiotelegraph Service. A year later, the World Telegraph Union and Radiotelegraph Service merged to become the International Telecommunication Union. It was through its membership in this new union and the postal union that Vatican City came into the international arena under the UN radar.

Soon after its formation, the United Nations invited these unions and their members to attend UN sessions on an ad hoc basis. The Roman Catholic Church dove right in. Starting in 1951, representatives of the Vatican and the Holy See began attending sessions of the UN General Assembly, the World Health Organization, and the UN Educational, Scientific and Cultural Organization as ad hoc observers. Five years later, the Holy See was elected as a member of the UN Economic and Social Council and became a full member of the Atomic Energy Agency. By 1957, "the Catholic Church" had also sent delegates—creating some confusion as to who took the lead between "Vatican City," "the Holy See," and "the Catholic Church." Despite this clever attempt to maximize its UN presence by having three different entities represent it, an agreement was reached with UN Secretary-General Dag Hammarskjöld that, henceforth, the Holy See would be the church's only entity at the UN.

The next power play occurred on March 21, 1964, when the Holy See informed UN Secretary-General U Thant that Pope Paul VI had dispatched its first permanent observer, Reverend Monsignor Alberto Giovannetti, to the UN's New York headquarters. U Thant accepted the move without referring it to the General Assembly or Security Council. But then, such a referral would have been unnecessary: non-member states could obtain permanent observer status simply by notifying the UN secretary general that they had appointed an observer. Unlike other entities, such as NGOs, they did not require an invitation from the General Assembly. So technically, if not ethically, the Vatican secretary of state was well within the rules when he gave U Thant this rather belated heads-up. On the other hand, according to a non-governmental organization seeking change of the Vatican's status at the UN:

> The bar was not set very high for U Thant's acceptance of the Holy See's permanent observer status. Because permanent observers are not formally recognized in the UN charter, the protocol for their admission developed by custom. U Thant noted of the criteria he applied in deciding whether to accept UN observers: "I have been following one line which

seems to be the only possible one, that is, to accept observers when such an arrangement is proposed in the cases where the country in question is recognized diplomatically in this form or that form by a majority of UN members."

It is not known exactly how U Thant did his number-crunching. Only fourteen of the eighty-two UN member states in 1959 had formal relations with the Vatican, and that proportion had not shifted significantly in five years. (By 1985, the figure was only fifty-three out of 159 member states.) No vote was ever taken on the Holy See's presence at the UN by the General Assembly, and—contrary to historical revisionism by the Vatican—the Holy See was never invited to join.[60] Of course, none of this would matter by the time John Paul II was pontiff. Ronald Reagan was so delighted to have a dedicated anti-Communist in Saint Peter's chair that, in 1984, the US established formal relations with the Holy See. From that point on, Rome got pretty much everything it wanted at the UN.

In 1999, a coalition of 700 non-governmental organizations around the world launched the "See Change" campaign, aimed at changing the Holy See's status at the UN. The campaign called for an official review of the Roman Catholic Church's status at

60 Pope John Paul II acknowledged that it was Pope Paul VI who set things in motion.

the UN, with the ultimate goal being a downgrade of the Holy See's status to that of non-governmental organization—the same status as the world's other major religions. It was not a group of atheists, Jews, or Muslims leading this campaign but Catholics For a Free Choice (CFFC), a group of pro-Vatican II Catholics. Already fighting their own internal battles with Rome over issues like women's reproductive rights, members of CFFC were ashamed of the fact that the Holy See had an international platform for its harmful, medieval policies on sexuality.[61]

What was it about the Holy See's unique Permanent Observer status that, since the 1950s, had caused such a groundswell of opposition to its status, from all corners of the earth (see *catholicsforchoice.org/campaigns/SeeChangeCampaign.asp*)? First, it's important to consider some of the UN organizations with which the Holy See has influence. In addition to its permanent observer stationed at the UN's New York office, the Vatican sends permanent observers to the UN's offices in Geneva and Vienna, as well as to the

+ UN Organization for Industrial Development
+ UN Food and Agricultural Organization
+ UN Educational, Scientific and Cultural Organization
+ Organization of American States
+ Office of the UN High Commissioner for Refugees

61 CFFC also had a more personal axe to grind with the Vatican: in 1995, the Holy See tried to ban the group's attendance at the Beijing Conference on Women.

- World Health Organization
- International Labour Organization
- World Organization of Tourism

It also sends representatives to the

- International Atomic Energy Agency
- World Organization of Commerce
- Council of Europe
- Organization for Security and Cooperation in Europe
- International Institute for the Unification of Private Law
- International Committee of Military Medicine

Finally, the Holy See is also a member of the UN Economic and Social Council (ECOSOC), the World Trade Organization, and the UN Industrial Development Organization.

One should not dismiss out of hand the genuine good that the Roman Catholic Church can do on a range of issues by using its UN platform. For example, the Holy See has spoken out against social and economic injustice while assisting in poverty reduction efforts in developing nations. And on most days, the Holy See's connection to the organizations listed above would cause barely a ripple. However, in 1968, a resolution by ECOSOC—of which the Holy See was a member—clarified that non-member states could be partners and participants at the UN through their observer status, while NGOs and religious organizations (i.e., other religions) were merely "consultants." The difference meant that the Holy See, unlike any other religion, could speak and vote at UN conferences. This distinction would have grim consequences under the papacy of John Paul II and his trusty theological lieutenant.

Crashing the Party

To describe the Holy See's role at UN conferences in the mid-1990s as "obstructionist" would be an understatement. Official documents of these events are filled with Holy See "objections" to the majority consensus. At the 1995 Beijing Conference on Women, for example, the Holy See insisted on expressing reservations to the Beijing Platform for Action, the conference's final report. It took issue with such concepts as "women's right to control their sexuality" and "women's right to control ... their fertility," asserting that these rights should refer only to "the responsible use of sexuality within marriage." Vatican representatives also condemned "family planning" as "morally unacceptable" and disassociated the Holy See from the consensus on the entire section about health, saying it gave "totally unbalanced attention to sexual and reproductive health" (the very issues other delegates considered most important at the conference). These official objections, based entirely on sectarian religious positions—rather than on governmental policy positions—were entered into the final report of the conference, serving only to weaken support for the conclusions of the majority.

The previous year, at the Cairo conference on population and development, things were no better. By the mid-1990s, 600,000 women a year were dying needlessly during pregnancy and childbirth. But in Cairo, the Holy See successfully led the effort to block the inclusion of safe, legal abortion on the list of basic reproductive rights for women. It used its voice to limit access to family planning, safe abortion—even in countries where abortion is legal—and emergency contraception—even for women who have been raped as an act of war. "As a result," notes Geoffrey Robertson, "a conference that should have discussed population policy and international aid was hijacked by a church masquerading as a state, preventing consensus being reached on any proposal that might possibly challenge the proposition that the only acceptable human genital contact was that between husband and wife for the purpose of procreation."

As for the UN's efforts in the fight against AIDS, the Holy See offered no solutions to a crisis that was killing 2.5 million people a year and infecting 5.8 million more with HIV. Instead, it repeatedly condemned the use of condoms and attempted to block international policy decisions that would make condom education and use a major tool in preventing HIV/AIDS. Apart from a few Catholic nations in Latin America and Africa, the Vatican typically relied on the support of rogue Arab states like Libya and Sudan, which do not support full human rights for women, and Islamic regimes such as Iran, which have openly promoted the death penalty for homosexuals. "From decrying emergency contraception for women who had been raped in Kosovo to burning boxes of condoms as AIDS ravages Africa, the hierarchy of the Roman Catholic Church has allowed out-dated doctrinal concerns to take priority over the lives of real people," Catholics For a Free Choice argued. "The Holy See insists on foisting its limited and largely rejected view of gender, sexuality and reproductive health on a world intent on creating a more progressive personal ethic that is respectful of the common good."

None of this has changed since the mid-1990s. Vatican diplomatic pressure has led to serious funding deficits for important UN programs like the UN Population Fund, which suffered massive reductions thanks to common cause between the Vatican, American evangelicals, and President George W. Bush (except for "abstinence" campaigns, of course). The month after Ratzinger's election as Pope Benedict, Catholic politicians in El Salvador were threatened with excommunication if they did not toe the church's line on contraception. So they passed a law requiring all condom packages to carry a deliberately erroneous "warning": that condoms offer no protection against AIDS. In Sydney, Australia, the pope personally intervened in the spring of 2010 to stop a life-saving needle exchange program run by nuns. In Brazil, where abortion is a crime, doctors were required to call the police when women came to hospitals bleeding from self-administered terminations.

The list goes on. Here's a brief compendium of the Vatican's—and Joseph Ratzinger's—outrages, on the world stage, in the name of Vatican "statehood":

- ◆ **1994**: After the Rwandan massacre, the Vatican allowed priests and nuns accused of burning and bulldozing Rwandan churches (with Tutsis inside them) to take sanctuary in parishes in Italy. The church obstructed efforts to have one of those priests surrender. (Father Athanase

Seromba, who hid for several years at a parish
near Florence under an assumed name, was
convicted of genocide by the the International
Criminal Tribunal for Rwanda in 2006 and
sentenced to fifteen years in prison. When he
appealed, the court found him even guiltier
than before, and sentenced him to life.)

♦ **1996:** The Holy See launched a campaign
against UNICEF, encouraging states to withdraw contributions because the organization
had sponsored a handbook for women in refu-
gee camps that included information on how to
access maternity and family planning services.

♦ **1998:** Holy See delegates at the Rome conference to establish the International Criminal
Court (ICC) were determined to water down
the draft language on crimes against humanity
by excluding rape. They were wary of any explosive term that might justify a victim's termina-
tion of an unwanted consequential pregnancy.
Thankfully, they failed to stop the inclusion
of rape (at least on a widespread or systematic
scale), or "forced pregnancy" (making women
pregnant with the intent of affecting the ethnic
composition of a population, as in the Serbian
rape of Muslim women). But they did get a
compromise: in countries where the church had

succeeded in getting abortions banned by law, women who were raped in war would be forced to carry the children of the enemy solider who had raped them (often after killing, in their presence, their husband and children).

That same year, as the ICC Treaty was being drafted, the Holy See led a campaign to add a clause to an Article 7(I)(h) provision on "Persecution" that included the phrase "on grounds of gender." The church, and various homophobic Catholic and Islamic states, successfully lobbied to include the following addendum: "For the purpose of this Statute, it is understood that the term 'gender' refers to the two sexes, male and female, within the context of society. The term 'gender' does not include any meaning different from the above." In other words, governments were free to persecute transsexuals, or anyone whose appearance does not conform to gender norms as Rome has defined them. In other words, gay men, lesbians, bisexuals, etc.

+ **July 17, 1998**: The Holy See refused to sign the ICC Treaty when its major proposal was rejected for inclusion in the final draft. The Vatican wanted a special clause exempting priests and their penitents from ever having to reveal secrets of the confessional, even if the penitent confessed to genocide or some other atrocity. (It also wanted drug trafficking made an international crime but, interestingly, said nothing about pedophile trafficking.)

◆ **1999**: Cardinal Ratzinger chastised the United Kingdom for its arrest of Chilean dictator and torturer Augusto Pinochet. Having failed in his efforts to use the high diplomatic channels the Holy See usually found so reliable to prevent Pinochet's arrest, the CDF prefect went public to "repeat to the world that at no time can the sovereignty of any state, big or small, be violated, stripping the local government of the power to judge a fellow national." (Of course, the Vatican was doing just that in the sex abuse scandals, by insisting on the exclusivity of canon law for its priests: stripping local governments of the power to judge fellow nationals. In any case, Chile could not have prosecuted Pinochet, who had given himself amnesty before leaving office.)

◆ **2000**: Cardinal Ratzinger launched a blistering attack on the UN's "New World Order" because one of its goals was to reduce the world's population. "At the base of this new world order," he wrote, with his typically sexist logic, "is the ideology of 'women's empowerment,' which erroneously sees the principle obstacles to a woman's fulfillment as the family and matrimony...Christians have the duty to protest."

♦ **2005:** After the ICC issued arrest warrants for the leaders of Uganda's brutal Lords Resistance Army, local Catholic clergy denounced the move as a threat to peace and a "western" imposition. The archbishop of Gulu then launched a campaign against the indictment of LRA leader Joseph Kony, whose international crimes (including the use of children as sex slaves) later exploded into a social media sensation. There was no censure from the Vatican.

In light of the Roman Catholic Church's disgraceful record at the UN, it seems darkly ironic that the only two UN human rights treaties the Holy See has ever signed are those which, it could be said, the church has fundamentally breached: the Convention Against Torture and Other Cruel, Inhuman or Degrading Treatment or Punishment (2002) and the Convention on the Rights of the Child (1990). Before signing the first, the Holy See was required to submit a report in July 2003, but failed to do so. The next report due date was July 2007, but that deadline came and went with no report forthcoming. Geoffrey Robertson and other human rights experts suggest that this may be because international courts have ruled that rape and child sex abuse can amount to torture when they serve such purposes as "intimidation, degradation, humiliation...control or destruction of a person." Under these terms, of course, adherence to the convention would expose the Vatican's sorry record on child abuse to further scrutiny, thus strengthening any case against Pope Benedict in terms of "command responsibility" for such crimes.

It is the Holy See's signing of the Convention on the Rights of the Child, however, that most exposes the Vatican to ridicule and contempt, given its record on child protection. The church's endorsement of that treaty should be seen in light of some other statements it has made. In the 1992 revised catechism, under "Offenses Against Chastity," here's the language Ratzinger approved for "Rape" (Section 2356): "Rape deeply wounds the respect, freedom, and physical and moral integrity to which every person has a right...It is always an intrinsically evil act. Graver still is the rape of children committed by parents (incest) *or those responsible for the education of the children entrusted to them.*"[62]

In Ratzinger's 2003 CDF document, *Considerations Regarding Proposals to Give Legal Recognition to Unions Between Homosexual Persons*, the CDF prefect cited the UN Convention on the Rights of the Child as an argument against adoption by gay or lesbian couples. "Allowing children to be adopted by persons living in such unions," he said, "would actually mean *doing violence to* [these children]"[63] because they would be deprived of one gender in the parenting. Recent history suggests that the adopted children of gay or lesbian parents are, statistically

62 Emphasis added.

63 Emphasis added.

speaking, much safer than children left alone with a Catholic priest.

If Pope Benedict was serious about defending the spirit of the treaty, he should have reflected more deeply on his words: "The best interests of the child, as the weaker and more vulnerable party," he said, in the same document, "are to be the paramount consideration in every case." An excellent point, and most appropriate for the child victims of priestly sex abuse. Their "best interests" would have been better served had the church taken immediate action to stop the abuse, authorize bishops to call the police and social service agencies, and offer counseling—rather than ignoring the victims' many pleas for help, as Ratzinger is widely reported to have done throughout his tenure at the CDF.

In addition to *Placing the Best Interest of Children First*, the UN Convention on the Rights of the Child also includes a section called *Duty to Investigate and Prosecute Child Sex Abuse*. This provision contains articles stating that parties shall take "all appropriate legislative, administrative," and other measures to protect children from abuse, "including sexual abuse." It is worth noting that the Holy See not only ratified the Convention; it added a solemn declaration that its ratification marked a "renewed expression" of the church's "constant concern for the well-being of children and families." (This is rather like BP's "solemn declaration" of the oil giant's concern for marine life in the Gulf of Mexico, or the US Bank's "solemn declaration" of regret at the misfortune of people whose homes it repossessed.) In its statement to the UN Special Conference on Children in 2002, the Holy See was at least saying the right thing: "Legislation is needed to protect children from all forms of exploitation and abuse, as in the case of incest and pedophilia ... these scourges are an affront and a scandal to humanity. These various forms of violence must not go unpunished."

There is more, so much more, empty hypocritical blather one could quote from the public record regarding the Vatican's "concern" for children. But the reader shall be spared. Instead, let us give the final word to Ratzinger, from his *Doctrinal Note on Some Questions Regarding the Participation of Catholics in Political Life* (2002): "A kind of cultural relativism exists today, evident in the conceptualization and defence of an ethical pluralism, which sanctions the decadence and disintegration of reason and the principles of the natural moral law." Ignoring, for the moment, Ratzinger's favorite sport of attacking abstractions ("cultural relativism," "ethical pluralism," etc.) one wonders how he could possibly have written the phrase "disintegration of reason" without irony, given everything he has done in defence of his so-called "truth."

"The Butler Did It": *The Vatican in Disarray*

If Pope Benedict XVI could always count on one thing, it was his control of the institution itself, his ability to command loyalty from the upper ranks of the curia to the Vatican's lowliest servant and his peculiar gift for staving off potential threats to his position. But in 2012, even that veneer of invincibility began to evaporate, with the Vatican itself appearing to fall off the rails. In February, the Italian daily *Il Fatto Quotidiano* published sensational details of a bizarre plot to assassinate the pope. In a letter dated December 30, 2011 and labeled "strictly confidential for the Holy Father," the anonymous writer reported several conversations that Cardinal Paolo Romeo, the archbishop of Palermo, had allegedly held with Italian businessmen in Beijing on a trip to China in November 2011. During one of these conversations, Romeo was said to have predicted that Benedict would be dead within twelve months and that his replacement would be Angelo Scola, the archbishop of Milan. The letter was subsequently dismissed as a hoax, a stealthy attempt to undermine both Romeo and especially Scola—whom Benedict himself was said to regard as a worthy successor. But who would do such a thing?

Il Fatto Quotidiano reported that the letter had been delivered in early January to Tarcisio Bertone and Georg Gänswein by Cardinal Darío Castrillón Hoyos of Colombia. The newspaper did not say how Castrillón Hoyos came into possession of the letter. Apparently, it was written in German to avoid attracting the attention of certain Vatican officials while communicating directly with close advisers to the German pope. The revelations seemed further proof that a power struggle was unfolding inside the Vatican. This followed news, earlier in February, that a former deputy governor of Vatican City had accused Vatican officials of corruption over how bids and contracts were being managed.

Archbishop Carlo Maria Vigano had been transferred to another post after blowing the whistle on cronyism in the awarding of contracts for construction work at the Vatican. Vigano had appealed directly to Benedict, pleading with him to block the transfer and let him stay in Rome to continue his anti-fraud work. "Holy Father," he had written, "my transfer at this time would provoke much disorientation and discouragement in those who have believed it was possible to clean up so many situations of corruption and abuse of power that have been rooted in the management of so many departments." But Vigano's plea went unanswered. Instead, Tarcisio Bertone sent him to Washington as papal nuncio. So, rather than becoming a champion of transparency at the Vatican, the archbishop was given the not-so-plum assignment of handling those multimillion-dollar lawsuits against US dioceses over clerical sex abuse. Now Vigano's letter to the pope had become public knowledge. Clearly, someone on the inside was leaking sensitive information in an attempt to discredit one Vatican faction to the advantage of another.

By the end of May 2012, the power struggle had exploded into a major scandal, a cloak-and-dagger whodunit that Vatican officials themselves began referring to as "Vatileaks."[64] That month saw the publication of a sensational book by Italian journalist Gianluigi Nuzzi, *Your Holiness: The Secret Papers of Benedict XVI*. Nuzzi, aided by a mysterious source named "Maria," disclosed a large bundle of private Vatican correspondence, much of it revealing allegations of corruption, cronyism, and clashes over management of the Institute for Works of Religion (IOR), or Vatican Bank. On May 24, IOR president Ettore Gotti Tedeschi was fired. His departure was a big failure

---

64 A nod to Wikileaks, the international online organization that publishes submissions of private, secret, and classified media from anonymous news sources, news leaks, and whistleblowers. Wikileaks and its founder, Julian Assange, gained international infamy in 2011 when an encrypted version of its huge archive of unredacted US State Department cables was revealed to be available, along with the decryption key, to those who knew where to look.

for Pope Benedict, since his appointment just three years earlier
had been aimed at bringing the secretive institution in line with
international transparency standards. (In 2009, the pope had
fired Tedeschi's predecessor, Monsignor Angelo Caloia, after
evidence emerged that Caloia had expanded money laundering
and kept secret accounts for favored politicians—a practice for
which the IOR had first become notorious in the 1970s. At that
time, Albino Luciani—a.k.a. Pope John Paul I—tried to clean it
up; he may have paid with his life in the attempt.) Nuzzi's book
revealed that many people of influence still had a direct line to
the Vatican "head of state" through the Vatican Bank.[65]

Meanwhile, Benedict had called for an investigation by
Vatican police and a committee of cardinals after that mysterious letter about an assassination plot was leaked to the media.
On May 25, the story took a bizarre twist when Vatican gen-
darmes arrested Paolo Gabriele, Benedict's butler. Gabriele, who
served the pope's meals, helped him dress, and sat in the front
seat of the pope-mobile for the pontiff's general audiences, was
found to be in possession of confidential documents. Suspected
of leaking private letters, some of which were addressed to the
pope, he was ultimately revealed as the anonymous "Maria"
source for Nuzzi's book and formally charged with illegal

---

65 According to a New York Times article of May 26, 2012, correspondence revealed in
the book included a letter from Bruno Vespa, Italy's best-known television host, who
sent a cheque for $12,500 USD to Georg Gänswein, "a small sum at the disposal of
the pope's charity," and asked when he could have a private audience. Giovanni Bazoli,
director of Italy's Intesa San Paolo bank, sent a cheque for $32,000 USD, "with my
most deferential salutations." Other letters to Gänswein included those from officials
in former Prime Minister Silvio Berlusconi's government to Mercedes Benz directors
responsible for maintaining the pope mobile. All sought "favors, recommendations, and
most of all, the pope's ear."

possession of secret documents. For the next two months, he was held in a "safe room" in the Vatican police station before being released into house arrest to await trial. Gabriele's lawyer claimed that he had acted alone (i.e., was not part of a wider conspiracy), and had done so out of love and concern for the pope and a desire to help him clean up the church.[66]

Some Vatican observers concluded that Gabriele was a convenient scapegoat for the Curia, who were eager to contain the scandal. As Paolo Rodari, a Vatican expert for the Italian daily *Il Foglio*, noted, so many documents had been leaked from the Vatican in 2012 that Gabriele could not have been the true—or only—source. "Many of the documents that came out didn't ever pass through the pope's apartment where he works," Rodari told the *New York Times*. Meanwhile, the one name that kept coming up—as it had in the sex abuse scandals and other intrigues involving Vatican power struggles—was that of Secretary of State Cardinal Tarcisio Bertone. Were the leaked documents an attempt to undermine Bertone because of his poor administration, his struggle to manage Benedict's scandal-ridden papacy? Bertone was widely criticized for his role in the firing of Ettore Gotti Tedeschi by the Vatican Bank's lay board of financiers. Tedeschi's defenders said he was trying to improve

---

66 Gabriele, after admitting in court that he had leaked papal documents to Nuzzi, was convicted of aggravated theft and sentenced to eighteen months in jail. He was freed before the end of the year when Pope Benedict visited him in his jail cell and granted him a "Christmas pardon." In a related trial, Holy See computer expert Claudio Sciarpelletti received a two-month suspended sentence for obstruction of justice, after having allegedly aided and abetted Gabriele's leak of documents and then changed his version of events several times under police questioning about his correspondence with Gabriele.

the transparency of IOR finances, but Bertone was impeding his efforts—just as he had done with former deputy governor Vigano, whom he had shipped off to Washington the moment the words "corruption" and "cronyism" left his lips.

The official Vatican spin on Tedeschi's firing was that he had become an obstacle to transparency and had "not carried out functions of primary importance for his role" at the IOR. But Italy's Carabinieri national police force, which detained Tedeschi in June 2012 as part of a corruption investigation, found intriguing evidence to suggest otherwise. An officer searching the banker's home found a dossier stuffed with files and ring binders that contained information about the Vatican Bank. This included references to anonymous numbered accounts and messages indicating how IOR officials got around European regulations aimed at combating money laundering. Was Tedeschi intending to go public? Whatever the case, the Vatican Bank was already suffering a severe credibility crisis that threatened to topple it.

On March 30, 2012, the Milan branch of the global investment bank JPMorgan Chase officially closed the Vatican bank's account due to concern that it was being used for money laundering. The account, opened in 2009, had transferred some $1.5 billion USD in funds to other Vatican accounts—mostly in Germany. But when Italian investigators began asking questions about the Milan account, JPMorgan Chase executives got nervous. When JPMorgan Chase asked Vatican officials where the money going through the account originated (and why so much of it had been moved in such a short time), the answers were unsatisfactory. So they closed the account. Despite having done business with the Vatican for thirty-five years, JPMorgan

Chase officials could hardly be blamed for getting cold feet: the previous September, tax police in Rome had frozen $33 million USD in Vatican assets due to concerns raised by a covert investigation about its accounting practices. What other dirt might be uncovered?

All of this hardly raised confidence in Pope Benedict's own efforts to clean up the IOR. In late 2010, he had launched an anti-corruption arm within the Curia aimed at improving the image of the Vatican's financial dealings. (The goal was to secure a place for the Holy See on the international Financial Action Task Force's "white list" of states adhering to international standards in the fight against corruption, tax fraud, and money laundering.) But in March 2012, the US State Department named the Holy See as a "jurisdiction of concern" for money-laundering practices in its annual International Narcotics Control Strategy Report. Despite the church's appearance beside countries like North Korea and Syria, Vatican officials declared the glass half full: being a "jurisdiction of concern" was better than being a "primary concern." Commenting in *Corriere della Sera* about the "Vatileaks" and banking scandals, Roman Catholic historian Alberto Melloni wrote: "Never has the sense of disorientation in the Catholic Church reached these levels. But now there is something even more: a sense of systemic disorder."

Dungeons and Dragons

Just when it seemed that things could get no worse for Pope Benedict, they did. When the Pope decided to launch an investigation into the "Vatileaks" scandal, the committee of three cardinals he appointed—Spanish Cardinal Julian Herranz, Cardinal Salvatore De Giorgi, a former archbishop of Palermo, and the Slovak Cardinal Jozef Tomko, who once headed the Vatican's department for missionaries—did a very thorough job. Eight months later, they had compiled two volumes of almost 300 pages based on "dozens and dozens" of interviews with bishops, cardinals, and lay people. Although Benedict had been kept apprised of the investigation with weekly meetings, he was not prepared for what appeared in print when the cardinals delivered their report to him on December 17, 2012.

What the report revealed was a detailed profile of the Roman Curia that did not spare even the Pope's closest collaborators. Its findings were so explosive that even the loquacious Vatican spokesman, Federico Lombardi—who normally didn't hesitate to issue fierce denials of a false rumor or an overblown theory—refused to comment. The most sensational of the contents would not be revealed until ten days after Benedict left office, in article published by *La Repubblica*. According to the leading Italian journal, the three cardinals uncovered an underground network of gay priests—clerics "united by sexual orientation"—whose members set up sexual liaisons in several locations. These included a villa outside Rome, a sauna in Rome's Cuarto Miligo district, a former university residence used by a provincial Italian archbishop, and even a beauty salon inside the Vatican. Since blackmail tends to thrive in homophobic environments, it was perhaps no surprise that some of these clerics had been subject to the "external influence" of laymen with links of a "worldly nature."

"It appears the people who procure these sexual services

have become greedy," said longtime Vatican observer John Cornwell. "They have been putting the squeeze on their priestly clients to launder cash through the Vatican. There is no suggestion that the bank has knowingly collaborated." But within weeks of this report's delivery to the Pope, Italy's central bank in January suspended credit-card activities inside Vatican City for "anti-money-laundering reasons." According to a *La Repubblica* source "very close" to the three cardinals, Benedict decided on December 17—the day he received the report—that he had no choice but to resign. In what Cornwell and others saw as a supreme self-sacrifice on Benedict's part, the Pope was taking "the biggest ever gamble in the Church": resigning to ensure that "the Filth" be cleansed from the Vatican, possibly in the hope that others (Sodano? Bertone?) would resign along with him.

Epilogue

International Criminal Court, The Hague
The Not-Too-Distant Future
Benedict XVI, the pope emeritus, sits quietly in the dock con-templating how he might answer the prosecutor's question. As the principal defendant on charges of obstruction of justice for crimes against humanity, he has been put on trial for command responsibility in the church's denial and cover-up of clerical sex abuse—particularly the priest-shifting and stonewalling of authorities that have been the hallmarks of the Vatican's response to the problem. For some reason, and despite the efforts of the Vatican's top lawyers, he has failed in his bid to avoid prosecution. (In this he lacks the good fortune of former Vatican Bank chief Paul Marcinkus, who managed to elude the clutches of Italian authorities after being indicted in the collapse of the Banco Ambrosiano.) And now, as he sits in the dock at The Hague, the television cameras transmitting his every ner-vous twitch to a global audience, he has begun to think about other aspects of his religious career, going back to his days at the CDF, and earlier. For the first time, he is feeling regret.

The experience of being in court, questioned by lawyers, and hearing the testimonies of abuse victims like Wilfried

Fesselmann, has deeply affected him. Being confronted by the tears of Fesselmann, in particular, has moved him so profoundly that he finds himself rethinking everything he has ever done in the Name of the Father. Benedict's Road to Damascus revelation occurs precisely at the moment that Fesselmann tells the court how horrified he was when Father Hullermann forced him, a small boy of eleven, to fellate him. Hearing these words, Joseph Ratzinger feels a lightning bolt of guilt and remorse shooting through his octogenarian veins. Fesselmann, weeping on the stand, repeatedly asks him why, as Cardinal Ratzinger, the retired pope had never defrocked Father Hullermann.

Ratzinger's entire life flashes before his eyes. Everything— from his ordination by Cardinal von Faulhaber and the speech he wrote at Vatican II attacking Cardinal Ottaviani, to the squabbles with Hans Küng, the demonization of Leonardo Boff, and the relentless psychological abuse of women and gay men—comes back to haunt him, begging for reassessment. Confronted with reality in a manner he never thought possible (if only because he has insulated himself from reality for so long), the former pope now begins to wonder what it all meant, what it was all about, this call to Augustinian "truth." What it was *for*. He knows his time on this earth is limited, that he is growing weaker and weaker. He wonders if he will truly be at peace as he approaches the pearly gates. When it comes time to face Saint Peter, will his passage to heaven be as smooth as his climb up the Vatican career ladder? Or will a small voice inside him plead for mercy, forcing him to beg forgiveness for his sins? Like Scrooge, in Dickens's *A Christmas Carol*, he prefers not to wait to find out. As he awaits the verdict, he breaks down in tears and apologizes to Fesselmann. He does this before the court, before the cameras, before the entire world.

Afterword

On February 28, 2013, Pope Benedict XVI said his final good-byes to Vatican officials gathered in the San Damaso courtyard of the Apostolic Palace. With a handsome young corps of Swiss Guards standing by at attention, he walked slowly toward his papal limousine and got inside. After taking the short drive to the top of the hill of the Vatican gardens, he boarded a white helicopter and—accompanied by his loyal secretary, Georg Gänswein—began the fifteen-minute flight to Castel Gandolfo, the summer palace where he would spend the next two months. To the thousands of Catholic faithful who crowded St. Peter's Square that day, the scene of the pope flying away from the Vatican, over the rooftops of Rome and the Tiber River, toward the Coliseum and beyond, was reminiscent of the crucified Christ: rising from the metaphorical "dead," their pope was sacrificing himself for the good of the Church. To less credulous observers, the scene was reminiscent of other, less poetic helicopter departures; more like US president Richard Nixon, fleeing the White House lawn in 1974 after besmirching his office with Watergate, or those final evacuees of the US embassy in Saigon a year later, getting out while they still could.

For any Roman Catholic who does not subscribe to the John Paul II personality cult (part of which requires total credulity surrounding his May 1, 2011 beatification and canonization, bereft of any suspicion that its occurrence a mere six years after his death was in any way opportunistic or self-serving for his successor); for any Roman Catholic who hasn't spent the last three decades cloistered in the Vatican and is not a member of Opus Dei, the Legionaries of Christ, or Communion and Liberation; and for anyone else who is not a Roman Catholic but has witnessed with dismay the gradual decline of the church since the early 1980s, it would be hard to avoid the conclusion that Joseph Ratzinger's over-all record—both as defender of the faith for twenty-four years and as Pope Benedict for nearly eight—was a disaster.

In 1969, Ratzinger was forty-two years old. At that time, he deplored the student protest movement, which he saw as evidence that society—not the church—was going to hell in a hand basket. Deeply threatened by the younger generation's contempt for the faith, he did not see this development as a temporary reflex, a trend that could have withered away under a more progressive church that embraced the reforms of Vatican II. Such a vision, for him, was a non-starter. Instead, he had a more apocalyptic vision: the church as doomed by relativism and secularism. This Mother Church would be stripped of all her wealth and the papacy of all its earthly power. This was Ratzinger's prophecy for the church, as shared with a German radio station that year: "She will be small and, to a large extent, will have to start from the beginning. She will no longer be able to fill many of the buildings created in her period of great splendor. Because of the smaller number of followers, she will lose many of her privileges in society. Contrary to what has happened until now, she will present herself much more as a community of followers ... It will make her poor and a church of the little people ... All this will require time. The process will be slow and painful."

One gets the impression that this is exactly what Ratzinger was hoping for: that he far preferred a church of the few—if those few shared the "true" faith of Augustinian fall and redemption—to a church of the multitudes that sold its soul by engaging with the modern world. To some extent this vision has come to pass, although not with the ultimate effect he might have preferred. Various figures put the world's Roman Catholic population today at 1.2 billion. But how many of those 1.2 billion souls actually belong to a parish or still consider themselves part of a faith community? How many see themselves as practicing Catholics any more? How many are "cultural" or "relativist" Catholics who detest the Vatican? How many have become atheists—at least in their hearts, if not out in the open?

In 2011, Pope Benedict lost Ireland. For the church, losing a country like Ireland—which lived and breathed its religion—is like losing a limb. Meanwhile, on the European mainland, a movement to secularize the continent was doing well. As for North America, the litany of bankrupt dioceses told the US and Canadian stories. Nowadays, the Vatican has little choice but to bank on its missions in Latin America, Africa, and even certain countries in Asia, to stay afloat. In the global South, where faith in God can be one of the few comforts in life, the Holy See aims to steer the church clear of "relativism." (To achieve this, it had better hope that clerical sex abuse in these countries remains under wraps.)

The part that's difficult to fathom is why the man who became Pope Benedict would stay in the game as long as he did. When John Paul II died, Ratzinger was seventy-eight years old. Why not just trundle off into the Bavarian sunset to enjoy the rest of his days in quiet contemplation? Why not rest on his laurels, savoring the constant triumph of his will over a half-century career? What was it about the papacy he found so appealing? Did he not anticipate how the abuse scandals that began on his watch at the CDF would explode by the time he was pope, leaving him to clean up the mess? Was his lust for power that insatiable? Less than eight years later, when he walked away from it all, he was wracked with arthritis but otherwise still in possession of his faculties as he approached his eighty-sixth birthday. He had wanted the papacy so badly, and had pledged to serve his Lord as most of his predecessors had—to the death. In the end, when he left, it was like surrender. One question would remain long after his departure: how could the Roman Catholic Church survive, or why should it, after Ratzinger's successful campaign to consign Vatican II to the dust heap and turn the church from a community of differences into a breeding ground for reactionary, ultra-orthodox conservatism?

On April 26, 2010, Hans Küng marked the fifth anniversary of Benedict's pontificate by writing a letter to the world's bishops. This was not a happy correspondence: it was a *cri de coeur*, declaring the church to be in its "worst credibility crisis since the Reformation." Once the two youngest theologians at Vatican II, Ratzinger and Küng were now two of its oldest surviving intellectuals. They had been through their wars in the 1960s and '70s but, in more recent years, had maintained a mutual, if distant, respect. Ratzinger had even invited Küng to the Vatican, shortly after taking office as pope. The two men enjoyed a friendly, four-hour conversation about the state of the church and the possibilities for renewal. But the five years since that meeting had been a disappointment for Küng. In his letter to the world's bishops, Küng cited a litany of missed opportunities on Pope Benedict's part, including this one: "to make the spirit of the Second Vatican Council the compass for the whole Catholic Church, including the Vatican itself." By imposing his own authoritarian version of theology onto the church, Küng charged, Ratzinger had disobeyed what canon law considers the highest authority in the Catholic Church, the Ecumenical Council. "Time and again," said Küng, Ratzinger had "added qualifications to the conciliar texts and interpreted them against the spirit of the council fathers." Now, he said, His Holiness was "increasingly cut off from the vast majority of church members who pay less and less heed to Rome and, at best, identify themselves with their local parish and bishop."

A year later, in a video address to a conference of the American Catholic Council, Küng likened Benedict's papal power to the absolute power of French monarchs, which the people of France revolted against in 1789. Küng was not overly hopeful of church reform, given the restorationist hierarchy that Benedict and John Paul II had set up for it. But, he added, "the world is moving on, going ahead, with or without the church. I believe the gospel of Jesus Christ is stronger than the hierarchy ... More priests will be leaving, more parishes will be without pastors, more churches will be empty." Küng concluded that more young people and women would also leave the church, or at least disassociate internally from it: "All these are indications, I think, that we have to change now." Toward the end of Benedict's pontificate, a series of television ads in British Columbia heralded a new campaign to bring disenchanted Catholics in Canada back into the fold: quoting a favorite saying, "Once a Catholic, always a Catholic," the folks at Catholics Come Home (an American organization that spearheaded similar campaigns in the US in recent years) appealed to stray members of the flock to recognize "that mysterious pull inside you, driving you to look into your faith once more," which "comes directly from God." But nothing about their campaign indicated that the church had done a single thing to merit a second look.

Real and lasting change for the Roman Catholic Church is unlikely. Ratzinger's conquest of his religion was so complete that perhaps only its total annihilation would allow something better to arise from the ashes. All the contenders to succeed Benedict XVI were cardinals whose appointments either he or Pope John Paul II had approved; all were arch-conservatives unlikely to set a new course for Roman Catholicism. Even the conclave itself—normally an occasion for Catholics to mourn their dead pope and respect the pontifical secrecy governing the selection of his successor—was dogged by controversy in 2013. The 115 cardinals voting in the conclave had already cleared the age restriction, with no one above the age of eighty allowed to cast ballots. Now they were expected to have clean records with regard to any kind of sex scandal.

With just three days remaining in his pontificate, Benedict accepted the resignation (thus, disqualification from the conclave) of Cardinal Keith O'Brien, former head of the Catholic Church in England and Wales. O'Brien's sin, which he confessed after the story broke in the media, was to have made "inappropriate" (i.e., sexual) advances toward young priests in the 1980s. But some scandal-tainted Cardinals refused to voluntarily skip the conclave. Cardinal Sean Brady, archbishop of Armagh, Cardinal Timothy Dolan, archbishop of New York, Cardinal Roger Mahony, archbishop emeritus of Los Angeles, and Cardinal Justin Rigali, former archbishop of Philadelphia, had all faced—or were facing—questions about what they knew about the abuse of children by priests. But all took the flight to Rome to participate in the conclave.

Then, on the day before the conclave began, *La Repubblica* unearthed yet another "Vatileaks" scandal: the Holy See had purchased a €23-million share of an apartment building in Rome that happened to house Europa Multiclub, the continent's biggest gay sauna. *La Repubblica* reported that Cardinal Ivan Dias, the head of the Congregation for Evangelisation of Peoples, lived in a twelve-room apartment on the first floor of the building "just yards from the ground floor entrance to the steamy flesh pot." The sauna's website promoted one of its "bear nights" with a video featuring a fat hairy man who strips down before changing into a priest's outfit, but "remaining in a thong, because he wants to expose body and soul." And the brains behind the 2008 purchase of this building? None other than the Vatican Secretary of State, Cardinal Tarcisio Bertone.

As evening fell on St. Peter's Square on March 13, 2013, white smoke began billowing out from the Sistine Chapel chimney. After only five ballots, the College of Cardinals decided to elect the runner-up from 2005 to become the Church's 266th supreme pontiff: Cardinal Jorge Mario Bergoglio, a seventy-six-year-old Jesuit from Argentina and the archbishop of Buenos Aires. The choice was surprising for a number of reasons, apart from the fact that Bergoglio was on nobody's list of frontrunners.[67] The son of Italian immigrants, he was the first pope from the New World, the first non-European in thirteen centuries, and the first Jesuit. Unlike his predecessor, he had spent almost no time in the Vatican and had enjoyed a lengthy pastoral career. And, unlike the bookish and aloof Ratzinger (who read his speeches in Latin), Bergoglio was a self-effacing man of the people, a "shoe leather priest" who offered home-spun homilies off the cuff and kissed the feet of AIDS patients. Catholic news agencies made much of the fact that he chose to live in a simple apartment rather than the sumptuous residence provided by the church, that he cooked his own meals, and that he gave up his chauffeured limousine in favor of public transit. When he first appeared on the balcony above St. Peter's Square, in his

---

67 He wasn't even among Vatican experts' top three choices for first Latin American pope, being passed over by the oddsmakers in favor of Brazil's Odilo Scherer, Honduras's Oscar Rodriguez, and fellow Argentinian Leonardo Sandri.

comportment an eerie hybrid of John XXIII and John Paul I, he greeted the crowd with a folksy "Brothers and sisters, good evening!" and instantly endeared himself by taking the name Francis—after Saint Francis of Assisi, the barefoot friar, great lover of animals, and champion of the poor.

Within minutes of his appearance on that balcony, however, social media made it possible to learn much more about Pope Francis—and get a clue of what kind of successor to Pope Benedict he might turn out to be—than what was on offer from *L'Osservatore Romano*. For all the accolades about his critiques of capitalism and his compassion for the poor, Cardinal Bergoglio was on public record as an orthodox traditionalist on all matters related to the faith—someone close to the doctrinally conservative Communion and Liberation movement, and clearly entrenched on the right wing of the Argentinian church. Under Pope Francis, no one was betting on fresh new dialogues about abortion, birth control, euthanasia, or same-sex marriage. On the latter issue, Bergoglio had been more than candid in his views, earning a public rebuke in 2010 from Argentinian president Cristina Fernandez de Kirchner. Opposing legislation to introduce equal marriage laws, he called same-sex marriage "a scheme to destroy God's plan" and "a real and dire anthropological throwback," also referring to gay adoption as a form of discrimination against children that threatened the survival of the family. De Kirchner described his tone as reminiscent of "medieval times and the Inquisition."

Of course, Bergoglio could not have become the first Argentinian pope as a man of his generation without a thorough vetting of his activities during the so-called "dirty war" of

1976–83. Because he rarely gave media interviews and was reluctant to contradict his critics (even when he thought their allegations against him were false), it was difficult to get Bergoglio on the record about the church's support of General Videla, whose crimes against humanity included the kidnapping, torture, and slaughter of thousands of his opponents and the selling off of their orphaned children. It was only in his 2010 book *The Jesuit* that Bergoglio broke a long silence about his role in the 1976 kidnapping, torture, and ultimate release of two Jesuit priests he had dismissed from the order. Bergoglio had expelled Orlando Yorio and Francisco Jalics for having ministered to residents of the slums, considered a hotbed of Marxist influence. The priests later charged Bergoglio with deliberately setting them up by withdrawing the Jesuit order's protection of them—a typical signal to fascist regimes that their enemies are up for grabs.

Sure enough, the two were kidnapped by government forces a few days after Bergoglio dismissed them. Imprisoned for five months at a clandestine detention center, they were later found lying drugged and semi-naked in a field. In *The Jesuit*, Bergoglio implied that it was his direct intervention with General Videla that led to the release of the pair, thus saving their lives. From this, one might conclude that the Jesuit leader had experienced a crisis of conscience about the fate of these priests as a result of his own actions. Adolfo Perez Esquivel, who won the 1980 Nobel Peace Prize for documenting the junta's atrocities, was asked about Bergoglio's record on the day he became Pope Francis. While the former Jesuit leader may have lacked the courage of other priests, said Esquivel, that was not the same as being a collaborator. "Bergoglio was no accomplice of the dictatorship," he said. "He can't be accused of that." Maybe not. But by twice invoking his right to refuse to appear in open court for trials involving torture, murder, and the theft of babies (and then giving evasive answers when he finally did testify in 2010), the future Pope Francis gave ammunition to critics who said he placed more importance in preserving the church's image than in preserving human rights. That impression was no doubt reinforced by the Vatican's first official denial under his papacy, which occurred less than forty-eight hours after he had become pope: Accusations that he had hadn't done enough to help the kidnapped priests were based on nothing more than "left-wing" and "anti-clerical" sentiment.

So what message were the cardinals sending by choosing Bergoglio as the new pope? He was already old and, with only one lung, presumably not up the rigors of a long term in office. He was no less doctrinally conservative than his two predecessors, having become a sort of leader of the opposition to progressive human rights law in Argentina, and was a Vatican neophyte to boot. Why was this the man to see the church through one of its most difficult periods in modern history? Was he merely another caretaker—a kinder and gentler Benedict, whose common touch would distract the masses but would ultimately do nothing to reform the church? Or would he take decisive action, in the time that he had, to solve the many problems dogging it? The world's 1.2 billion Catholics were about to find out.

In the spirit of *aggiornamento*, or "bringing up to date" with which Pope John XXIII heralded the dawning of Vatican II, I humbly offer a "Top Five" wish list to Pope Francis, on matters of grave importance to the church and its flock. The first two are conceivable under his pontificate, though unlikely; the other three are, admittedly, the stuff of fantasy.[68]

1. Clean house: When Benedict spoke of "the Filth" infecting the Vatican, he may have been talking about those guilty of the clerical sex abuse of children. But it's also quite possible that he was including good but flawed gay men who got caught in the blackmail trap—and thus became an inconvenient embarrassment for the church. Notwithstanding his own homophobic world view, Pope Francis needs to be clear that by "the Filth," what he is referring to are the priest-shifting bishops and cover-up cardinals; the curial members who profit from money-laundering, the clerics doing favors for unsavory political or underworld figures, and so on. Hypocrisy has become the Vatican's oxygen, crucial to its very survival. The new pope needs to change the culture of the Roman Curia so that such hypocrisy no longer governs its every act.

2. Rewrite *Crimen Sollicitationis*: In addition to

---

68 But not necessarily; in an earlier draft of this book, the top of this wish list proposed what seemed, at the time, like another fanciful notion: the resignation of Pope Benedict.

opening the CDF archives and approving a full investigation of sex abuse cases in cooperation with civil authorities, the new pope should declare that *Crimen Sollicitationis* is to be completely rewritten. In the new *Crimen*, all references to "pontifical secrecy" should be removed. The new instruction should have clear guidelines on how to refer a case of alleged child sex abuse to civil authorities. Priests and other church employees found to be credibly accused of criminal offenses should be turned over to civil authorities, with those convicted permanently defrocked. As well, bishops, archbishops, cardinals—even future popes—found guilty of "priest shifting" or obstruction of justice should, under the new canon law, also be defrocked. Victims and families unable or unwilling to take their cases to court should have the option of seeking justice and closure through church-sponsored Truth and Reconciliation commissions at the diocesan level. Such an approach would stop the bleeding of billions of dollars in lawsuits, and—if successful—prevent suicides, saving the lives of victims by helping to restore their dignity.

3. Convene Vatican III: Pope Francis should call a Third Vatican Council, to pick up where Vatican II left off. It should convene in 2015, on the fiftieth anniversary of the adjournment of Vatican II. Vatican III, which would run for three years, should have a broad-reaching mandate that includes a sweeping

review of Vatican II documents and a re-assessment of them in light of the previous half-century. For example, to address the recruitment and retention crisis facing the priesthood, Vatican III should include a review of canon law with regard to provisions on mandatory celibacy and female ordination. It should also include proposals for a new theological review board and an amnesty program that would allow theologians and others disciplined for "wrong thinking" since 1981 to seek reinstatement and/or reconciliation. (This, perhaps, should be subject to a liability waiver: the church, having taken a beating in the sex abuse scandals, could not suffer the additional burden of a raft of lawsuits to compensate for the lost wages and employment opportunities of everyone Joseph Ratzinger fired between 1981 and 2005.) Finally, it should include a Papal Commission on Reproductive Health and Human Sexuality, which would deal with the wide range of issues under this theme that the church has made a habit of pronouncing on since 1965. The composition of this commission should be similar to that which dealt with birth control at Vatican II, but in this case the majority report should be considered binding.

4. Decentralize power: A few days before the 2013 conclave, Cardinal Cormac Murphy-O'Connor, former head of the Catholic Church in England, spoke for many concerned Catholics when he

declared that the Vatican must "put its own house in order." Clearly taking aim at the papacy and the Curia, the cardinal said: "There is no doubt that today there needs to be renewal in the church, reform in the church, and especially of its government." Vatican II called for the devolution of power from Rome and the delegation of several church decision-making powers to the diocesan level. The all-powerful Curia has become a bloated monster since the mid-nineteenth century, when the Vatican lost its papal territories. Neither Popes John Paul II nor Benedict XVI were very interested in cleaning up the Curia. The former was too busy globetrotting; the latter buried in his books. Pope Francis could enhance his populist appeal by taking on this project.

5. End Vatican statehood: One of the final results of Vatican III should be a papal decree declaring the end of statehood for the Vatican and, therefore, the pontiff's own status as head of state. This would have several implications. First, in keeping with Joseph Ratzinger's vision of a "church for the little people" (and in the interests of helping pay off the sex abuse lawsuits), all Apostolic Nunciatures would be closed, their properties sold and their papal nuncios recalled to Rome, where they would be asked to seek alternative employment. All foreign ambassadors would be sent home. Finally, the Holy See would submit two resolutions to the UN General Assembly: the first

seeking to dissolve its status as a non-member state permanent observer, the second requesting status as a non-governmental organization.

Should Pope Francis preside over most or all of these changes, he would likely become a candidate for the Nobel Peace Prize. More importantly, he would secure a legacy worth celebrating: such progress in the church's governance would restore the faint hope, for many of the disillusioned, that social justice is truly a core value of Roman Catholicism. It would be clear evidence that—contrary to the self-serving, manipulative cultishness of the "Catholics Come Home" campaign—the church was serious about calling back its flock. And they would come. Slowly at first in Europe and North America, but they would come. Under such a regime of change, there would also be more theological choices available for Catholics in the global South. Particularly in Africa and Latin America, which form the vast majority of today's flock, there would be less intimidation, less pressure to conform, and more diversity of expression in interpreting the gospels. I'm not saying I would go back. There's been too much water under the bridge for that. But the church I grew up in before Joseph Ratzinger shattered my illusions was a pretty good place. If, for some reason, a miracle occurred and Pope Francis embraced Vatican II, I would not rule out the odd peek through a cathedral door now and then. But I am not holding my breath.

Acknowledgments

The author would like to thank the following for their inspiration, advice, assistance or other acts of kindness in the service of this book: Pierre Beaulne, David Beers, Dennis E. Bolen, Alexandre Boulerice, Carellin Brooks, David Chariandy, Sharon Davidson, Marc Gawthrop, Terry Glavin, Thammarath Jamikorn and Klaus Wallner, Don Larventz, Daniela Lorenzi, Edmund Lynch, Erin Mullan, Troy Myers and Ginger Gosnell, James Oakes, Stan Persky, Barbara Pulling, Walter Quan, and Alexandra Youngberg.

The author also expresses his gratitude to the BC Arts Council, for the grant that helped him finish a first draft of the book; to the Canadian Union of Public Employees, for the leaves of absence that allowed him to complete it; and to several family members, friends, and CUPE colleagues not named here, for their interest and support.

Special and warm thanks go to Brian Lam and Robert Ballantyne, not only for believing in *The Trial* but for agreeing to publish it on short notice. Kudos as well to their extraordinary team at Arsenal Pulp Press—associate editor Susan Safyan, proofreader Linda Field, production manager Gerilee McBride, marketing manager Cynara Geissler, and Jennifer Abel Kovitz and Missi Smith of 45th Parallel Communications—who made it all come together so seamlessly.

Finally, thanks to the author's husband, Aung Htwe Nyunt Saw ("Lune"), whose very presence is a daily refutation of Ratzingerian thought.

Selected References

Books

Allen, John L. Jr. *The Rise of Benedict XVI: The Inside Story of How the Pope was Elected and Where He Will Take the Catholic Church.* New York: Doubleday, 2005.

Anonymous. *Against Ratzinger.* New York: Seven Stories Press, 2008.

Bardazzi, Marco. *In the Vineyard of the Lord: The Life, Faith, and Teachings of Joseph Ratzinger, Pope Benedict XVI.* New York: Rizzoli International Publications, 2005.

Bonavoglia, Angela. *Good Catholic Girls: How Women Are Leading the Fight to Change the Church.* New York: Regan Books, 2005.

Briggs, Kenneth. *Double Crossed: Uncovering the Catholic Church's Betrayal of American Nuns.* New York: Doubleday, 2006.

De Roo, Remi. *Chronicles of a Vatican II Bishop.* Toronto: Novalis, 2012.

Fox, Matthew. *The Pope's War: Why Ratzinger's Secret Crusade Has Imperiled the Church and How It Can Be Saved.* New York: Sterling Ethos, 2011.

Fox, Thomas C. *Sexuality and Catholicism.* New York: George Braziller, 1995.

Gillis, Chester, ed. *The Political Papacy: John Paul II, Benedict XVI, and Their Influence.* St. Paul: Paradigm Publishing, 2008.

Halter, Deborah. *The Papal "No": A Comprehensive Guide to the Vatican's Rejection of Women's Ordination.* New York: Crossroad, 2004.

Hofmann, Paul. *The Vatican's Women: Female Influence at the Holy See.* New York: St. Martin's Press, 2002.

Kaiser, Robert Blair. *A Church in Search of Itself: Benedict XVI and the Battle for the Future.* New York: Knopf, 2006.

Küng, Hans. *Infallible? An Inquiry.* New York: Doubleday, 1971.

———— and Leonard Swidler, eds. *The Church in Anguish: Has the Vatican Betrayed Vatican II?* San Francisco: Harper & Row, 1987.

————. *The Catholic Church: A Short History.* New York: Modern Library, 2001.

Lynch, Father Bernard. *A Priest on Trial.* London: Bloomsbury, 1994.

Manning, Joanna. *Is the Pope Catholic? A Woman Confronts Her Church.* Toronto: Malcolm Lester, 1999.

Maguire, Daniel C. "The Shadow Side of the Homosexuality Debate." In *Homosexuality and the Priesthood and the Religious Life*, edited by Jeannine Gramick. New York: Crossroad, 1989.

Nugent, Robert. "Priest, Celibate and Gay: You Are Not Alone." In *A Challenge to Love: Gay and Lesbian Catholics in the Church*, edited by Robert Nugent. New York: Crossroad, 1986.

Perito, John E. *Contemporary Catholic Sexuality: What Is Taught and What Is Practiced.* New York: Crossroad, 2003.

Quattrocchi, Angelo. *The Pope is NOT Gay.* London: Verso, 2010.

Ranke-Heinemann, Uta. *Eunuchs for Heaven: The Catholic Church and Sexuality.* London: Andre-Deutsch, 1990.

Ratzinger, Joseph. *Milestones: Memoirs 1927–1977.* San Francisco: Ignatius Press, 1998.

————. *Values in a Time of Upheaval.* San Francisco: Ignatius Press, 2006.

————. *Maria: Pope Benedict XVI on the Mother of God.* San Francisco: Ignatius Press, 2009.

Robertson, Geoffrey. *The Case of the Pope: Vatican Accountability for Human Rights Abuse.* London: Penguin, 2010.

Ruether, Rosemary Radford. "John Paul II and the Growing Alienation of Women from the Church." In *The Church in Anguish: Has the Vatican Betrayed Vatican II?*, edited by Hans Küng and Leonard Swidler. San Francisco: Harper & Row, 1987.

————. *Catholic Does Not Equal the Vatican: A Vision for Progressive Catholicism*. New York: The New Press, 2008.

Schoenherr, Richard A., and Lawrence A. Young, *Full Pews and Empty Altars: Demographics of the Priest Shortage in United States Catholic Dioceses*. Madison: University of Wisconsin Press, 1993.

Seewald, Peter. *Light of the World: The Pope, the Church and the Signs of the Times*. San Francisco: Ignatius Press, 2010.

Thavis, John. *The Vatican Diaries: A Behind-the-Scenes Look at the Power, Personalities, and Politics at the Heart of the Catholic Church*. New York: Viking, 2013.

Winter, Miriam Therese. *Out of the Depths: The Story of Ludmila Javorova, Ordained Roman Catholic Priest*. New York: Crossroad, 2001.

Yallop, David. *In God's Name: An Investigation into the Murder of Pope John Paul I*. New York: Carroll & Graf, 2007.

Periodicals

Adams, Guy. "Brazil Rocked by Abortion for 9-Year-Old Rape Victim." *The Independent*, March 9, 2009. http://www.independent.co.uk/news/world/americas/brazil-rocked-by-abortion-for-9yearold-rape-victim-1640165.html.

Adil, Shakil. "Religious Leaders Across Mideast Rage Against Pope's Comments on Islam." *Information Liberation*, September 15, 2006. http://www.informationliberation.com/index.php?id=15763.

Akerson, David. "Should the ICC Prosecute the Pope?," *Denver Journal of Law & Policy*, September 29, 2011. http://djilp.org/1047should-the-icc-prosecute-the-pope/.

Allen, John L. Jr. "Pope Tells Ratzinger More Collaboration Needed." *National Catholic Reporter*, February 1, 2002.

————. "Vatican Asks Condoleeza Rice to Help Stop a Sex Abuse Lawsuit." *National Catholic Reporter*, March 3, 2005. http://www.national catholicreporter.org/update/bn030305.htm.

————. "Hans Küng and Pope Benedict, Old Friends and Archrivals, Have a Cordial Meeting." *National Catholic Reporter*, September 26, 2005. http://nationalcatholicreporter.org/update/bn092605.htm

————. "Profile: New Pope, Bergoglio, Was Runner-Up in 2005 Conclave." *National Catholic Reporter*, March 3, 2013. http://ncronline.org/blogs/ncr-today/papabile-day-men-who-could-be-pope-13.

Blaine, Barbara. "Why the Pope Must Face Justice at The Hague." *The Guardian*, September 17, 2011. http://www.guardian.co.uk/commentisfree/cifamerica/2011/sep/17/pope-clergy-sex-abuse-hague.

Butt, Riazat. "Pope Claims Condoms Could Make African Aids Crisis Worse." *The Guardian*, March 17, 2008. http://www.guardian.co.uk/world/2009/mar/17/pope-africa-condoms-aids.

Carbery, Genevieve. "The Breakup: Why Ireland Is No Longer the Vatican's Loyal Follower." *Time*, July 27, 2011.

Cornwell, John. "Gay Sex Rings, 'The Filth' Corrupting the Vatican … and Why the Pope REALLY Quit." *The Daily Mail*, March 2, 2013. http://www.dailymail.co.uk/news/article-2287074/Pope-resigns-2013-Gay-sex-rings-The-Filth-corrupting-Vatican--Pope-REALLY-quit.html.

Davies, Lizzy, John Hooper and Kate Connolly. "Pope Benedict XVI Resigns Owing to Age and Declining Health." *The Guardian*, February 11, 2013. http://www.guardian.co.uk/world/2013/feb/11/pope-benedict-xvi-resigns-age.

Day, Michael. "As Cardinals Gather to Elect Pope, Catholic Officials Break Into a Sweat Over News That Priests Share €23m Building with Huge Gay Sauna." *The Independent*, March 11, 2013. http://www.independent.co.uk/news/world/europe/as-cardinals-gather-to-elect-pope-catholic-

officials-break-into-a-sweat-over-news-that-priests-share-23m-building-
with-huge-gay-sauna-8529670.html.

D'Emilio, Frances and Winfield, Nicole. "Pope Says Condoms OK to Use in
Some Cases." *The Star*, November 21, 2010. http://www.thestar.com/news/
world/2010/11/21/pope_says_condoms_ok_to_use_in_some_cases.html.

Donadio, Rachel. "A Vatican Whodunit, a Punch Line of a Suspect." *New
York Times*, May 26, 2012.

"Election of Pope Francis Stirs Argentina's 'Dirty War' Past, and Role of
Church in Deaths of Thousands." *National Post*, March 14, 2013. http://
news.nationalpost.com/2013/03/14/election-of-pope-francis-stirs-argenti
nas-dirty-war-past-and-role-of-church-in-deaths-of-thousands.

Filteau, Jerry. "Hans Küng Urges Peaceful Revolution against Roman
Absolutism." *National Catholic Reporter*, June 11, 2011. http://ncronline.
org/news/faith-parish/hans-Küng-urges-peaceful-revolution-against-ro
man-absolutism.

Gibson, David. "Pope Benedict XVI and the Anglican Outreach." *Washington
Post*, October 25, 2009. http://www.washingtonpost.com/wp-dyn/con
tent/article/2009/10/23/AR2009102302403.html.

————. "Vatican Orders Crackdown on American Nuns." *USA Today*,
April 19, 2012. http://usatoday30.usatoday.com/news/religionstory/
2012-04-18/american-nuns-vatican/54396560/1.

Goodstein, Laurie. "Abuse Victims Ask Court to Prosecute the Vatican." *New
York Times*, September 13, 2011. http://www.nytimes.com/2011/09/14/
world/europe/14vatican.html.

————. "American Nuns Vow to Fight Vatican Criticism." *New York
Times*, June 1, 2012. http://www.nytimes.com/2012/06/02/usnuns-speak
-about-vatican-criticism.html?_r=0.

Henao, Luis Andres. "'Papa Villero' Hailed in Buenos Aires."
Vancouver Sun, March 16, 2013.

Hitchens, Christopher. "Bring the Pope to Justice." *Newsweek*, May 3, 2010.

"Irish PM Slams Vatican 'Dysfunction' on Child Abuse." *The Telegraph*, July 21, 2011. http://www.telegraph.co.uk/news/religion/8651160/Irish-PM-slams-Vatican-dysfunction-on-child-abuse.html#mm_hash.

Israely, Jeff and Howard Chua-Eoan. "Why Being Pope Means Never Having to Say You're Sorry: The Sex Abuse Scandal and the Limits of Atonement." *Time*, June 7, 2010.

Jouault, Catherine. "Predator Priests to Answer to Pope." *The Province*, July 16, 2010.

Kasim, Nsimbe. "Speaker Kadaga Receives Blessings from Pope." *New Vision*, December 13, 2012. http://www.newvision.co.ug/news/638115-speaker kadaga-receives-blessings-from-pope.html.

Kenny, Mary. "Is Ireland Divorcing from the Catholic Church?" *The Telegraph*, July 26, 2011. http://www.telegraph.co.uk/news/worldnews/europe/ireland/8663451/Is-Ireland-divorcing-from-the-Catholic-Church.html.

Llenas, Bryan. "On Eve of Conclave, Latin American Catholics Hope for One of their Own to Lead the Church." *Fox News* (Latino), March 11, 2013. http://latino.foxnews.com/latino/news/2013/03/11/before-conclave-latin-american-outsider-could-change-everything/.

Manthorpe, Jonathan. "Pope Benedict Tries to Purify Scandal-Ridden Vatican Bank." *Vancouver Sun*, July 4, 2012.

Murphy, Brian and Warren, Michael. "Pope Francis: Simple Image, Complex Past." *Yahoo News/Associated Press*, March 13, 2013. http://news.yahoo.com/pope-francis-simple-image-complex-past-000732533.html.

Nadeau, Barbie Latza. "JPMorgan Chase Closes Vatican Bank Account." *The Daily Beast*, March 21, 2012. http://www.thedailybeast.com/articles/2012/03/21/jp-morgan-chase-closes-vatican-bank-account.html.

O'Shaughnessy, Hugh. "The Sins of the Argentinian Church." *The Guardian*,

January 4, 2011. http://www.guardian.co.uk/commentisfree/belief/2011/jan/04/argenitina-videla-bergoglio-repentance.

"Oct. 27 Set as Date of Assisi Gathering for World Peace." *Catholic News Agency*, April 4, 2011. http://www.catholicnewsagency.com/news/oct.-27-set-as-date-of-assisi-gathering-for-world-peace.

Papenfuss, Mary. "Vatican Cracks Down on 'Liberal' US Nuns." *Newser*, April 19, 2012. http://www.newser.com/story/144364/vatican-cracks-down-on-liberal-us-nuns.html.

Pentin, Edward. "Cardinal Bergoglio Hits Out at SameSex Marriage." *National Catholic Register*, July 8, 2010. http://www.ncregister.com/blog/edward-pentin/cardinal_bergoglio_hits_out_at_same-sex_marriage.

"Pope Denies Feeling Alone Over Holocaust-Denying Bishop." *ABS-CBN News.com*, March 17, 2009. http://www.abs-cbnnews.com/world/03/17/09/pope-denies-feeling-alone-over-holocaust-denying-bishop.

Pullela, Philip. "Abandon the Pride of Wanting to Become God." *Globe and Mail*, April 18, 2011.

Reese, Thomas J. "The Hidden Exodus: Catholics Becoming Protestants." *National Catholic Reporter*, April 18, 2011.

Rychlak, Ronald J. "Accusing Pope Benedict," *The National Review*, September 28, 2011. http://www.nationalreview.com/articles/278540accusing-pope-benedict-ronald-j-rychlak.

Sandri, Luigi. "Vatican Attempts to Clarify Jesuit's Stance on Religious Pluralism." *Christianity Today*, February 1, 2001. http://www.christianitytoday.com/ct/2001/februaryweb-only/55.0c.html.

Saunders, Doug. "The Pope and the Junta: in Search of the True Story." *Globe and Mail*, March 16, 2013.

"Sexual Abuse By Clergy a 'Mystery,' Pope Says." *CBC News*, June 17, 2012. http://www.cbc.ca/news/world/story/2012/06/17/pope-declares-child-abuse-mystery.html.

Spencer, Kent. "Catholics Come Home," *The Province*, December 18, 2012.

Strasser, Annie-Rose. "Church Excommunicates Doctor and Mother of 9-Year-Old Rape Victim—But Not the Man Who Raped Her." *ThinkProgress*, May 25, 2012. http://thinkprogress.org/health/2012/05/25/490171/brazil-excommunication-for-abortion/.

Sullivan, Andrew. "Sin or Crime?" *The Atlantic*, March 25, 2010. http://www.theatlantic.com/daily-dish/archive/2010/03sin-or-crime/188912/.

Tóibín, Colm. "Among the Flutterers," *London Review of Books*, August 19, 2010.

Valente, Gianni. "Tradition and Freedom: The Lectures of the Young Joseph." *30 Days*, March 2006. http://www.30giorni.it/articoli_id_10284_l3.htm.

"Vatican Officials Told Irish Not to Report Child Abuse." *BBC News*, January 19, 2011. http://www.bbc.co.uk/news/world-europe-12222612.

Walsh, Jason. "Why the ICC Likely Won't Charge Pope Over Catholic Church Sex Abuses." *Christian Science Monitor*, September 15, 2011. http://www.csmonitor.com/World/Europe/2011/0915/Why-the-ICC-likely-won-t-charge-pope-over-Catholic-Church-sex-abuses.

Winfield, Nicole. "Pope Makes Saint of Woman Who Died after Refusing Abortion." *The Independent*, May 17, 2004. http://www.independent.co.uk/news/world/europe/pope-makes-saint-of-woman-who-died--after-refusing-abortion-6169679.html.

Websites

Küng, Hans. "Church in Worst Credibility Crisis since Reformation, Theologian Tells Bishops." *Clerical Whispers Blog*, April 16, 2010. http://clericalwhispers.blogspot.ca/2010/04/church-in-worst-credibility-crisis.html.

Sipe, Richard. "Paedophiles and Celibacy." *Celibacy, Sex & Catholic Church*, March 18, 2010. http://www.richardsipe.com/Miscl/vatican_connection. htm.

Media

In Good Conscience: Sister Jeannine Gramick's Journey of Faith. DVD. Directed by Barbara Rick. New York: Out of the Blue Films, 2009.

Tuchman, Gary. *What the Pope Knew*. CNN, Aired September 25, 2010. (Transcript available at: http://transcripts.cnn.com/TRANSCRIPTS /1009/25/siu.01.html.)

Reports

Catholics for a Free Choice. *The Catholic Church at the United Nations: Church or State?* See Change briefing paper, 2000.

Center for Constitutional Rights. *Victims' Communication: Pursuant to Article 15 of the Rome Statute Requesting Investigation and Prosecution of High-level Vatican Officials for Rape and Other Forms of Sexual Violence as Crimes Against Humanity and Torture as a Crime Against Humanity*, 2011. (Full text available online at: http://www.bishop-accountability.org/news2011 /09_10/2011_09_13_CCR_Victims_Communication.pdf)

Sheehan, Thomas. "Fortress Vaticana." Stanford University, 2000.

Vatican Documents

Crimen Sollicitationis: Instruction on the Manner of Proceeding in Cases of Solicitation. The Vatican Press, 1962.

Congregation for the Doctrine of the Faith. *Letter to the Bishops of the Catholic Church on the Pastoral Care of Homosexual Persons*. October 1, 1986.

————. *Some Considerations Concerning the Response to Legislative Proposals on the Non-Discrimination of Homosexual Persons*. July 22, 1992.

————. *Circular Letter to Assist Episcopal Conferences in Developing Guidelines for Dealing with Cases of Sexual Abuses of Minors Perpetrated by Clerics*. May 3, 2011.

Letter to the Irish Catholic Bishops' Advisory Committee from Apostolic Nuncio Luciano Storero. January 31, 1997.

Letter to Cardinal Ratzinger, Pontifical Legate in Ecuador, from Pope John Paul I. September 1, 1978.

The Regensburg Lecture: Apostolic Journey of His Holiness Benedict XVI to Munchen, Altotting and Regensburg (September 9–14, 2006). Meeting with the Representatives of Science, Lecture of the Holy Father. Aula Magna of the University of Regensburg. September 12, 2006.

Index

DANIEL GAWTHROP is the author of four previous books, including *The Rice Queen Diaries* (Arsenal Pulp Press) and *Affirmation: The AIDS Odyssey of Dr. Peter* (New Star Books). A self-professed "lapsed Catholic," he lives in Vancouver. Follow him on Twitter: @dgawthrop

www.danielgawthrop.com